JOHN WOO

INTERVIEWS

CONVERSATIONS WITH FILMMAKERS SERIES
PETER BRUNETTE, GENERAL EDITOR

Photo credit: Erik Unger

JOHN WOO
INTERVIEWS

EDITED BY ROBERT K. ELDER

UNIVERSITY PRESS OF MISSISSIPPI / JACKSON

www.upress.state.ms.us

The University Press of Mississippi is a member of the Association of American University Presses.

Copyright © 2005 by University Press of Mississippi

All rights reserved

First edition 2005

∞

Library of Congress Cataloging-in-Publication Data

John Woo : interviews / edited by Robert K. Elder.— 1st ed.
    p. cm. — (Conversations with filmmakers series)
  Includes index.
  ISBN 1-57806-775-8 (cloth : alk. paper) — ISBN 1-57806-776-6 (pbk. : alk. paper)
  1. Woo, John, 1948– —Interviews. 2. Motion picture producers and directors—China—Interviews. I. Elder, Robert K. II. Series.
  PN1998.3.W655J65 2005
  791.4302'33—dc22   2005001469

British Library Cataloging-in-Publication Data available

CONTENTS

Introduction   vii

Chronology   xv

Filmography   xix

John Woo: Early Oral History   3
    HONG KONG FILM ARCHIVE

John Woo: Movie by Movie, 1968 to 1990   16
    ROBERT K. ELDER

John Woo's *A Better Tomorrow*   59
    KAREN FANG

The Killer: Criterion Collection Commentary Track Interview Excerpts   73
    DAVID CHUTE, MARK RANCE, ET AL.

Hard Boiled: Criterion Collection Commentary Track Excerpts   81
    JOHN WOO, TERENCE CHANG, AND DAVE KEHR

Star Director, With a Bullet: Hong Kong's John Woo Aims for Piece of U.S. Action   89
    RICHARD CHRISTIANSEN

The Hard Road to *Hard Target*   94
    BARBARA SCHARRES

ACTION! Woo Said It! 108
MARK CARO

The Woo Dynasty Comes to Hollywood 114
TED ELRICK

Look Woo's Talking 121
MAUREEN "MO" RYAN

Honor, Loyalty, and Chivalry 125
MICHAEL SINGER

Wooing Hollywood 140
AMY WU

Number One with a Bullet 143
ANNE THOMPSON

From *The Actor's Encyclopedia of Casting Directors* 155
KAREN KONDAZIAN

The Two Sides of John Woo 162
ROBERT K. ELDER

John Woo: Hot-handed God of Hong Kong Film Directors 168
PATRICK MACIAS

John Woo at the Gene Siskel Film Center 174
BARBARA SCHARRES AND BOB BALABAN

Index 185

INTRODUCTION

WHEN I TALKED TO BARBARA SCHARRES, programmer of the Gene Siskel Film Center in Chicago and friend to John Woo, about putting together this collection of interviews, she made an intriguing observation. She believes too much has been made of the Western world's impact on Woo's work, that it has been misunderstood or exaggerated.

"He always talks about Scorsese and Truffaut, but I've always thought the biggest influence on John's films has always been his own imagination, his own life, his own sense of rhythm," Scharres said.

As you read the interviews in this volume, I believe Scharres's statement bears out, especially when you consider Woo's own biographical and philosophical connection to recurring themes throughout his films. When I chose interviews for this book, I tried to select pieces that would bring the roots of these themes to light.

When I told John I was assembling and editing a book about him, he was cautious. "There are so many untrue things out there," he said. "So much wrong."

So I set out with a rather ambitious goal: to create the single most accurate, authoritative source on Woo's films and biography. That was my promise to him. In effect, I wanted to be as meticulous with Woo's life and career as he is with each frame of film.

Editing *John Woo: Interviews* turned out to be a more intense, time-consuming experience than I had anticipated. Not only were there issues of simple fact-checking (multiple published dates of birth, etc.)—but also issues of transliteration and John's English skills and memory.

In matters of his early childhood and Hong Kong career, much chronological confusion comes from that fact that Woo's mother lied about his age to place him in primary school. Born Wu Yu-Sheng in Guangzhou, China, in October 1946, Woo had a difficult, tumultuous childhood. His family fled Guangzhou in 1950 to escape Communist rule, only to find poverty, overcrowding and gang violence in Hong Kong.

But in 1954, following a year of being homeless after a neighborhood fire, Woo's family received assistance from the Lutheran Church and Woo was put back in school. His age (nine years old) was reduced by two years so he could catch up academically, and thereafter Woo is often confused about how old he was during different points in his life.

In interviews, Woo doesn't hide this part of his life. If anything, he's proud of his parents and family, how they persevered and kept him on "the right track." He speaks freely and openly when prompted about his childhood, as with most subjects. But especially in the Western press, his early years as a filmmaker get lost, possibly because so few of those movies have made it to the West on DVD.

To fill in the gaps, Woo was good-spirited enough to grant me several hours to interview him about his Hong Kong career. All the facts and dates were double-checked by Woo himself, and where his memory proved murky, his assistant Brittany Philion and the amazing Law Kar at the Hong Kong Film Archive stepped in.

Still, Woo has an amazing memory for details, if not dates. And his passion for the cinema was unbridled, even early in life, as he told the Hong Kong Film Archive in an oral history interview in 2001. In one story that Woo tells, he and his brother used to sneak into the movies with adults, since children got in free with parents.

"At that time, I carried my brother on my back and my hand was holding someone else's coattail," Woo said. "While I was walking up the stairs, an attendant caught me. I therefore told him that I was that man's son and the attendant challenged me that I did not look like that man. He then slapped my face a few times and pushed me and my brother down the stairway and chased us out of the cinema."

Growing up poor in Hong Kong was a daily battle, and both the church and the cinema provided refuge. Often in interviews Woo talks about his loyalty to the church and the roughness of those times, though he has to be pressed for specific anecdotes. Once he was taken to the hospital after someone threw hot ashes in his face while he was carrying his toddler brother.

"The place we lived in was pretty awful; we were living in hell. If you wanted to survive, you had to be strong. I got beat up almost every day," he told me in a Chicago jazz club in 2002. "Whenever I went out of the house or the alley, I had to grab something as a weapon for protection. I had to fight really hard to survive. I never gave up, I fought back."

It's not surprising then that the adult Woo abhors violence. "I'm a peace-lover, and I hate war. I hate to see people killing each other," he told David Chute in 1994.

In fact, like his cinematic hero Martin Scorsese, Woo also felt a calling to serve the church. "My first dream was to become a pastor," he told the Hong Kong Film Archive in 2001. "I had never thought of becoming a director in the future. I received a lot of help from the church since I was a child. And I adored and worshiped the universal love of Jesus and his philosophy. I admired the wholehearted devotion of pastors and their love and kindness in helping others. . . . Therefore, I hoped that one day I could return the favor to society and all those people who had helped me before."

Yet, he has built his career on flamboyantly violent films and become the master of "bullet ballets." Nicolas Cage gives this explanation: "Maybe the more violent your art is, the more peaceful your life is because you're getting that [expression] out," he told me in 2002. "It's sort of a weird contradiction. What you hate can actually become something very interesting to you artistically. You get power over it."

And power over it, he has. Although Woo started his career with comedy, kung fu films, and even a successful adaptation of an opera, he's firmly established himself in the West as the master of action cinema. But, Woo says on the commentary track for *The Killer*, he has "never taken violence seriously in my films. All I'm concerned with when I'm making violent scenes is that it has to be based on emotion. . . ."

In the commentary track for *Hard Boiled*, film critic Dave Kehr explains Woo's carnivals of carnage this way: "I think the mistake that people make is assuming that there's only one kind of violence in movies, and that's very far from the truth. There are dozens and dozens of ways of filming violence and treating violence, and thinking about what it can mean in the context of the story," Kehr says. "I think in

John's films . . . violence becomes a way of these men relating to each other. It's able to express these very intense feelings that they wouldn't be able to express in any other way, certainly not verbally, certainly not physically, but through passionate violence. . . . John's films are this kind of celebration, a kind of breakthrough, in that they use this very stylized violence to achieve that."

Still, Western journalists tend to focus on Woo's portrayal of violence, sometimes at the expense of overlooking his other themes, such as faith and a strong commitment to friends and family. Even a casual reader of this book will notice how important friends and family are to the director. Woo honors his friends, collaborators, and influences by crediting the impact their work has had on his career. He's constantly espousing his admiration for his mentor, Chang Cheh, and praising director and producer Tsui Hark for his friendship and belief in him, especially at a time when Woo was at an extremely low point in his career. Much has been made of the influence François Truffaut, Sam Peckinpah, and Martin Scorsese have had on Woo's work, and in the following pages you'll find the director himself passionately praising his heroes.

Previously in interviews, he's always preferred to keep his children's names out of the press, wanting to protect their privacy and give them some semblance of a normal upbringing in Hong Kong. Only in this book, for the first time, has Woo shared their names and new family details (including his father's reasons for leaving their ancestral home).

It was Woo's dedication to family and the handover of Hong Kong from Britain to China that caused the family to move again, this time to America. "In Hong Kong, we worked like crazy. We work seven days a week, almost over 18 hours a day. And I never had any time for my children. . . . They didn't even want to talk to me. When they needed a father or they need to see my face, [there wasn't time]. I love my family and I love my children and I wanted it to be normal," he told Scharres of the Siskel Center in 2004. Moving to the West, however, did not make him more understood as a director. There were other problems. Often, especially early in his Western career, journalists would simply misquote John, sifting through his tangle of prepositions and misunderstanding his references to foreign movies. Add to this the problem of transliteration, wherein each translator invented English spellings of

Cantonese and Mandarin names. Then, of course, many Chinese filmmakers have Westernized names in addition to these other names. Even the name John Woo is an amalgamation of his Mandarin, Cantonese, Christian, and Shanghainese names.

In this book, we've standardized his multiple names with Woo's preferred spellings. His Mandarin name is Wu Yu-Sheng. His Cantonese name is Ng Yu-sum. We've also resisted (and in fact, opposed) the trend by Internet movie databases and other sources to Westernize Chinese names. We've kept the surname, or family, name in front, as is traditional for Chinese names; e.g. Chow Yun-Fat will never be listed as Yun-Fat Chow, and we struggled to maintain this style for all Chinese names, using multiple sources to confirm the proper order, when available.

Also, a word about editing this book. As you will read in proceeding pages, we did not always edit Woo's wordy, run-on sentences, in an effort to maintain the richness of his storytelling abilities and speaking style. Grammar isn't often corrected, except in areas where an intended preposition or added article produced clarity. Some of Woo's favorite phrases ("At that time" or "I was so shocked") are still there, although we've cut down their frequency. We wanted to maintain the spirit, as well as the flavor, of Woo's speech.

The director's English continues to improve and grow more sophisticated, and he's long since abandoned having interpreters sit in on interviews with Western journalists. He's become more confident in his English. Woo has changed in other ways as well, says friend and producer Terence Chang. "If he's changed at all, I don't think it's America [that's changed him]," Chang told me in 2002. "It's age. . . . Our roles have sort of reversed now. He used to be the temperamental guy and I always smoothed relationships over. Now I say what I want, and he's the diplomat."

The transition to the Hollywood system, however, wasn't smooth at first. His debut American production, the Jean-Claude Van Damme action vehicle *Hard Target*, was recut several times to get an R rating, and Woo's crew was afraid of him. In Hong Kong, his crew even took to calling the unsmiling Woo "the Black-faced God." "Of course, I screamed and yelled sometimes," Woo said in the same piece. "In America, I like to work in a friendly way. People are so nice to me. They really make me change. If I yell and scream, it won't help at all. It only makes things worse."

Since his Hong Kong days, he's not abandoned his Christian ideals or symbols. His use of both freeze frame (a nod to François Truffaut) and the dove motif stay intact, even through his more commercial films such as *Mission: Impossible 2* and *Paycheck*.

In 2000, he spoke with *Premiere*'s Anne Thompson about his signature doves. "I love doves. I am a Christian. Doves represent the purity of love, all kinds of beauty. They're spiritual. Also the dove is a messenger between people and God. When I was in high school I used to draw posters for the church, they had topics like Jesus dying . . . but I used to draw a picture of a dove."

At the writing of this introduction, Woo is planning to break out of the action genre and make a musical. There has even been talk of a Chinese and American epic, either called *The Divide* or *Men of Destiny*, about the Irish and Chinese workers building the transcontinental railroad. Whatever his subject, however, doves are sure to appear. Also present will be his frenetic editing and fascination with duality and the conflicts of faith and honor.

Veering from the conventions of the Conversations with Filmmakers Series, the interviews in this volume have been arranged to reflect the order of Woo's filmography rather than the dates the interviews were conducted. The first in-depth interviews with Woo coincided with his arrival in the United States in the early 1990s and were focused on his current films. In reordering the interviews, I've begun the volume with later interviews that went back to discuss Woo's pre-Hollywood career, thus providing the detail and background needed to fully understand Woo's complicated biography and artistry.

In keeping with Woo's sense of loyalty and honor, it would be unforgivable to not acknowledge the principal players who helped make this book a reality.

Thanks are due to Peter Becker at the Criterion Collection, who gave us permission to use invaluable excerpts from Criterion's *The Killer* and *Hard Boiled* commentary tracks. Angela Tong, Angel Shing, and Mable Ho at the Hong Kong Film Archive allowed us to translate one of John's oral histories, and again I thank them for their good will in this cross-cultural exchange. Additional support from Anthony C. Ferrante at

Cinescape Magazine, Jeff Black at IFILM, and Barbara Scharres and Karen Cross Durham at the Gene Siskel Film Center in Chicago was much appreciated.

John Woo: Interviews was a massive undertaking that could not have been realized without the help and guidance of the following people: Peter Brunette, David Chute, Mark Gallagher, Roger Garcia, James Hathaway, John Horn, Delphine Ip, Law Kar, Kathleen Rowe Karlyn, Dave Kehr, Tien-Tsung Lee, Li Cheuk-to, Carmen Rivera, Bill Ryan, Herman Sanchez, Tim Sika, Adrienne Smith, Sean Smith, Erik Unger, Jian Wang, Tony Williams, and Randy Weissman.

My gratitude as well for the support given to me by my editors at *The Chicago Tribune*: Lilah Lohr, Tim Bannon, Mary Elson and Jim Warren. Special thanks also to superstar copy editor Betsy Edgerton and my unshakeable editor at University Press of Mississippi, Walter Biggins. This volume would have been riddled with mistakes and misspellings were it not for the sharp eyes of Alison Knezevich, assistant to the editor, and the tenacity of assistants Alexis Crawford, Michelle Edgar, and Michael Hirtzer. My gratitude goes to them for hunting down errors missed by my dyslexic brain.

An equal bow of appreciation goes out to Woo's assistant, Brittany Philion, whose eternal grace and patience were tested many times during the process of putting *John Woo: Interviews* together.

Lastly, without the time and kindness of the director himself, this book would not have been possible. So, thanks John, I'm honored by your belief in me and your friendship.

RKE

CHRONOLOGY

1946   John Woo is born Wu Yu-Sheng in Guangzhou, China, during the end of October. He is born to Wu Chuk-wen, second secretary to a general and a former high school history teacher, and housewife Liu Mei-ying. Woo is the oldest of three children, two boys and a girl. Later, Woo's mother tells primary school officials her eldest son was born in September of 1948, so he can start in the first grade at age nine. Woo's name in Mandarin, the language spoken in mainland China, is Wu Yu-Sheng. His name in Cantonese, spoken in Hong Kong, is Ng Yu-sum. The birth date on Woo's passport is September 22, 1948.

1949   At age three, Woo develops an unknown, agonizing back infection. Woo's father finds a German-trained doctor who cures Woo.

1950   Woo's family moves to Hong Kong for political reasons during the Communist Party's rise to power. His experience with poverty in Hong Kong colors many of his movies.

1953   A fire destroys the Woo home and the family is forced to live on the streets for the next year.

1955   At age nine, Woo begins attending a Christian school with the financial support of an American family. At school, an English teacher asks Woo to change his name to something easier to pronounce; he chooses John, after John the Baptist. Woo finds refuge from street violence and poverty in the church. Woo paints images on glass and shines a flashlight

	through it to project images, a precursor to his future filmmaking. He also begins to work as an extra on Hong Kong films. His first role is as a dead Japanese soldier.
1962	When Woo is sixteen, his father dies of tuberculosis, after being hospitalized for nearly ten years. Woo writes, directs, and stars in several high school plays. He finishes his formal education at Concordia Lutheran High School and Matteo Ricci College, but Hong Kong has no film school. Still, Woo is determined to teach himself about film and even resorts to stealing books from the library.
1964	He meets with friends at a sister missionary school of Concordia Lutheran High School to discuss art, culture, and religion.
1967	Joins a student film group, College Cine Club, to discuss experimental film ideas. Writes poems and a short article for the *Chinese Student Weekly*. During his twenties, Woo is greatly influenced by French New Wave filmmakers, Japanese director Akira Kurosawa, and U.S. filmmakers Sam Peckinpah and Stanley Kubrick.
1968–70	Woo joins the Cathay Organization. He makes his first experimental films, *The Evil One, Learning by Doing, Accidentally*, and *Death Knot*, with friend Sek Kei.
1969	Woo becomes a script supervisor for the Cathay Organization, his first major industry job.
1970–71	Lands a job at Shaw Brothers studio as an assistant director and script supervisor to director Chang Cheh.
1973	Begins directing his first feature, *Farewell Buddy*, with Peter Wong. Woo hires a young Jackie Chan as the original stunt coordinator on the film, after working on a previous movie with him under Chang Cheh. Lui's Film Company, an independent film company, finances the movie. The government censor board deems it too violent, and the movie gets shelved. But executives at Golden Harvest studio see promise in the film, pay for reshoots, and release it under the name *The Young Dragons* more than a year later. Woo signs a three-year contract with Golden Harvest.
1974	Woo travels to Korea to direct *The Dragon Tamers*.

CHRONOLOGY   xvii

1976   On March 5, Woo marries Chun-lung Niu, a former script supervisor of his mentor, Chang Cheh. Her English name: Anne (pronounced "Annie") Woo. *Countdown in Kung Fu* (also called *Hand of Death*) is released, featuring martial arts star Jackie Chan in one of his first major roles. *Money Crazy* is released and Woo becomes recognized as a comedy director. This is the first time he uses the name John Woo in his film credits, but as "John Y. S. Woo." His first daughter, Kimberly Hsiang-fong Woo, is born in Hong Kong.

1978   Woo directs *From Riches to Rags*. This is the first commercial movie in which Woo feels he has the freedom to express his own ideas. Woo meets director Tsui Hark. Overlooking the Hong Kong Harbor, they vow to improve the Hong Kong film industry and the movies it produces. Woo's second daughter, Angeles Fei-shai Woo, is born. She is named after the city of her birth, Los Angeles, where her parents are visiting relatives.

1981   *Laughing Times* is released, a movie Woo shoots under the name Wu Hsiang-Fei, a pseudonym that combines the middle names of his daughters. The success of the film helps set up new studio Cinema City.

1982   Woo makes his first war movie, *The Sunset Warrior*, but it isn't released until after the success of *A Better Tomorrow*. In 1986, the film is recut and additional footage is shot, then it's released under the name *Heroes Shed No Tears*. Woo's third child and only son, Frank Yee Fong Woo, is born in California, when Anne is visiting family. Woo gets the news while shooting the end sequence of *Plain Jane to the Rescue*.

1983   Leaves Golden Harvest; joins Cinema City which breaks its promise to allow Woo to make more personal films, including a much dreamed-about gangster genre film. He is sent to Taiwan, essentially exiled, to manage Cinema City's office in the country. He films *The Time You Need a Friend*.

1985   Woo teams with producer/director Tsui Hark to make *A Better Tomorrow*.

1986   *A Better Tomorrow*, starring Chow Yun-Fat, is released and becomes Hong Kong's highest grossing film.

1987	*A Better Tomorrow* is shown at the Toronto Film Festival.
1989	*The Killer* is released. It gathers box office momentum and international acclaim.
1992	Woo moves to the United States.
1993	*Hard Target*, his first American-made film, opens. Woo has to edit the original version six times to avoid an NC-17 rating for violence.
1994	Forms WCG Entertainment, a production company, with Terence Chang and Christopher Godsick.
1996	Receives CineAsia's Lifetime Achievement Award in Filmmaking.
1997	*Face/Off* is released. It wins the Jury Grand Prize at the Sweden Fantastic Film Festival. It grosses over $100 million at the box office. Woo wins two MTV Movie Awards for *Face/Off*; they are his first-ever American awards.
1999	Woo becomes a citizen of the United States on January 12, 1999. *Mission: Impossible 2*, starring Tom Cruise, is released. Woo forms Lion Rock Productions with producer Terence Chang.
2002	*Windtalkers*, with Nicolas Cage, is released.
2003	*Paycheck*, starring Ben Affleck and Uma Thurman, is released.
2004	Woo films the pilot for a new *Lost in Space* television series in Canada. Chicago's Gene Siskel Film Center honors Woo as the first-ever recipient of its Visionary Award for Innovation in Filmmaking.
2005	March, Woo travels to Hong Kong to shoot a short film in support of charitable organization United Nation Children Fund (UNICEF). Woo's contribution is part of a two-hour feature titled *All the Invisible Children*, which will be jointly completed by Woo, Ridley Scott, Spike Lee, and three other directors. Woo's chapter is called "Song Song and the Little Cat."

FILMOGRAPHY

Student/Experimental Films

1968
THE EVIL ONE
Director: **John Woo**
Screenplay: **John Woo**
Cinematography: Lam Chak
Cast: **John Woo**, Chow See-men, Lo Men
8 mm, B&W, silent
approx. 20 minutes

SECRET KILLER
Director: **John Woo**
Screenplay: **John Woo**
Cinematography: Lam Chak
Cast: **John Woo**, Ching Nai-gun
16mm, B&W
approx. 6 minutes

1969
LEARNING BY DOING
Director: **John Woo**
Screenplay: **John Woo**
Cinematography: Chiu Tak-hak
Cast: **John Woo**, Cheung King-hung, Sek Kei (a.k.a. Wong Chi-keung)
16 mm, B&W
approx. 14 minutes

ACCIDENTALLY/OURAN
Director: **John Woo**
Screenplay: **John Woo**
Cinematography: Sek Kei
Editing: **John Woo**
Cast: **John Woo** (Young Man)
B&W, silent
8 minutes

DEATH KNOT/DEAD KNOT/SIJIE
Director: Sek Kei
Screenplay: **John Woo**
Editing: Sek Kei
Cast: **John Woo** (Young Artist), Cho Chung-lang, Chan Kai-yat
16mm, B&W
18 minutes

Professional Career

As Director
1974
THE YOUNG DRAGONS/TIE HAN ROU QING
Golden Harvest
Director: **John Woo**
Screenplay: **John Woo**
Cast: Fung Hark-on, Lau Kong, Tien Ni, Yu Yang
Color

THE DRAGON TAMERS/BELLES OF TAE KWON DO/NU ZI TAI QUAN QUN YING HUI
Golden Harvest
Director: **John Woo**
Screenplay: **John Woo**
Music: Joseph Koo
Cast: Ji Han Jae, James Tien, Carter Wong, Yuen Wah
Color

FILMOGRAPHY xxi

1975
COUNTDOWN IN KUNG FU/HAND OF DEATH/FISTS OF THE DOUBLE K/FIST TO FIST/HONG KONG FACE-OFF/STRIKE OF DEATH/SHAOLIN MEN/SHAO LIN MEN
Golden Harvest
Producer: Raymond Chow
Director: **John Woo**
Screenplay: **John Woo**
Cinematography: Leung wing-gut
Editing: Peter Cheung, Yuan Tung-chun
Music: Joseph Koo
Cast: Jackie Chan (Tan Feng), Chang Chung (Zorro), Sammo Hung (Officer Tu Ching), James Tien (Shih Shao-Feng), John Woo (The Revolutionary)
Color
95 minutes

1976
PRINCESS CHANG PING/DINU HUA/PRINCESS CHEUNG PING
Golden Harvest
Producer: Raymond Chow
Director: **John Woo**
Screenplay: **John Woo**, based on the Cantonese opera by Tong Tik-sang
Cinematography: Cheung Yiu-jo
Editing: Peter Cheung
Production Design: Louis Sit
Music: Joseph Koo
Cast: Lung Kim-sung (Chow Shih Hsien), Mui Shuet-shi (Princess Chang Ping)
Color
102 minutes

1977
MONEY CRAZY/THE PILFERER'S PROGRESS/FA QUIAN HAN
Golden Harvest
Producer: Raymond Chow
Director: **John Woo** (as John J. S. Woo)

Screenplay: **John Woo** (as John J. S. Woo)
Cinematography: Tsin Yu
Editing: Chang Yau Chung (also credited as Peter Cheung, Chang Yau-chung or Cheung Yiu-chung)
Production Design: Louis Sit
Music: Chen Hsun-chi
Cast: Richard Ng (Dragon Ng), Ricky Hui (Poison), Angie Chiu, Lan Law (Mrs. Chang)
Color
92 minutes

1978
HELLO, LATE HOMECOMERS/HA LUO, YE GUI REN
Golden Harvest, Cinema City
Producers: Lau Tin-chi, Louis Sit, **John Woo**
Directors: Lau Tin-chi, Louis Sit, **John Woo**
Screenplay: Lau Tin-chi, Louis Sit, **John Woo**
Cast: Angel Chan, Fung Hark-on, Hoi San Lee, Louis Lo, Yik Ka

FOLLOW THE STAR/DA SHA XING YU XIAO MEI TOU/THE HULK AND THE LITTLE GIRL
Golden Harvest
Producer: Raymond Chow
Director: **John Woo**
Screenplay: T. C. Lao, **John Woo**
Cinematography: Chi Ming Chiang
Editing: Yau Chung Chang
Production Design: Louis Sit
Music: Hsun Chi Chen
Cast: Roy Chiao (Drunken Sheng), Rowena Cortes (Miss Chen), Fung Hark-on, Kuo Sheng (Thug #1), **John Woo** (Miss Chen's father)
Color
90 minutes

1980
FROM RICHES TO RAGS/MONEY TALK/QUIAN ZUO GUAI/IT'S ALL BECAUSE OF MONEY

Golden Harvest
Producer: Raymond Chow
Director: **John Woo**
Screenplay: **John Woo**
Cinematography: Bill Wong
Editing: Yau Chung Chang and Peter Cheung (a.k.a. Cheung Yiu-chung)
Music: Sam Hui
Cast: Jo Jo Chan (Jo Jo), Ricky Hui (Ricky), Johnny Koo (Fatso), Lam Ching-Ying (Kung Fu Hitman), Tong Ching, Yik Ka
Color
101 minutes

LAST HURRAH FOR CHIVALRY/HAO XIA
Golden Harvest
Producer: Raymond Chow
Director: **John Woo** (as John Y. S. Woo)
Screenplay: **John Woo** (as John Y. S. Woo)
Cinematography: Cheung Yiu-jo
Editing: Peter Cheung
Cast: Wei Pei, Liu Sung Jen, Liu Chiang , Wai Chu-xia
Color
102 minutes

1981
TO HELL WITH THE DEVIL/MO DENG TIAN SHI
Golden Harvest
Producers: Raymond Chow, Leonard Ho
Director: **John Woo**
Screenplay: Szeto Chuek-Hon, **John Woo**
Cinematography: Bill Wong
Editing: **John Woo**
Production Design: Alex Ma
Music: Goblin, Tang Siu-Lam
Cast: Chan Pak-cheung (Rocky), Fat Chung (The Devil), Paul Chun (Priest), Fung Shui-fan (Imp), Sye Hse (Peggy)
Color
88 minutes

LAUGHING TIMES/HUA JI SHI DAI
Cinema City Film Productions
Producer: Karl Maka
Director: **John Woo** (as Wu Hsiang-Fei)
Screenplay: **John Woo** and Raymond Wong
Cinematography: Ming Ho
Editing: Tony Chow
Cast: Hoi San Lee (Thug), Karl Maka (Master Thug), Dean Shek (The Tramp), Raymond Wong (Man Eating Bananas), Wong Wai
Color
94 minutes

1982
PLAIN JANE TO THE RESCUE/LAM AU CHUN NO. 3/BA CAI LIN YA ZHEN
Golden Harvest
Producers: Raymond Chow, Josephine Siao, Louis Sit
Director: **John Woo**
Screenplay: Chan Wang Lau, **John Woo**
Cinematography: Lau Hung-Chuen
Editing: Fan Kung-wing
Production Design: Alex Ma
Music: Tang Siu-Lam
Cast: Chen Sing (Chen), Charlie Cho (Sand's Son), Ricky Hui (Fang), Norman Law (Himself), Michael Lee (Sand)
Color
86 minutes

1984
THE TIME YOU NEED A FRIEND/XIAO JIANG
Cinema City
Producers: Karl Maka, Dean Shek, Raymond Wong, **John Woo**
Director: **John Woo**
Screenplay: Raymond Wong, **John Woo**
Cast: Lau Shui-Kei, Sun Yueh (Ku Ren), David Tao (Shen Bien)
Color
91 minutes

1984
RUN TIGER RUN/LIANG ZHI LAO HU
Cinema City
Producers: Karl Maka, Dean Shek, Raymond Wong, **John Woo**
Director: **John Woo**
Screenplay: Raymond Wong
Cast: Bin Bin (Babe Steak, Benny Shit), Frank Hsu, Teddy Robin Kwan (Teddy Shit), Pan Yin-tze (Miss Mary Lee), Ting Hsiao-hui (Mortal Lips), Tsui Hark (Grandpa Steak)
Color
91 minutes

1986
A BETTER TOMORROW/YING HUANG BOON SIK
Cinema City
Producers: Tsui Hark, **John Woo**
Director: **John Woo**
Screenplay: Chan Hing-Ka, Leung Suk-Wah and **John Woo**
Cinematography: Wong Wing-hang
Editing: Kam Ma, David Wu
Production Design: Lui Chi-leung
Music: Joseph Koo
Cast: Ti Lung (Ho Tse Sung), Leslie Cheung (Kit Sung), Chow Yun-Fat (Mark Gor/Mark Lee), Emily Chu (Jackie), Waise Lee (Shing), **John Woo** (detective)
Color
91 minutes

HEROES SHED NO TEARS/THE SUNSET WARRIOR/YING XIONG WEI LEI
Golden Harvest/Paragon Films
Producers: Peter Chan, John Woo and Raymond Chow
Director: **John Woo**
Screenplay: **John Woo**
Cinematography: Naragawa Kenichi
Editor: Peter Cheung

Music: Chung Siu Fung, Tang Siu-Lam
Cast: Eddy Ko (Chan Chung), Lam Ching Ying, Chen Yue Sang, Lau Chau Sang, Phillip Laffredo, Cecile Le Bailly
Color
82 minutes

1988
A BETTER TOMORROW II/YINGHUNG BUNSIK II
Cinema City
Producer: Tsui Hark
Associate Producers: Paul JQ Lee, Alawn Lai
Director: **John Woo**
Screenplay: Tsui Hark, **John Woo**
Cinematography: Wong Wing-hang
Editing: David Wu
Production Design: Andy Lee, Chi Fung Lok
Music: Joseph Koo, Lowell Lo
Cast: Dean Shek (Si Lung), Ti Lung (Ho Tse Sung), Leslie Cheung (Kit Sung/Billie), Chow Yun-Fat (Ken Gor/Mark Lee), Emily Chu (Jackie Sung)
Color
105 minutes

1989
THE KILLER/DIE XUE SHUANG XIONG
Golden Princess/Magnum Films
Producer: Tsui Hark
Director: **John Woo**
Screenplay: **John Woo**
Cinematography: Peter Pau, Wong Wing-hang
Editing: Fan Kung-wing
Music: Lowell Lo
Cast: Chow Yun-Fat (Joe in Cantonese/Jeffrey in English), Danny Lee (Insp. Li), Sally Yeh (Jennie), Kong Chu (Sydney), Kenneth Tsang (Sgt. Randy Chang)
Color
104 minutes

JUST HEROES/TRAGIC HEROES/YI DAN QUN YING
Magnum Films
Producers: Chang Cheh, David Chiang, Danny Lee, Tsui Hark
Directors: **John Woo**, Wu Ma
Screenplay: Tommy Hau, Ni Kuang
Cinematography: Cho Wai-ki, Yee Tung-lung
Editing: Choi Hung
Production Design: Ringo Cheung, Andy Lee
Music: Romeo Diaz, James Wong
Cast: Chen Kuan-tai (Tai), David Chiang (Wai), Chiu Lui, Stephen Chow (Jacky), Paul Chu (Tsou)
Color
97 minutes

1990
BULLET IN THE HEAD/DIE XUE JIE TOU
Golden Princess/John Woo Productions
Producers: Catherine Lau, Patrick Leung, John Woo
Director: John Woo
Screenplay: Janet Chun, Patrick Leung, John Woo
Cinematography: Wilson Chan, Ardy Lam, Chai Kittikum Som, Wong Wing-hang
Editing: John Woo, David Wu
Production Design: James Leung
Music: Romeo Diaz, James Wong
Cast: Tony Leung Chiu Wai (Ben), Jacky Cheung (Frank), Waise Lee (Paul), Simon Yam (Luke), Fennie Yuen (Jane), Yolinda Yam (Sally Yen)
Color
126 minutes (United Kingdom)
136 minutes (Hong Kong)

ONCE A THIEF/ZONG HENG SI HAI
Golden Princess/Milestone Pictures
Producers: Terence Chang, Linda Kuk
Director: **John Woo**
Screenplay: **John Woo**, Clifton Ko, Janet Chun
Director of Cinematography: Poon Hang-seng

Cameraman: William Yim
Editing: David Wu
Cast: Leslie Cheung (Jim), Chow Yun-Fat (Joe), Cherie Chung (Cherie), Kenneth Tsang (Chow)
Color
103 minutes

1992
HARD BOILED/HARD-BOILED/HOT-HANDED GOD OF COPS/LASHOU SHENTAN
Golden Princess/Milestones Pictures
Producers: Terence Chang, Linda Kuk
Associate producer: Amy Chin
Director: **John Woo**
Screenplay: Barry Wong, from the story by **John Woo**
Cinematography: Wong Wing-hang (a.k.a. Wang Wing-Heng)
Editing: Kai Kit-Wai, **John Woo**, David Wu
Stunt coordinator: Philip Kwok
Production Design: James Leung
Music: Michael Gibbs
Cast: Chow Yun-Fat (Tequila), Tony Leung (Tony), Teresa Mo (Teresa Chang), Philip Chan (Mr. Pang), Philip Kwok (Mad Dog), Anthony Wong (Johnny Wong), Bowie Lam (Ah Lung), Kwan Hoi-shan (Hui), **John Woo** (barman in jazz club)
Color
126 minutes

1993
HARD TARGET
Universal Studios
Producers: Terence Chang, Sean Daniel, Moshe Diamant, James Jacks, Daryl Kass, Chuck Pfarrer, Sam Raimi, Robert G. Tapert, Eugene Van Varenberg
Director: **John Woo**
Screenplay: Chuck Pfarrer
Cinematography: Russell Carpenter
Editing: Bob Murawski

Production Design: Phil Dagort
Music: Graeme Revell
Cast: Jean-Claude Van Damme (Chance Boudreaux), Lance Henriksen (Emil Fouchon), Yancy Butler (Natasha "Nat" Binder), Wilford Brimley (Uncle Douvee), Kasi Lemmons (Carmine Mitchell), Arnold Vosloo (Pik Van Cleaf)
Color
92 minutes

1996
BROKEN ARROW
Twentieth-Century Fox
Producers: Bill Badalato, Terence Chang, Joe Gareri, Christopher Godsick, Mark Gordon, Brad Lewis, Dwight H. Little, Michele Maples, Allison Lyon Segan
Director: **John Woo**
Screenplay: Graham Yost
Cinematography: Peter Levy
Editing: Joe Hutshing, Steve Mirkovich, John Wright
Production Design: Holger Gross
Music: Harry Gregson-Williams, Don Harper, Hans Zimmer
Cast: John Travolta (Maj. Vic Deakins), Christian Slater (Capt. Riley Hale), Samantha Mathis (Terry Carmichael), Delroy Lindo (Col. Max Wilkins), Bob Gunton (Pritchett), Frank Whaley (Giles Prentice), Howie Long (MSgt. Kelly)
Color
108 minutes

1997
FACE/OFF
Paramount Pictures
Producers: Terence Chang, Michael Colleary, Michael Douglas, Christopher Godsick, Raul Julia-Levy, Jonathan D. Krane, Jeff Levine, Barrie M. Osborne, David Permut, Steven Reuther, Mike Werb
Director: **John Woo**
Screenplay: Mike Werb, Michael Colleary
Cinematography: Oliver Wood

Editing: Steven Kemper, Christian Wagner
Production Design: Neil Spisak
Music: Andrew Farriss, Gavin Greenaway, Michael Hutchence, John Powell, Michael A. Reagan
Cast: John Travolta (Sean Archer/Castor Troy), Nicolas Cage (Castor Troy/Sean Archer), Joan Allen (Dr. Eve Archer), Alessandro Nivola (Pollux Troy), Gina Gershon (Sasha Hassler), Dominique Swain (Jamie Archer), Nick Cassavetes (Dietrich Hassler)
Color
139 minutes

2000
MISSION: IMPOSSIBLE II
Paramount Pictures
Producers: Terence Chang, Tom Cruise, Michael Doven, Paul Hitchcock, Amy Stevens, Paula Wagner
Director: **John Woo**
Screenplay: Robert Towne
Cinematography: Jeffrey L. Kimball
Editing: Tony Ciccone, Steven Kemper, Christian Wagner
Production Design: Thomas E. Sanders
Music: Klaus Badelt, Fred Durst, Lisa Gerrard, Kirk Hammett, James Hetfield, Jason Newsted, Lalo Schifrin, Lars Ulrich, Mel Wesson, Hans Zimmer, Rob Zombie
Cast: Tom Cruise (Ethan Hunt), Dougray Scott (Sean Ambrose), Thandie Newton (Nyah Nordoff-Hall), Ving Rhames (Luther Stickell), Richard Roxburgh (Hugh Stamp)
Color
123 minutes

2002
WINDTALKERS
MGM
Producers: Arthur Anderson, Terence Chang, C. O. Erickson, Tracie Graham-Rice, Caroline Macaulay, Alison R. Rosenzweig, John J. Smith, Richard Stenta, Stephen Traxler, **John Woo**
Director: **John Woo**

Screenplay: John Rice, Joe Batteer
Cinematography: Jeffrey L. Kimball
Editing: Jeff Gullo, Steven Kemper, Tom Rolf
Production Design: Holger Gross
Music: James Horner
Cast: Nicolas Cage (Sgt. Joe Enders), Adam Beach (Pvt. Ben Yahzee), Christian Slater (Sgt. Ox Henderson), Peter Stromare (Gunnery Sgt. Hjelmstad), Noah Emmerich (Pvt. Chick), Mark Ruffalo (Pvt. Pappas)
Color
134 minutes (theatrical)
153 minutes (director's cut)

2003
PAYCHECK
Paramount Pictures/DreamWorks SKG
Producers: Arthur Anderson, Terence Chang, John Davis, Michael Hackett, Keiko Koyama, Stratton Leopold, Caroline Macaulay, David Solomon, **John Woo**
Director: **John Woo**
Screenplay: Dean Georgaris
Cinematography: Larry Blanford, Jeffrey L. Kimball
Editing: Christopher Rouse, Kevin Stitt
Production Design: William Sandell
Music: John Powell, James McKee Smith, John Ashton Thomas
Cast: Ben Affleck (Michael Jennings), Aaron Eckhart (James Rethrick), Uma Thurman (Dr. Rachel Porter), Paul Giamatti (Shorty), Colm Feore (John Wolfe)
Color
119 minutes

As Producer Only
SUPER CITIZEN (1985)
LOVE, LONE FLOWER (1985)
THE PEACE HOTEL/HEPING FANDIAN (1995)
SOMEBODY UP THERE LIKES ME/LANG MAN FENG BAO (1996)
THE REPLACEMENT KILLERS (1998)

THE BIG HIT (1998)
BULLETPROOF MONK (2003)

As Actor Only
THE THIRTY MILLION DOLLAR RUSH/HENG CAI SAN QIAN WAN (1985)
STARRY IS THE NIGHT/GAM YE SING GWONG CHAAN LAAN (1988)
REBEL FROM CHINA/YONG CHUANG TIAN XIA (1990)
PARTY OF A WEALTHY FAMILY/HAOMEN YEYAN (1991)
TWIN DRAGONS/SHUANG LONG HUI (1992)
TASK FORCE/YIT HUET JUI KEUNG (1997)

As Director for Television
ONCE A THIEF (the TV series) (1996)
BLACKJACK (1998)
LOST IN SPACE (2004)

JOHN WOO
INTERVIEWS

John Woo: Early Oral History

HONG KONG FILM ARCHIVE/2001

I AM NG YU-SUM. My actual date of birth should be around the end of October in 1946. When I was young, my family was so poor that I could not attend primary school (first grade) until I was nine. Nine was well beyond the official age to start primary school and for that reason, my mother changed my birth date to the end of September in 1948. On the other hand, my family was quite traditional and they used the lunar calendar to count days.

I was born in Guangzhou, but my family's hometown [also translated as "ancestral home"—ed.] is Pingnan city, Guangxi province. I am a Guangxian. I remember when I was five, my family moved from mainland China to Hong Kong. Due to poverty, my dad suffered from tuberculosis and my whole family lived in the wooden sheds at Shek Kip Mei. In those days, a lot of people in Hong Kong were actually not doing too well either, many of whom came from mainland China.

In the '50s, there was a big fire, the so-called "Shek Kip Mei Big Fire." That fire burned up the whole area of wooden sheds, including our house. For one year afterward, we lived on the streets as homeless people. I remember many people had similar experiences as we did, and we all lived in temporary tents on Pak Ho Street.

Our living was supported by the Social Welfare Department and the churches. As a result, we waited until the government built the first

From the Hong Kong Film Archive oral history interview with John Woo (2001), www.lcsd.gov.hk/CE/CulturalService/HKFA/. Reprinted by permission. Translated from Cantonese by Annisa Lee, with fact checking by Law Kar.

temporary housing projects, commonly called the temporary two-story shelters, before we had a chance to live in a building.

Although we were very poor, our parents still hoped that I could receive a good and proper education. Unfortunately, there were no opportunities around. Finally, I was lucky to get help from the church. Through the help of the Chinese Christian Church, an American family sponsored my study. I was grateful to them. Since I was already nine years old then, my mother asked me to take off two years from my age when I reported to school so that I could have a chance to study in the first grade in primary school. My school was called Heep Woh Primary School, and it was located on Prince Edward Road. It was a very good school. The teachers took very good care of us and treated us as family. The American family also sent us money and presents every Christmas. I remember I was very happy then. Due to the fact that there were English lessons taught by English teachers who had problems memorizing Chinese names, which are also hard to pronounce, my English teacher suggested to me to have an English name. Since I was a Christian myself and I admired John the Baptist, I chose John as my English name.

When I was young, my family was very poor, but my mother still loved to go to watch movies. Every time she went to see movies, she would take me along. Ironically, my dad [a teacher—ed.] did not like movies because he thought that movies were all fake. He assumed that only literature was official and only life itself is real. Obviously, my mom ignored his theories. I remember that my mom loved to watch Cantonese and Western films, and every time we followed her to the cinema. In those days, each parent was allowed to bring one child to the cinema. Sometimes when our parents had no free time, other children and I would wait at the entrance of the cinema and follow others' coattails to get into the cinema. Or, we would beg others to pretend that we were their kids in hopes that they would take us into the cinema. We pretended to be others' kids to gain our access into the cinema. Sometimes we met some kind people and they were willing to take us into the cinema. After we got into the theater . . . those cinema attendants were very mean in those days and they always inspected inside the cinema with their flashlights. Therefore, after we entered the cinema, we needed to take care of ourselves and find a place to hide. Some of us would hide under the seats and some beside the bathroom because whenever the attendant caught us, they would kick us out of the cinema.

I remember one time, I carried my brother on my back and followed someone's coattail to the cinema. . . . In those days, I was already very picky. I did not like to sit in the front; I only loved to sit in the balcony. That time, I remember it was in the Palace Cinema. The dress circle in that cinema was situated on the second floor. At that time, I carried my brother on my back and my hand was holding someone else's coattail. . . . While I was walking up the stairs, an attendant caught me. I therefore told him that I was that man's son and the attendant challenged me that I did not look like that man. He then slapped my face a few times and pushed me and my brother down the stairway and chased us out of the cinema. [Even though we were chased out], many times, I still peeked through the cracks into the cinema. I liked movies to a point that I became quite addicted. Not only I loved to watch Cantonese movies, I also loved to watch musicals, Western movies, and cops/crime films—almost every genre of film.

Among all, my favorite films were musicals. Due to the very harsh environment I lived in, I often felt like I was living in hell and there were a lot of unjust and sinful things happening around me. At the same time, there were many protests and violent outbursts in the society. Too many disappointing events and all these made me feel that life was hopeless. In those days, there were two places I often went to: the church and the cinema. Whenever I met something unhappy, or when my mood was bad, feeling lonely and disappointed, I would love to go to the church. The church had become like my refuge and it made me feel calm. I also learned a lot of things there. Another place was the cinema. Every time when I watched a musical, I would be fascinated by the world created by it. In musicals, the songs were good to listen to and the story and characters were perfect.

I remember the first musical I saw was *The Wizard of Oz* starring Judy Garland. That film brought me immense happiness and hope. Even today, I still deeply remember that film. Besides this, I also liked many, many other musicals starring Gene Kelly and Fred Astaire. Besides musicals, I also liked to watch Western and crime/gangster films, especially the latter, which influenced me the most because I had been living in a world that was filled with crime and injustice. I had also experienced different scenarios of life and death and even witnessed some gangster fights in the streets. Because of that, I personally was interested in the crime and gangster movies. I admired Humphrey Bogart and some French films. Just because I loved movies when I was young, I became a temporary extra after I graduated from primary school. My roles were usually a shoeshine boy, a Japanese soldier or a street child wanderer. But I thought it was really fun and I loved to hide behind the props and peeked at my admired stars and saw how the directors made films. [Friend Law Kar remembers Woo worked as an extra on King Hu's *Sons of Good Earth* (1965), a Shaw Brothers film, when Woo was seventeen years old—ed.]

I remembered when I was almost eleven, I already liked to use glass . . . and used calligraphy pens to draw some visuals on glass. I have tried to draw General Kwan [from the historical novel *Three Kingdoms* or *Romance of the Three Kingdoms*], some Western cowboys and cartoon characters such as the Monkey King on glass. I would cover my whole body with a blanket and make the surrounding area really dark like the theater. After that, I would use my left hand to hold the glass and then use the flashlight to shine on the glass. The figure on the glass will be projected on the wall. I would then move the flashlight back and forth or up and down to create an effect of movement of the characters on the wall. They were sometimes big, sometimes small, sometimes on the right, sometimes on the left. I felt like I was watching movies when they were moving. It was really fun and I loved that trick for quite a long time.

After I graduated from primary school, I started secondary school at Heep Woh Secondary School. Heep Woh Secondary School was operated by the Lutheran Church. I really liked that church, and I became a member of the Lutheran Church. It was a very good school. Not only did it emphasize cultivating knowledge in students, it also stressed the disciplines of conduct, wisdom, unity, and beauty. The school and especially the church organized a lot of activities, including classical and folk dances, music and literature classes. By that time, my first dream was to become a pastor. I had never thought of becoming a director in the future. I received a lot of help from the church since I was a child. And I adored and worshiped the universal love of Jesus and his philosophy.

I admired the wholehearted devotion of pastors and their love and kindness in helping others. That was a great spirit. Therefore, I hoped that one day I could return the favor to society and all those people who had helped me before. I also wanted to help those in need. In those days, there were a lot of injustices in the society and many conditions of inequality of wealth distribution. There were a lot of people needing help and comfort. However, later I discovered my preferences were more on the artistic side. I liked arts such as music, drawing, poetry, and films. Therefore, none of my friends, including myself, believed that I could concentrate on the study of theology. Many advised me to give up the dream of becoming a pastor and continue my study in the arts.

At school, I participated in a drama club and I really liked to act, and I dreamed of becoming a movie star. Therefore I decided to become an actor and I started as a theatrical actor. I did a few small theatrical performances and I directed one or two theatrical projects. I acted as a rebellious teenager in a number called *The Parents' Heart*. I was like James Dean and the story was like the prodigal son. I thought I did a great job but my best acting, according to my memory, was in the *Ching Dynasty Feud*. I acted as Lee Lin Ying, a eunuch. That character was easy to act and was likable.

When I was in secondary school, my most admired Mandarin directors were Chang Cheh, King Hu (Hu Chin Chuan), and Lung Kong. Actually in those days, I loved to watch all kinds of films except Cantonese operas. Since I liked to watch the kung fu movies, I therefore particularly liked Chang Cheh and King Hu. Director Lung Kong made a few good films. Besides *The Story of a Discharged Prisoner*, he made a few films regarding social issues. He is a very advanced, skillful director who emphasized inner thoughts/internal emotions. For Western films, I liked to watch French and Japanese films. I especially admired directors Jean-Pierre Melville, François Truffaut, and Federico Fellini. I also liked Japanese gangster movies such as those made by Akira Kurosawa, Kobayashi Masaki, Kon Ichikawa, and Teruo Ishii. The ones who influenced me the most were Jean-Pierre Melville and Akira Kurosawa. Regarding American films, I like those made by Sam Peckinpah and Stanley Kubrick.

Besides movies and theatres, I also liked to read *Zhongguo Xue Sheng Zhou Bao*, the *Chinese Student Weekly*. It had influenced me deeply and helped me most significantly. It had inspired me a lot, not only about life, literature, but also about films. I remembered when I was sixteen, I wrote my first article, which was published in the *Chinese Student Weekly*. The topic was "killing a dog." The reason for me to write the article was because I lived in the government projects and I had a lot of neighbors who had killed dogs and sold dog meat. They usually killed the dogs in public places and I felt that such acts were very cruel. Therefore I decided to describe the process and adopted a compassionate way to illustrate the nightmare with painful feelings. I was very happy that the article was published and because of that periodical, I began to truly understand movies.

When I was nearing graduation, I reckoned that only films could blend all kinds of arts together. Before that, I had learned about music and guitar, drawing, writing poetry, and dancing. But I was not successful in any of them. I thought it was because I was not consistent and I had not found one skill that could completely express my inner thoughts. Later, after I knew more about films, I realized that only films could bring all different artistic elements together and express thoroughly my feelings. As a result, I decided to concentrate my efforts to learn about filmmaking.

I barely graduated from high school, and originally I wanted to go abroad to study filmmaking. That was due to the fact that there was no film school in Hong Kong. However, my mother told me that she was not able to afford my study. My family was still not doing too well in those days. My dad had lung problems and he died when I was sixteen. My mother left to work on her own in a quarry bay. She cut stones and moved the stones in construction sites. She also worked as a seamstress and seller on the street to support me and my brother and sister. Of course, I was grateful to my mom and I understood her situation. I could not continue to study filmmaking. The only method remaining was to watch more films and learn more from watching films. I tried to continue my university study in a cinema.

In those days, Hong Kong was doing really well. The best thing was I could see any movie anytime, anywhere. The movies were from all over the world. Not only were those commercial films, I was able to see a lot of artistic films, such as the French avant-garde films, the realism films from Italy, and many good movies from Japan. They were great films made by Akira Kurosawa and Ozu Yasujiro. I had also many chances to watch

American films. Besides watching films, my best help was joining the College Cine Club [sometimes referred to as University Life Film Club—ed.] organized by the *Chinese Student Weekly*. I really appreciated that opportunity. . . . I was really grateful to the club manager of the *Chinese Student Weekly*, Mr. Lam Yuk Han. He also started the Chuan Kin Experimental College.

[Editor's note: The Chuan Kin Experimental College is not a formal educational institution, but "rather an experimental one," says Law Kar. It applied "the sort of studying/teaching method similar to the Western 'teach-ins' of the '70s," he explains. "Students were not required to have proper qualifications to be enrolled and paid just a nominal tuition fee to take any course."]

I remembered in those days, he started the Chuan Kin Experimental College at Dorset Street, Kowloon Tong. There were many different classes such as movies, dramas, literature, drawing, poetry, etc., in the college. . . . Different people taught the classes and they allowed all young people who had a heart to learn literature and moviemaking to have a chance to learn something there.

The days in the College Cine Club were the happiest days in my life. Not only did I get to know a lot of friends who loved movies, I also learned a lot of true knowledge about movies from them. I really appreciated my good friends Wong Chi-keung [also known as film critic Sek Kei—ed.], Ada Lok, Joe Chan, Law Kar, Lin Nien-tong, Chiu Tak Hak, Chan Keung Yeung, and Chan Kai Yat, especially Luk Nai, Law Kar, and Kam Ping Hing who wrote a lot of movie-related articles and translated much film literature and criticism for the *Chinese Student Weekly*. Through their articles, I got to learn more about cinema theory and many other things about films. Not only did I get to know more about my friends, I made some experimental films with Wong Chi-keung and Chiu Tak Hak. I was really happy then. Although we were not rich, all of us were addicted to films. We would try our best to find a job and then used all our savings to buy film. In those days, we used 16 mm and 8 mm film to make experimental movies. Whoever had money bought the film and that person would be the producer. After we had a producer, whoever then wrote a script would become the scriptwriter. Wong Chi-keung or I would be the directors. After all, we had so much fun together and we made experimental films together.

In those days, I made around four to five so-called experimental films. However, my productions were not mature in those days. I remember one film called *Accidentally* and another one called *The Evil One*. My favorite one is *Death Knot* that I made with Wong Chi-keung. *Death Knot* was directed by Wong Chi-keung [again, Sek Kei—ed.] and I was the screenwriter and producer for that film. It was a playful story and Wong was outstanding in his cinematography. I liked his camerawork. At the same time, his emotions were very intense. Maybe it was due to his skills in painting and superb knowledge in literature because his visual design was appealing.

I also appreciated many good friends such as Ada Lok and Sai Sai. They frequently translated some French literature and knowledge about films and introduced all French New Wave films to us. Because of them, I got to know about French movies. In those days, I remembered I deeply fell in love with Jean-Pierre Melville's films, such as *Le Samourai* and *Red Circle* (*Le Cercle Rouge*). I also like François Truffaut and all the films made by the French New Wave directors. In those days, the French New Wave movies had not only changed the cinematic world, but they also influenced me a lot. I had a feeling that I could do what the French New Wave directors did. Therefore, I would say, the inspiration they gave me was really great. Honestly, I thought the Hong Kong movies were not too good in those days and they had many problems such as plagiarism and they needed much improvement. I was thinking in my heart, that if we could have the spirit of the French directors, we could change the Hong Kong film industry. I believed that was a viable method and so I was determined to become a director because I hoped to contribute to the movie industry in Hong Kong. Except . . . I worked as an assistant of secretary Joe Chan in the College Cine Club, and learned from him the essence of film literature. Chan was talented in writing and his skills were very good. Even now, I am still mesmerized by my good old days in the club and my friends there. Besides the people I just mentioned, there were also Tai Tin and Wu Kuk Yan. It was the best time in my life and it impacted my life the most.

When I was around nineteen, twenty years old, I wanted to join the filmmaking industry, but it was a very difficult time to enter into the movie world when you had no connections. The film industry was still very conservative in those days, it was operated like a family business. Therefore, if you did not have anyone to introduce or recommend you, nor did you have any relationship with the insiders, it was very difficult to get into that world. But I was very lucky, I met Dr. Sun Kar Man from the Cathay Organization.

At that time, Sun Kai Man was the production manager of the Cathay Organization. He studied film in Italy and was a movie producer with a lot of foresight and creativity. He was the first educated young man who was willing to be open-minded and who loved filmmaking, so he was also the first person willing to invite people like us into the film industry. At that time he invited several friends such as Lam Lin Tung and Kam Bing Hing to be screenwriters, assistant directors, and artistic designers in the Cathay Organization.

He was also a man with a mission: He wanted to bring changes to Mandarin films so that there will be a fresh look, a new era. Because of this I was fortunate enough to become a log keeper at the Cathay Organization. I was very happy just to get a job. However after I joined the Cathay Organization, I saw many bad things about Hong Kong moviemaking; for example, sloppy production and many other undesirable practices. . . . Then, I threw myself into learning about filmmaking. I paid a lot of attention to how the cameramen and workers design and make arrangements for various shots, and I was particularly interested in how the director directed a scene. When I was twenty-one, I finally had the opportunity to become an assistant director. I remember the first time I was assistant director the film was *Little Apple*, co-directed by Cheung Sum and Mr. Wong Ping. In the process of working as an assistant director I gained a deeper understanding of the overall production of a movie. At that time, I was very happy, but unfortunately after the film was finished, the Cathay Organization went out of business and we again became unemployed.

I happened to make the acquaintance of Mr. Chiu Gang Jian through the introduction of a friend. He was an outstanding screenwriter from Taiwan who had made experimental films. He was also a movie fanatic. At that time he was, I think, the head of the screenwriters department in Shaw Brothers. We became hooked to each other immediately and became good friends. I was a great admirer of Mr. Chang Cheh and liked his films very much. Besides having this spirit of the loyalty and heroism, his films were also very personal. At the same time he was the innovator of many film techniques so I was very eager to learn from him and take part in his work. Because Mr. Chiu Gang Jian had written several screenplays for Chang Cheh, they were also good friends. I got to know Chang Cheh through Chiu Gang Jian.

Chang Cheh was not only an excellent director, he was also a *true* intellectual. Besides being a very creative moviemaker, he was very willing to give rookies a chance. After I became a member of Chang Cheh's team I was at first the log keeper and the second assistant director. Then after I had worked for him for over a year, I became good friends with actors whom I admired such as Jiang Dawei [also known as David Chiang or John Chiang—ed.] and Ti Lung.

To go back to the New Wave of French films, besides the films of François Truffaut, I also loved the musical dramas of Jacques Demy such as *The Umbrellas of Cherbourg* and *The Young Girls of Rochefort* or *Les Demoiselles De Rochefort*. These films taught me what romance and love were. The element of romanticism is very strong in his films. In his so-called French romanticism, besides poeticism there is also a touch of melancholy. In a nutshell, his films are romantic, they have love and a touch of melancholy. Also, the songs and music in his films are quite perfect. When I watched his movies, I felt I was reading a poem. So, not only did I like his movies, but I was also very much influenced by them.

As to why I like the films of Federico Fellini, his movies are very rich. Every image was like a painting and the message of every image was like a portrayal of his inner world. At the same time, his techniques and the use of images made a great impact on me, especially in the design of visual effects.

I also like François Truffaut very much, because his films are so full of love and every film of his is a new experiment. His movie techniques are full of freedom, very bold and uninhibited.

As for American films, I personally like Sam Peckinpah and Stanley Kubrick. *The Wild Bunch* by Sam Peckinpah is one of my favorite westerns. I liked the way he used the slow motion shooting. It conveys an extra sense of romanticism. Of course I like the films of Akira Kurosawa because his films are often full of the spirit of humanitarianism. Another thing is the great impact he makes when he describes the loyalty and heroic spirit of the character. So, I like the series of heroic warrior films he made such as *The Seven Samurai, Yojimbo,* and *High and Low*. Almost all of his works are equally outstanding.

I learned a lot when I was assistant director to Chang Cheh. Actually he had two to three assistant directors. I guess I was the second assistant director. Actually, I was pretty lazy when I worked for him because I didn't like to go to the scene of the shooting. I often slipped away to the editing room to do the jobs that came after the shooting. I felt I could learn more in these areas and enrich my experience in the practical side of moviemaking. Chang Cheh had a lot of trust in me and let me be in charge of the "after shooting" jobs such as editing, dubbing, etc. The way he filmed was rather like the directors of the West: he would shoot from many different angles and made good use of his shots. But that also meant that editing would take more time and effort. Through working with the editors I learned many kinds of moviemaking techniques and got to know how to make the best use of shots to create different types of atmosphere and feelings.

Though I seldom went to the scenes of the actual shooting, whenever I did go, I liked to hang out with Jiang Dawei, Wong Chung, Ti Lung, etc. On several occasions when I demonstrated how to play a scene to the actors, Jiang Dawei, etc. would say I looked like I had a lot of acting potential. So he and Ti Lung often encouraged me to take up acting.

I remember once Chang Cheh was making a movie called *Young People* and he needed a second male supporting actor to play the part of the villain. Jiang Dawei and Ti Lung urged Chang Cheh to let me play the part. But Chang Cheh was noncommittal. So Jiang Dawei and Ti Lung arranged a tryout for me. But just when everything was ready and the shooting was ready to start, Chang Cheh came over and put a stop to it. Jiang Dawei and his friends were not happy and insisted that I was perfect for the part, so why wasn't I given the chance? Then Chang Cheh said to them, "It is better for Ng Yu-Sum to concentrate on directing."

This remark of his became an incentive for me to pursue a career in directing. At that time I was not sure where my abilities lay and what direction I should take in the film industry. Chang Cheh is usually a rather reticent person but he was very observant. He could tell that I could not be a good actor but I could be a good director. I am extremely grateful to him.

Besides learning a lot from Chang Cheh, I also learned many things from the two kung fu advisers Tong Kai and Lau Kar Leung. We admired them so much, because not only did they improve the way Hong Kong action films were made, but they also came up with numerous new methods of expression and techniques. They were the pioneers who drew from Western boxing techniques and Japanese action skills to blend with Chinese kung fu and created a new mode of action techniques.

Not only did I appreciate the beauty and technique of the action sequences Tong Kai and Lau Kar Leung designed, I was also inspired by them. As a result, when I later made action movies I paid a lot of attention to the design of movements. I learned dancing before, so although I never learned kung fu, I was fascinated by dancing because I learned classical dances, folk dances, and tango, etc., when I was in high school. I even once taught dancing in church. I was very familiar with the beauty of dance, its romantic aura and techniques. When I made action movies I would blend Chinese kung fu with dance (like Lau Kar Leung did) and create a new mode of aesthetically pleasing movements.

When I was Chang Cheh's assistant director I never dreamed that I could become a director so soon, because I was hoping to gain more practical experience. I was not afraid of waiting for ten years or so, or even waiting 'til I was old, before I became a director. It did not matter to me. But towards the end of my time with Chang Cheh I began to feel some intangible pressure on me. At that time, Chang Cheh made many films. He could make up to four films a year and at the same time he would co-direct with other people. So he told all the assistant directors and his co-directors to give regular reports to me.

On the other hand, we would often view films together. When we found a scene that needed to be re-shot I would be the one to convey the bad news to the people concerned. Inadvertently, I became the detestable go-between. Under too much pressure and too many such incidents, I felt I could not bear it anymore. So as not to give a wrong impression or even give rise to misunderstanding, I handed in my resignation to him. Nevertheless, I was very grateful to him for allowing me to learn so much about filmmaking; he gave me a real understanding of the spirit of loyalty and heroism of Chinese movies.

I left Chang Cheh when I was twenty-three, twenty-four and joined an independent film company called Fu Kwok. At that time Yuen Woo Ping and I were the assistant directors and log keepers.

After that I was the assistant director for several films. At that time, I was a bit lost—I did not know whether I should direct my energies towards making artistic films or make commercial movies. I had a lot of inner struggles concerning this. In the end it came to my mind that both artistic and commercial films were, after all, films, so even in a commercial film it is possible to do something new or convey new messages. In the same way, one can create all kinds of moods in a commercial film. So, I realized that no matter what kind of film it was, as long as I had the opportunity to make it, the result was the same. Ever since then, I was not picky anymore and so long as the opportunity offered itself, I would do my best to learn and develop my talents to the best of my ability.

In 1973, I did not know which way to turn. I had a good friend Wong Hoi Yi who worked together with me at Shaw Brothers. He was the nephew of director Bao Hok Lai [credited in Shaw Brothers films as Pao Hsueh Li—ed.] and he had a good friend Lui Chi Ho who was very interested in investing in the movie industry. Mr. Lui provided financial backing for Wong Hoi Yi to start an independent movie company. So Wong became both the boss and the producer. On the other hand, he was not very familiar with producing a movie so he got me involved in the hope that the two of us could co-direct a film.

This was a big break for me and I am very grateful to my friend and also to Mr. Lui who was willing to invest in a movie under such conditions. I was about twenty-six, twenty-seven at that time. That movie was called *The Young Dragons*, an action film set in the early years of the Republic of China. The production cost was actually not very high, but we still managed to get Mr. Ni Kuang to write the screenplay for us. I am very grateful to him.

John Woo: Movie by Movie, 1968 to 1990

ROBERT K. ELDER / 2004

ROBERT K. ELDER: *The goal here is to talk about each one of your early films, because as an American audience, we don't have access to or know much about your work from 1968 to 1990. To start off, I just got done watching your short film* The Evil One, *the first film you directed and starred in.*

JOHN WOO: Ohhhh . . . that was bad. It was fun, a lot of fun—but it wasn't a great one. Kind of like a practice. Not a real experiment. I just tried to show a concept but I didn't experiment with anything.

Q: *For people who haven't seen it, what was the plot?*

JW: It's a portrait of romance that [my character] has. There's a little romance. It was romantic memories. I just met a girl I really loved and tried to keep her to myself. And then I didn't realize she also had her own life. We met coincidently and then separated in silence. Sometimes you really want to love somebody but it's all . . . fate.

Q: *This was your first time working as an actor in front of the camera. What was that experience like?*

JW: Yeah, yeah. It was the first time. It was pretty fun. Actually I was in love with that girl in the film but she didn't know. She was the daughter of the minister.

Q: *I've seen references that this film was in 1968 . . . but when did you go to the Cathay Organization in Hong Kong?*

Printed with permission by Robert K. Elder <www.robelder.com>.

JW: I worked in the studio when I was twenty years old [in 1966]. [*The Evil One*] was 1968.

Q: *You do realize, that short film you just described as* The Evil One, *is called* Accidentally *on the* Hard Boiled *Criterion DVD?*
JW: Hmmmm. Maybe I gave them the wrong information.

Q: *So was this filmmaking after or before or during your involvement with Chinese Student Weekly?*
JW: I joined the film club, what they called the University Life Film Club [commonly known as College Cine Club—ed.]. So I joined them and we studied film and watched artistic films and made 16 mm or Super8 films. Then I also wrote some poems and some short articles for the newspaper.

Q: *How many of those early, experimental films did you make?*
JW: I made four. The order goes *The Evil One, Learning by Doing, Accidentally,* and *Death Knot*.

Q: *Were all of those made in 1968?*
JW: '68, '69, and '70.

Q: *Now, there's another experimental short Law Kar told me about called* The Secret Killer. *Is that one we forgot about?*
JW: Yeah, maybe. I forgot about it. I don't quite remember that one. Law Kar, maybe he knows better than me. We worked together on some little things.
[Law Kar says: "What I know about *The Secret Killer* is that it really exists and I have the credits of the film . . . they were handwritten by John Woo himself in the late 1960s along with credits of his other experimental films. I've not seen the film and have not seen any descriptions of it. . . ." —ed.]

Q: *We talked before about* The Evil One, *but can you talk to me about* Learning by Doing?
JW: *Learning by Doing* is a pretty violent story about an intellectual kid. He had nothing to do with this world—very quiet and innocent.

Somehow he got influenced by a bad person and learned every bad thing from him—how to kill people. The bad person was like the devil, the most evil thing in the world. At the end, the young kid ended up turning what he had learned against the evil, to kill the evil.

Q: *What was after* Learning by Doing?
JW: *Accidentally*. It was made while I was working at Shaw Brothers. [In the movie], I meet a girl when I'm crossing the road. I'm in love with her at the first sight. It's a pretty short moment. I look around and see her, with the camera turning 360 degrees. We turn 360, the camera comes back to me and she's gone. . . .

The last one was called *Death Knot*. I was the writer and producer for that, directed by Sek Kei.

Q: *When that movie lists you as co-director, that's incorrect?*
JW: Yes. I just produced and wrote it, but I didn't direct it. It was directed by Sek Kei. It was a pretty fun thing, a very different thing. It was about a young guy. He had a nightmare—he was being chased by evil, and evil had never let him go. Evil was kinda like a symbol, kind of like a conqueror.

And he was in love with another beautiful girl, but the beautiful girl never exists. It's kind of like a man who is confused between homosexual and normal sex. It's between the evil and the angel—that kind of thing. It's hard to explain. But actually, the topic wasn't about the homosexual theme. It was just good versus evil.

Q: *Was homosexuality an explicit theme?*
JW: No, it just felt like it. I didn't make a homosexual movie.

Q: *In 1966 you were twenty, but you didn't direct until 1973, so tell me about the chronology between the short films and when you first started working at age nineteen at the Cathay Organization?*
JW: When I was about nineteen, twenty years old, I worked with the Cathay Organization as a supervisor and as assistant director.

Q: *How did you get your foot in the door there?*
JW: The chairman [Law Kar says "production manager" is a more exact title—ed.], Dr. Sun Kar Man was the first one who had studied film in

Italy. So he had great knowledge of movies and he was so open. He was the first one who opened the door then advised us—a kind of intellectual film person—into the business. So they hired a few of my friends. My group of friends made experimental films together, intellectual films. Some of them became assistant directors, a screenwriter, film director and I worked as a supervisor and assistant director.

Q: *What was the name of your friend that got you in?*
JW: The friend of mine is now a film critic, Sek Kei, and Law Kar. Sek Kei and Law Kar and Chiu Tak Huk. Chiu Tak Huk is in France right now. So I worked for the Cathay Organization for a couple of years and then they closed down because they made a lot of failed movies. They couldn't make any more money so that's why they had to close down.

Then in 1971, I had the opportunity to meet my mentor, Chang Cheh. A friend of mine, he was also the screenwriter called Chow Chang Chen, and he recommended me to Chang Cheh. I worked for him as an assistant director for three years. After I worked for several of his movies, I learned [a lot]. I was greatly influenced from his work. I admired his martial arts movies, *One-Armed Swordsman*, part one [1967] and part two [*One-Armed Swordsman Returns*, 1969]. He got famous from those films. *The Assassin* and *The Boxer from Shantung* [too].

Then after that in 1973, a friend of mine, Peter Wong—he also was an assistant director—got financing for a very low budget independent film and he invited me as a co-director. It was a kind of a typical kung fu movie, *Farewell Buddy*. Since I was so young, a lot of people didn't feel good about me. Some people even said in the newspaper, "This young guy has no experience. He only had a pretty short period working for a studio." And they didn't think I could make a movie. This was in 1973, I was about twenty-six, twenty-seven at the time. I was pretty young, the only young director in Hong Kong. At that time, the average age for a director was from forty-five to sixty-five, seventy.

But when I shot the film, even though it was still a stereotypical kind of kung fu movie, for a drama sequence, the love story, I used a similar technique from my first experimental film, *The Evil One*.

The story was about a man and a woman in love. Somehow they got separated. The beautiful woman was captured by the bad guy. Though they were living in different worlds, they still thought about each other.

They were missing each other. [But] somehow they did similar things in separate places. Like when I shot the main character, he was thinking of her while he's putting his hand on a flowerpot. Then I cut to the girl, who was putting her hand on a flowerpot. The girl has some sort of movement and then we cut to the young man who is also continuing her movement—using intercutting for an emotional touch. And actually, it was from my first experimental film.

In my first experimental film, when a girl disappeared, I intercut [my character] thinking of her, then cut to the flower. What I had done for the experimental film was very useful. That kind of technique was pretty unusual for a Hong Kong kung fu movie, only that little part. But after the movie finished, it was abandoned.

Q: *Because it was too violent, right?*
JW: Because of violence, there were so many rumors about it. But then we sold the movie to Golden Harvest. After the chairman had seen it, all of a sudden I got a call from the boss who called me for a meeting. The chairman and the president from the studio saw the movie and loved it. Then one of the chairmen, Mr. Leonard Ho (Ho Guan Chuen), said to me what they liked about the movie was the way I shot the romantic moments, the intercutting with the two different [characters], that little touch. . . . He thought it was very unusual for a kung fu movie. Also they had prepared a three-year director contract for me at Golden Harvest and then they asked me to sign it. I had to sign it right away because I was broke and didn't know my future. I didn't know what to do. I slept in someone's office at night and was wandering in the street at daytime. No food, no money. It was lucky.

The original name [of the film] was *Farewell Buddy*, but Golden Harvest changed the name to *The Young Dragons*.

Q: *Your co-director was Peter Wong, but why were you given sole credit?*
JW: The studio found I was the one who actually directed the whole movie, so they only used my name. After that, they gave us more money to reshoot some scenes, some of the action sequences and then they could pass the censors. Later, [it] became history.

Q: *This movie is famous for two reasons. One, you hired Jackie Chan to design some of the fight sequences. . . .*
JW: He was the stunt coordinator for that film.

Q: *What was that like? Where did you find him?*
JW: We knew each other before I made the movie. I always liked his work. He was such a hardworking guy and always had some good ideas. At the time he liked to imitate Bruce Lee. The way he fought, his choreography was pretty much like Bruce's action. Besides that, I also liked him. I worked with him on *The Manchurian*, [in which] he was one of the main characters. I was the assistant director for that film so we actually worked together in a film before *The Young Dragons*.

Q: *This film was famous for one other thing . . . the villain had a special glove. Can you tell me about that?*
JW: Actually that was my idea; the idea came from those motorcycle gangs, they're usually wearing those gloves but without the needles. I added needles, really sharp needles, on the glove. It was something to show the bad guy's evilness, [how] that kind of thing really hurts people. That also was the [central] reason the movie was abandoned. The people from the censorship [board] said that young people could learn from it, so that's why the Cathay Organization abandoned it.

Q: *They were afraid other kids would make gloves with razor blades and nails?*
JW: Yeah, yeah. . . .

Q: *What was that experience like? You're a young, hot director, 26, you have a whole crew? What's that like as a 26-year-old?*
JW: Of course I was extremely excited, but I also had a lot of difficulty making the film. The first thing was, like I said, a lot of people couldn't sign me. People said I was too young to be a film director. A lot of people doubted me, my abilities to direct a film.

Another thing was at the time, for the Hong Kong film [industry], everyone [shot movies] in a very simple way. There were no DPs [directors of photography], no production designers, no costume designers either. We were a very small group, so we had to figure out everything by ourselves. We only had a cameraman and a lighting man. The cameraman told the lighting man how to light. For the costumes, we just hired a guy who could make the costumes—we had to pick the color and the style. We didn't have a production designer. We only got a set dresser, so we had to find the real old temple, old house from the countryside. We could only afford to use one camera to shoot everything.

To be a film director you had to handle everything, every little detail, by yourself. It was pretty tough. When I had the chance to sign a contract with Golden Harvest, and I had to change the whole system. I was suggesting we learn from Hollywood. We needed to have a real DP [director of photography] and a real production designer and costume designer. We needed a real screenwriter to make a real movie. And actually, I was the first one who started to do a thing like that.

Also, I wanted to start using a Panavision camera. Before that we were using a Arriflex camera. At the start, everything was so hard. From the studio's point of view they wanted to save money. They didn't want to spend any more money to do other things. But I had to go step-by-step. Then after I made a couple movies for them, they realized we really needed to make a change.

Q: *So your next two films were* The Dragon Tamers *and* Countdown in Kung Fu *[also called* Hand of Death, Fist to Fist, Hong Kong Face-off, *or* Shaolin Men*] which were made in Korea?*
JW: Both films were with [the Golden Harvest] film company because they were low budget movies. At that time they were pretty popular, the Hong Kong studio liked to share production credit with the Korean film company, which would be responsible for half the production fee.

We spent less than $50,000 for *The Dragon Tamers*, then the Korean company was responsible for the other half of the budget. The only condition was that we had to hire a Korean crew and hire a Korean actor in the film. The funny thing was, I was only twenty-eight years old and had long hair—long hair like a hippie. I was so skinny and dressed like a hippie. We had to shoot the entire film in Korea, and after I arrived the people from the Korean production company were so shocked by my look. They were also shocked by my age. They were all old guys, over fifty, sixty. The producer, chairman, and assistant director were all pretty old. They had a lot of doubts about me and didn't even believe I could direct a movie.

Before the first day of shooting, they invited me to a dinner with over twelve people. I was the only young man from Hong Kong. They didn't give me any relaxation time because they had so much stuff for me.

When they started drinking, in the Korean custom, they'd do a drink with a little sake cup. For the custom, one of them had to finish a drink by themselves and then had to hand over a cup for me and fill it up full. And I had to "bottoms up"—finish it in one shot. Then I handed the cup back to him and filled it for him. After, he finishes the drink and hands it back . . . it could be non-stop for no matter how many people. So the cup is passed around to each person. There was no chance to eat the food . . . everyone kept drinking. I kept drinking over the night and I drank just like them and I didn't get drunk. We drank so many bottles of Korean wine. It was a hard liquor and I drank even better than them. Then one of the old guys said, "Oh, this guy can drink. It means he's qualified to be a director." So after the drinking, I convinced them a little bit.

So, the first day shooting, the next day, I set up a long tracking shot, using a dolly. It was pretty new for a Korean producer. Usually they didn't shoot a movie using a dolly because of economic reasons. They also made films with a very low budget, so they only shot everything in static shots. After I set up a long dolly shot, they said, "Oh . . . this guy could be a good director because he knows how to use the track." So that was a pretty fun thing.

Q: *That story about drinking, that shows up in* Bullet in the Head?
JW: Yeah, several of my gangster films, *Bullet in the Head* and *A Better Tomorrow*. It's a symbol of mine.

But I've learned so much from the Koreans. The people are so emotional. They're pretty nice people. That was my first experience working with some people from other countries.

Q: *What was* The Dragon Tamers *about?*
JW: It was actually copying the Japanese TV series. There was a very famous Japanese series about judo, so the studio asked me to make a movie just like that. So we made up a story, a Korean Tae Kwan Do movie. It was about a Chinese guy, who came to South Korea to teach kung fu, but he had learned . . . Korean Tae Kwan Do. [It was] also a

love story because there was a beautiful Korean Tae Kwan Do girl in love with him and then there was some evil Tae Kwan Do bad guy who tried to challenge them. He tries to take away the girl, so the hero had to fight with him. It was a mixture of Tae Kwan Do and a Chinese kung fu movie.

Q: *Do you remember what the name of the Japanese judo TV series was?*
JW: *Sugata Sanshiro* [*Judo Saga* or *Judo Story*—ed.], it was from one of Akira Kurosawa's earlier films. He made a really popular judo movie. It was the same thing almost. Because it was so successful, he made it into a TV series.

Q: *Your next film in Korea was* Countdown in Kung Fu. *So tell me about the second Korean film and tell me how long it took to shoot?*
JW: Two or three months. Pretty short, about two and half months. It was made in 1974 and released in '75 or something like that. *Shaolin Men* is the Mandarin title.

Q: *So the second Korean film with Jackie Chan, what was that experience like?*
JW: Actually, Jackie Chan was a stunt man and a stunt double. Then we brought in two famous Hong Kong famous actors, Tan Tao-liang and Chung Chang. I also brought in Sammo Hung as the stunt coordinator. With Yuen Bill and Jackie Chan and several stunt guys who became famous action directors, stars right now.

We had to use major Hong Kong actors and hired some major actor in Korea. After we arrived, I found out one of the Korean actors was a little too old and he couldn't do much of the action. But that character had to fight and knew how to fight very well. I suggested firing the Korean actor and tried to find another one. Then I found Jackie Chan. I liked him so much. He was pretty quiet but I truly loved his talents. I thought he was not only good in action but he had a good sense of humor and he was pretty tough. He was not afraid. He could fall on rocks with his bare back and he didn't mind getting cut. Then he could jump off a slope and slide down the hill. He could fall off a horse and continue running. So he knew how to and could do so many crazy things.

Another thing I found was some kind of loneliness; he didn't talk to other people much. [No one had] discovered his real talents—that kind of loneliness. I suggested to the studio, fire the Korean actor and let Jackie take over this role. They agreed with me. I changed the script right away, changed the old guy to a younger guy and made his part even bigger than the main character. He did it well. Everybody loved him and was so proud of him, but in the meantime he was working also as a stunt double.

There was a scene for the ending fight and Jackie Chan was the double for the bad guy. The scene was the bad guy jumped up in mid-air and [received] a Tae Kwan Do side kick, a real kick to the stomach. And he fell onto the ground. I just wanted to emphasize the impact, to make a powerful reaction, so I used the cable on Jackie. He would jump up on a trampoline and let the good guy kick him in the chest. We were using six guys pulling the cable wire directly backward and he fell to the ground. It looked pretty strong. We did it several times and I was never satisfied with it. There was always some mistake, the timing was wrong and I got a little mad [Woo laughs]. I pushed them pretty hard, and Sammo Hung and Jackie Chan—they all wanted to do it one more time. All the action was a new experiment for the stunt people.

I was learning from all the westerns. When they showed the Indian and cowboy shoot at each other, when the Indian gets shot—they were using a cable to drag him backward. I was using it the same way. So after about seven times, I'm asking people to drag him harder. After he got kicked in the chest, the six people dragged him backward—he falls onto the ground, his head bumps on a sharp rock on the ground. The back of his head slammed on the rock; it got bloody. He almost got killed—within an inch—because the rock was sharp like a triangle and he hit a sharp place. He passed out. We were so panicked, we hugged him, slapped him trying to wake him up. After thirty seconds, he woke up. He was crying, he didn't know where he was and didn't even know his name.

Can you imagine what six people dragging him back would do? It was just like a rocket, just like a rocket slamming into a rock—the power of that kind of thing. So after that moment, we all [stopped].

We also did a lot of new experiments for the action sequences. And after I finished the movie, I went back to the studio and I talked to the chairman, Dr. Ho. I talked to him and I said, "This guy is gonna be a star. You have to sign him." The studio liked him but they didn't want to pay too much money for him. Jackie Chan was just asking to have one thousand Hong Kong dollars more but the studio didn't want it.

He was so upset that he flew back to Australia and he wanted to retire. He thought he would never have another chance, never have any chance. After my movie was shown, the film director Lo Wei saw the movie and he loved it and he loved Jackie Chan. And he signed him up right away. He could give him one thousand Hong Kong dollars, a little more than that. So he brought him back to Hong Kong and started making movies. After Lo Wei saw the movie, he was really impressed with Jackie Chan and thought this guy is doable and thought he could be a big star. So it proves I was right [Woo laughs]. And after he made several movies for Lo . . . and all of a sudden he becomes a superstar and I was so happy, so happy for him.

Q: *I was able to track this film down a little while ago—you didn't tell that you were in it and that Jackie Chan's character saves your life!*
JW: [laughing] I forgot that!

Q: *I think it's interesting that two Hong Kong legends are in the same scene, and it's a very early scene. Nobody knows about it in the U.S. because it's so hard to find.*
JW: I was playing a revolutionary and I was wanted by the Ching government. They wanted to kill me. So I had to keep on running. There was a group of patriots, fighters who were saving me, helping me go through all kinds of dangerous situations. There was a moment when I almost got killed, but Jackie Chan sacrifices himself to save me.

Q: *The way it plays out is: there's a guy running at you with a spear, and Jackie puts himself between you and the spear, right?*
JW: Right.

Q: *Just before this film you met your future wife, Anne. Where did you meet her?*
JW: Hong Kong. She came from Taiwan and worked in Hong Kong for my mentor, Chang Cheh, as a script supervisor. She was also getting training from Mr. Chang's film school. One day, Mr. Chang was shooting

a film outside of our studio. So I met her. I knew Mr. Chang and I knew his crew, so they introduced her to me.

Q: *Do you remember the name of the film he was making?*
JW: I don't remember. The film was produced by his own company.

Q: *How long did you date before you got married?*
JW: I met her in 1975, right before I went to Korea to shoot my second Korean film. I met her once, and after I finished the film, I came back.

Q: *What do you remember about her? Were you the one chasing her, or was she the one chasing you?*
JW: It was a little of both. She was so pretty, innocent, and full of life. I liked her. The first time we met, I was dating her at a dim sum restaurant. I found she had painted fingernails. I talked to her, I said, "I've never liked girls with painted fingernails."

The second time we met, she was hiding her hands underneath the table. After a few minutes of conversation, she raised both of her hands and showed me: no paint on her fingernails. They were all clean. I was so happy.

Actually, that moment I learned from *Bonnie and Clyde*. All my life, I've been living in the movies. In *Bonnie and Clyde*, there was a scene after Warren Beatty met Faye Dunaway. After they did their first holdup, they were in a hamburger restaurant. They were just starting to get to know each other, and he said, "Change your hairstyle. I don't like your hair."

Then she pulled her hair behind her ears, she made a little change, and Warren Beatty smiled. And I had a similar moment.

Q: *What did she want to change about you then?*
JW: Oh, she didn't want me to smoke. She didn't want me to drink too much. A lot of things. [laughing]

Q: *If I remember right, you still smoke, but you don't drink so much.*
JW: Yeah, it's pretty tough.

Q: *Well, the next movie you did was the Cantonese opera called* Princess Chang Ping. *Tell me about that—it was a hit, right?*
JW: Yeah, that one was a big hit in Hong Kong, but only in Hong Kong and Singapore. It was from a very famous stage play. It also had been

made a movie in black and white about twenty years ago before mine. It was a remake. *Princess Chang Ping* was made in 1976 and released in '77.

I had just finished *Countdown in Kung Fu* and all of a sudden I had a call from the chairman and he says they want me to direct this movie. I was surprised because even though I love opera, I didn't know much about it. I loved watching it and I grew up with the Chinese opera. I'd wanted to try, but at that time, there were a lot of people in the business who didn't like the idea. They kept asking why the studio didn't hire a much older and much more experienced director to make the film. Some people even said, "How could a violent director make a Chinese opera?"

And *Princess Chang Ping* is pretty much like the story of *Romeo and Juliet*—that kind of a romantic, sad story. There was no action and it was a pure opera, an artistic piece. Some people criticized me and said I was too young and inexperienced. They said, "He made a lot of violent movies" and they didn't think I had the heart. So I was hurt.

When we prepped the movie, I talked to the actors. The supervisor was a former huge star and they all had high hopes for me. The people in the film business all gave me a lot of pressure. And one of my producers even wanted to take over my job. He wanted to direct by himself. He worked with the actors and the supervisor closely and gave his ideas. He even made a shot list for the crew, not for me. I was so mad.

We had to spend a lot of money because it was a pretty big budget piece for the studio. They had to spend over 1 million Hong Kong dollars—at that time it was pretty big—and that was for the pre-production. We had to build a real set and everything's so real and so big. Then I tried to make the stage play more like a movie, so we built everything in the movie way. We spent a lot of money. But I was so upset because of what other people were saying. Some people wanted to take over my job. Then I talked to the studio—I wanted to quit.

Q: *You wanted to quit?*
JW: Yeah, I wanted to quit because I didn't want to be involved with such a situation. It so embarrassed me. I knew I could make the film, but I didn't want to take all kinds of pressure from everywhere. It wasn't worth it, so I told them I had some other thing I wanted to do. The chairman gathered everyone, all the actors, the producers, the cameramen, the supervisor, in a room and he talked to everybody.

He said, "If this movie is not directed by John Woo, I will close down the movie right away and I don't care! I don't care how much I've spent on pre-production" and actually, he had spent 2 million Hong Kong dollars on everything and he didn't care about losing all this money. He said, "It's got to be directed by John Woo."

Q: *Once you got everybody in line, was it easier then to film or was it still a struggle to film?*
JW: It was both. After the chairman's meeting, nobody said a word. They all kept quiet, you know. Dr. Ho trusted me, he always liked the way I treated drama. And he knew I could make a movie more emotional, he knew I was a very emotional person. He knew I could handle all those romantic love and emotional moments pretty well. He believed in me and he didn't care what people said.

So after that, all the actors and the supervisor worked with me closely. They had to rehearse every scene for me and they explained the art of the opera. I was also getting some notes and some suggestions for the movie. And a movie is unlike the stage, the movie has got to be natural. So it's kind of a combination. They had to compromise with me a little bit and I adjusted their performance a little bit.

We had a pretty tough schedule . . . we had to release the movie for the Chinese New Year. It was a pretty big thing for Hong Kong, you know. So we had to work harder and longer hours and never stop. After the movie was made, it was big hit. It was a big hit for two reasons. It was very well-received by the young audience. The young had a great admiration for the actors and it broke all the records for the Chinese opera movie. The other thing was, it didn't look like a stage play, it looked pretty much like a movie. So the people loved it. Most of the critics said that the good thing about the movie was that it looked like a movie.

That was my first big success, it had made over 3 million Hong Kong dollars at that time. It was pretty big . . . it was a pretty big number for Hong Kong at that time. I was about twenty-nine.

Q: *How did you take success as a young man?*
JW: Well, I was very happy. I felt successful. I was giving money to my mom and I was helping my family. [I thought] I could talk to the studio, you know, do whatever I wanted. After *Princess Chang Ping* in the year

1977, I wanted to make a police story, a gangster movie, but they didn't let me do it.

I didn't know what to do because I wanted to make a movie like *Le Samourai*, kind of a gangster movie, but the studio didn't want me to do it. The studio kept saying that I should follow the trends, and that meant whatever was popular. At that time, the only popular topic for the film market was what we called "the fist and the pillow"—it means violence and sex.

They said no one would care about a police story, especially because I wanted to make a tragic gangster movie. They all said no. I was pretty upset. I found a couple movies to do, but only kung fu movies—it was hard to do a higher-level movie.

There was another actor who was just coming up called Michael Hui. He was making his first film called *Games Gamblers Play*, a comedy. He was a first-time director and he was so dedicated. I was a good friend of his younger brother Samuel Hui. They asked me for help, so I helped him. I truly admired Michael Hui and his brother Samuel Hui was a huge superstar, a singer. So I helped them to make a film, as a producer and helper. He was a first-time director; he had some technical problems like setting up cameras and I was helping him control the whole set. I learned so much from his work. I found making a comedy pretty interesting.

So after I helped him to make the *Games Gamblers Play*, the movie came out and it was huge success. It broke all the records. It made history and it also made Michael Hui become a huge star. So after that, the studio asked me to make a comedy. I said to them that comedy wasn't my expertise; I only wanted to make a gangster movie. They said, "You've learned so much from Michael Hui. Why you don't want to make one?"

I was so much an admirer of Jerry Lewis. I love Jerry Lewis; he was my hero at the time. I loved him and also Mel Brooks, Charlie Chaplin and all those great comical actors. So, I wanted to try. So in 1977, I only spent two weeks to write a script. I used a very small budget to make my first comedy, called *Money Crazy*.

At that time the successful comedies were pretty realistic, but my kind of comedy was much like a cartoon, very cartoonish. After I made the movie, everyone said, "This movie is so awful, everything's over the top like a Hong Kong Jerry Lewis or Mel Brooks type of movie and it doesn't work."

But it worked and it became a big hit, just a little under Michael Hui's movie, and all of a sudden I became a big comedy director.

Q: *One of the Hong Kong newspapers called you "The new golden boy of Hong Kong film comedies."*
JW: Yeah, yeah I remember that. But we were using an unpopular star and it was very low budget, shot in a very short time. And actually, I was the one who started the comical kung fu action in a movie. In all the fights, I made fun of kung fu. It was so influential for Sammo Hung and Jackie Chan, for their later work, to make all the action very comical, the funny fighting.

Q: *What was the plot of* Money Crazy?
JW: Oh, the plot was pretty simple. It's a story about a little guy who is looked down on by people. He's kind of like a failure, never had a chance. And all of a sudden, he is in love with a girl. He tried to steal a diamond from a rich guy, a little bit like *The Sting*. He tries to con the rich guy and the rich guy hired a killer, a crazy killer to chase after him. Everybody is crazy about money.

Q: *So is this the first movie you made under the name John Woo?*
JW: I think it started with *Money Crazy* . . . [Woo used the named "John Y. S. Woo" on *Money Crazy*—ed.]
Well, I had made several movies for the studio. Since the studio had some very, very big successes. They had made international movies like the Bruce Lee movies and a couple movies [1974's *Hong Kong Hitman*, 1975's *The Man from Hong Kong* and 1976's *A Queen's Ransom*—ed.] with George Lazenby [one-time James Bond actor—ed.], and even with Robert Mitchum [1977's *The Amsterdam Kill*—ed.].
Anyway, after they made several international movies and got into the international market, the chairman Mr. Shum Sham said to me, "John, this is our movie for the international market."
So there was a chance for me to have an international name. Wu Yu-Sheng was hard for the foreign audience to pronounce. Since we were in Hong Kong, our last name is translated into English usually based on the Cantonese pronunciation. And in Cantonese my last name is Ng so usually they would translate into the English "N-G" or "ing." And then

in Mandarin, I had to pronounce it "wu," spelled "Wu." My last name pronounced in Shanghainese—Shanghainese is a different language—is "woo," using the spelling "W-o-o." He said, "Woo is easy for reading."

I said good, fine. I also didn't like the "Ng" pronunciation. And then they suggested to me to use my Christian name, John, so that's how I became John Woo.

Q: *You had made your name under Wu Yu-Sheng and now you were John Woo. So what was it like to be two famous people at once? Or did people know who you were?*
JW: The Hong Kong audience, they didn't care about the English name. People still called me Wu Yu-Sheng. Even after I made a successful movie like *A Better Tomorrow*, some foreign press interviewed me and in the paper called me John Woo. Some Hong Kong journalists were saying, "Who the hell is John Woo?" They had never heard of a John Woo because they only knew, only cared about my Chinese name.

After awhile, when John Woo was getting more attention, then I explained to people that actually I had used the name for a long time. I think it was pretty funny.

Q: *The next movie after that is* Follow the Star.
JW: *Follow the Star* starred the old actor Roy Chiao. He was in the second *Indiana Jones* movie. He played the Chinese boss, a pretty funny character. He was very famous at the time, but he's passed away now.

The story is about a big old guy who took care of a very young singer who was only about fifteen years old. Her name was Rowena Cortes [also called Lu Yun Na—ed.]. It's pretty much like a father and daughter kind of relationship. All of a sudden a real bad guy chases after the young singer and wants to kidnap her. And the old guy helps her to solve her problem. It's pretty much like a cartoon—too cartoonish because when I saw the film, I went crazy. That film didn't work. It was awful. Even though some of the action moments were pretty funny, it was way too over the top and the people couldn't accept it.

After that, I talked to the studio and I really wanted to make a gangster movie. I even hired a writer to work on the script. But they still didn't let me do it, they just wanted me to keep making comedy and action. So I was really unhappy. I had so much anger.

So I came up with the idea to make a movie called *From Riches to Rags*. I was a big movie lover. I tried to do ten different scenes as a tribute to some of the movies I love.

The story is about two young kids, poor workers delivering soft drinks who all of a sudden get rich from a lottery ticket. One of the guys was always dreaming about wanting to be rich. But after he got rich, he fell in love with a girl and it changed his real character. He became more rich and corrupt and at the end, they are all sent to a mental institution. They go insane because of all the money, like [in] a Jerry Lewis movie.

Q: *Do you remember which movies and scenes you paid homage to?*
JW: In the hospital, there's a huge monument of gold in the middle of the hall and people keep circling around it. The idea was a tribute to *2001: A Space Odyssey* with the huge, dark monolith and all the monkeys circling around it.

Other movies, *The Deer Hunter*, etc. There was also some crazy guy saying, "The horror, the horror," like from *Apocalypse Now*.

Q: *In* Ten Thousand Bullets: The Cinematic Journey of John Woo, *Christopher Heard writes that* Riches to Rags *is one of your favorite movies because you had some freedom. Is that right?*
JW: Yeah. I had some freedom and was trying to send a message. At that time, I felt that people were going crazy because of money. Everybody chased after money and then they go crazy and then it's a crazy world.

I watched *It's a Mad Mad Mad Mad World* and I really love that movie. People all lost their minds because of money. I was so much concerned about the whole society. The rich people were always very rich and the poor people were always getting poorer and didn't have anybody that cared about them.

In that film, I just wanted to point out there's a lot of problems in this society that really need help and we really need to care about others. I also felt, especially in the church, that some good ministers never got a good church. They were always in the countryside or some island where there were not many people. Not-so-good ministers were always getting elected to higher positions.

Everything made me so mad, so I put my anger into my comedy. So that's why I was so happy with *From Riches to Rags*. . . . At least I could express myself.

Q: *The next one then is* Last Hurrah for Chivalry. *Was this one filmed before or after* Riches to Rags?
JW: After. The film was made in 1979. I asked a friend of mine to write a script. It was a police story and the studio still didn't want me to do it and didn't let me do it. They just wanted me to make another action movie. I was so unhappy, so that's why I made up my mind that I wanted to make a movie as a tribute to Kurosawa.

Last Hurrah for Chivalry was also a tribute to my mentor, Chang Cheh. I wanted to make up a story that could have a little bit of Chang Cheh's chivalrous spirit—a movie about honor and loyalty. I also wanted to have a little bit of the stylish look from Kurosawa's film. Me and my writers were working on the script, and it was pretty risky because there were not many people who cared about those movies anymore.

The people only went for the comedies or action comedies. They didn't like to watch any of the classical types of movies. But I really wanted to make that kind of story. I really wanted to make a classical swordplay movie.

The other idea, I tried to make it like a staged play. The whole movie looked like a stage. I didn't try to use any modern technique, just tried to make it like a traditional, classic movie. We had a very good story but I had made a pretty big mistake. We had been told we would have to use some modern terms, modern dialogue but in a classical movie.

I thought it could attract a young audience, so we were using some pretty bad modern language in the film but it didn't match. I really liked the performers, the action and a couple of swordfight duels. It looked pretty classic.

But it wasn't a success. For the box office, it was just OK. But some of the scenes were pretty good and actually, I had established a heroic character.

Q: *Is he inspired by Jing Ke, the guy who tried to assassinate Emperor Qin?*
JW: Yeah. It was inspired by this character.

The character who was played by Damian Lau, the guy with the sword, the wanderer, he's helping people—that character is similar to Chow Yun-Fat in *A Better Tomorrow*. It's the kind of heroic character willing to sacrifice himself, who is helping others. He has a code of honor, that kind of character. And also I could tell you another side story?

Q: *Please.*
JW: When I worked on *Hard Target* for my first American movie, two of the producers were Sam Raimi and Robert Tapert. We were very good friends; we worked together so well. After that movie, we tried to work on some other project together, then we talked a lot. They wanted to develop a TV series, a new action series and that was called *Hercules*.

I was suggesting, "Why don't you . . . I always wanted to make a western and combine it with kung fu." That gave him this idea. I asked them to watch *Last Hurrah for Chivalry*. They watched it again and again and they learned from my action sequences. So they used it in *Hercules*. They especially liked the swordfight between the good and bad guy by the water. They liked that kind of rhythm and action.

Q: *Is there a specific episode or did it influence the whole series?*
JW: The first few couple episodes, so afterwards they used it again and again. They made the idea work so well. It became a huge success.

Q: Last Hurrah for Chivalry *was also famous because it has the sleeping wizard, the master who fights while he's asleep.*
JW: Ha ha—I forgot, totally forgot about that!

Q: *There have been drunken masters and all sorts of masters but I've never heard of a master who fights while he's asleep.*
JW: Oh yeah. It was already in the script but it was a pretty rough idea. But I built it up more on the set. [I was] doing lots of drinking at that time . . .
[Laughter]
. . . but I never drank on the set. When I was young I would drink more and I would get more ideas. . . .

Q: *Well, you were young. You could do that.*
JW: Not anymore, I'm on good behavior.

Q: *Were you married then?*
JW: I married in 1977, a little bit before I made the movie *Money Crazy*, after I made *Princess Chang Ping*.

Q: *Did getting married change you any?*
JW: I didn't change much, because even though I got married, I was still fully concentrated on my work. In the years 1976 to '80, I was kind of like a searcher. I was searching for something, I was looking for something. I wanted to do something for myself, I wanted to do a movie that could really establish my character, [where I] really could express myself. I was kind of like the Lone Ranger.

I started pretty young and I wanted to change the whole system. I wanted to make a lot of changes and all I could do was [a little], step by step. In the late '70s, I found that there were a lot of young talented filmmakers who were working on television—like Tsui Hark, Ann Hui, Ringo Lam, Ronny Yu, Patrick Tam. A Hong Kong New Wave.

But they didn't have a chance to work on movies. I felt pretty lonely. I was struggling for almost eight years and I suggested to the studio that we should hire all those young upcoming filmmakers into the business. But they were so afraid and they always said, "Now we have John Woo. It's good enough." They didn't want to take a risk using a newcomer.

And I said, "No, no, no. For the whole business, if you want to change the Hong Kong movie industry and want to make Hong Kong movies look good, we have to use some new blood." I highly recommended Tsui Hark and Ann Hui, Patrick Tam and Kurt Wong, all those television directors for film. The studio didn't listen to me for two years, so I felt lonely. They were only interested in taking a stake with some older filmmakers. They didn't want to take a risk.

I wanted to have some friends. I wanted to have some people of the same age to exchange experiences, try to work together and do some different things to improve Hong Kong movies.

The year was 1979 and I met Tsui Hark. I didn't even know anything about him, I just saw some of his clips, some of the pieces of his work and it looked fantastic. It made me so much admire him.

We met and talked about art, about movies and I questioned him a lot, I really appreciated his work. He was very artistic. We had a very good conversation and then we looked at the Hong Kong harbor and there was a very beautiful sunset. We both looked at the Hong Kong harbor, and we swore together, we said together, "We *have* to find a way to make Hong Kong movies look good," to make a better kind of movie.

Q: *After what movie did you have this conversation?*
JW: *Last Hurrah for Chivalry*. After that film, I went back to comedy again and I made *To Hell with the Devil*.

Q: *Yes,* To Hell with the Devil *but doesn't* Hello, Late Homecomers *come earlier?*
JW: Oh yeah, I was a co-director with other guys. There was this kind of a popular midnight talk show; it was all about sex. It was still pretty conservative but for that time it was a pretty popular—they did some sex jokes. They wanted to make a movie [version] and went to the studio to make a film. Then [the studio] hired two directors, one was the original writer. It was pretty big job for them. Also, it was their first time and they wanted to co-direct with me. So, I just did one part. Each director directed one-third of the movie.

Q: *Like* New York Stories. . . .
JW: Yeah, yeah, yeah—three different stories.

Q: *What was your story?*
JW: I hardly remember . . . it's a story about somebody who wanted to kill his wife. He set up a lot of traps—the door would connect with a wire and bomb, and when she opened the door, it would blow up. He put poison in her drink. . . . Somehow the wife finds out in a letter to her husband and she makes him stay in the room and makes him do all the things [spring all the devices].

Q: *So she turns the tables on him?*
JW: Yeah, she turns the tables on him. Pretty funny, and it had a little sex. At that time, it was pretty subtle—just a sexy moment. But after I made my story, the other two didn't know how to direct it and they

asked me to finish their work for them. So that's why they used my name, they only used my name. I didn't have a problem with it; it was fun.

Q: *The next one was* To Hell with the Devil *and was that more of a surreal comedy?*
JW: Not a real comedy. The idea came from *Faust*, where the main character—he sells his soul to the devil.

Q: *Were you influenced by* Bedazzled, *the Dudley Moore, Peter Cook movie?*
JW: Yes, yes, yes.

Q: *So was that your version? Or simply an influence?*
JW: An influence. At this time, I tried to finish the contract with Golden Harvest and they wouldn't let me go because I had another three years with them. So I put that emotion, I put that idea into the movie. It's a young guy who would sell his soul to the devil, a trade for three wishes. But somehow, his [situation] got worse and worse. At the end of the movie he yelled at the devil and said, "I want my contract back! I just want to end it!" And that was how I used to yell at my boss at the studio. I wanted to throw it out. At that time, I was in contact with other people at Cinema City. They promised me if I moved over to them they would let me make the movie I wanted to make, to make my dream.

Q: *How did Golden Harvest feel about being portrayed as the devil?*
JW: Of course they were unhappy and they knew what it meant in the movie. That movie wasn't that bad but the ending scene was too over the top. When he's fighting with the devil, the devil blinks his eye—and lasers come out, shooting and blowing up things.

When I made the film it was pretty interesting. There were a lot of special effects, visual effect moments. When the main character got knocked out, he had a lot of stars spinning above his head. The whole ending was like a video game.

But we had no money. We didn't know how to make it. But then I came up with an idea. Because I knew the camera and lens pretty well, I was thinking I could use a mirror in front of the camera, get a reflection from a neon light on the side of the camera, then match the angle with the actors. When the devil blinked, then I turned on the neon light.

The neon light reflected into the mirror and from the mirror into the lens. I used that kind of technique to shoot the entire ending scene—the eyes shooting the laser beam with reflection into the lens. It looked like a special effect when actually it was not.

When Tsui Hark made this movie called *Sin* [English title: *Zu: Warriors from the Magic Mountain*—ed.] he had hired two visual effects people from *Star Wars*. [He brought them] to Hong Kong to work on his movie. Those two guys wanted to know how we made the visual effects and the studio sold them the film. For the scene with the laser beams, shooting and explosions—they were pretty surprised—they were asking, "How much is that?"

And I told them, "Eh, about five hundred to one thousand Hong Kong dollars." They were shocked. Just five hundred Hong Kong dollars to buy the neon lights and the mirror, some color filters and that was it. They were shocked. They thought we had spent a fortune to make all those effect shots.

Q: *In* To Hell with the Devil *you have references to* Gone with the Wind, The Exorcist, *and* Close Encounters of the Third Kind, *is that right?*
JW: Yeah, yeah, yeah.

Q: *What were those scenes? What did you do to pay homage to them?*
JW: I don't quite remember.

Q: *Next was* Laughing Times. *Was that 1981?*
JW: *Laughing Times* was copying Charlie Chaplin's movies. We were copying his character and look. It was made with a very low budget.

Q: *Who stars as the Charlie Chaplin character?*
JW: Dean Shek.

Q: *What made you want to make that type of film? What attracted you to Charlie Chaplin?*
JW: It wasn't my idea. I was actually trying to help a friend. At that time Dean Shek and Karl Maka [also known as Karl Mak—ed.], they wanted to start a company called Cinema City but they didn't have money. They wanted to make a movie financed by Golden Princess.

If the movie worked, then Golden Princess would support them, build their company. But if it didn't work, then they wouldn't support them. So they wanted me to help them to direct the film because at that time, I had fame from comedies. So I had to use a false name to help them. I used John Woo, the same English name, but a different Chinese name, Hsiang-Fei. [Woo used the middle names of his two daughters to create this pseudonym—ed.]

I still had a contract with Golden Harvest, so working for the other company, I had to use a false name. Everybody worked on the film without pay. They came up with a story, tried to make a Hong Kong style movie. We shot it in the countryside, on a very poor budget—but it worked and it was quite a hit. Since the movie was a big hit, it got support from Golden Princess. That's how they started Cinema City.

Q: *You later made two films for them in Taiwan, right?*
JW: In 1983 and '84, *The Time You Need a Friend* and *Run Tiger Run*.

Q: *But first was* Plain Jane to the Rescue *in 1982. Was that the first time you had a female star?*
JW: No, the second time. The first time was the *Princess Chang Ping*, but this was the first one with a big female star.

Q: *How did you find working with female leads? You're known as a "guy's director." How was it different?*
JW: I had a wonderful feeling, so much joy working with Josephine Siao Fong-fong [also known as Josephine Siao—ed.]. She was one of the biggest teenaged stars in the 1960s. She was extremely popular and smart, intelligent, intellectual, and full of great ideas. One of the smartest actresses in Hong Kong. When we worked together, it made things so much easier because she was also the producer of the film. She worked with the writers and came up with a lot of good ideas, a lot of great jokes. Her character was very funny and popular at the time.

Q: *What was the movie about?*
JW: It's a continuation of the same character of a very famous TV show that was created by her, for herself. They had made two movies before *Plain Jane to the Rescue*, mine was the third one.

In the movie, she was a tutor and a helper for a rich old man. The old man's son was very ambitious. He wanted to buy all of the Hong Kong property and become a money king. He didn't care much about this old man, and wanted to take over his fortune. Plain Jane wanted to help this old man.

At that time, there were a lot of rumors about Hong Kong. It was just after the British government had a meeting with the Chinese leadership to return Hong Kong to China. People started getting panicky. People were pretty upset and depressed about the future—they knew Hong Kong could be finished. There was not much hope for [positive] change. There was a lot of frustration at the time.

Josephine Fong-fong and I came up with the idea, at the end of the movie, everyone is stuck in a tunnel because of a little car accident. There are a lot of people stuck in the tunnel. All the cars are stopped and they couldn't move. Everyone was trying to find a way out, it was a big disaster.

So, it's symbolic of the future of Hong Kong. In 1997, people were going to be stuck in one place. They wanted to break through; they wanted to be free. But at the end, all the people found only one solution—helping and caring for each other. I guess I was the first one to put that kind of message into a film about 1997, [the year of] the transition. People learned how to come together and help each other, still keeping the dream, keeping hope. At the end, they all found hope—it brought everyone together. So that was the main concept for the movie.

At that time, my wife, she was living in the United States, and my son was born.

Q: *What was Anne doing in the United States?*
JW: Nothing. She was a housewife. I didn't want her to work too much [being pregnant]. Her family had emigrated to the United States, and she was flying back and forth.

In 1982, we were filming *Plain Jane to the Rescue*—on the last day, I was shooting the last scene and my son was born. She called me and I was so happy, and I put that [in the film]. It gave me the idea to send another new message in the scene. At the end of the scene, there was a pregnant woman who [gives birth]. Jane helps deliver the baby. Jane holds up the baby in the air and everyone applauds. Everyone was happy about the newborn baby. It was symbolic: Hong Kong was going to have a new life, and a new hope. Everybody gets back hope.

Q: *So you got a phone call that Frank was born—do you remember what you said? What your reaction was?*
JW: I jumped up in the air. I was very happy. Because we were shooting the scene, we were stuck on set. We didn't have a good conclusion for the end of movie. All of a sudden, it was the last day and we had to finish the movie. But I really wanted to send a good message with the film, even though it was a comedy. But at that time, everyone was very emotional about 1997. There was a lot of frustration, a lot of panic.

Then I got the phone call from my wife, and she told me my son was born. That made the idea click—a newborn baby, with Plain Jane holding him up in the air. I always feel, no matter what happens to Hong Kong, there is always hope, always new life. I never thought of the worst, I only think of the good. The future is going to be fine.

Q: *I know your daughter Angeles is named after Los Angeles, the city of her birth—but where does Frank's name come from?*
JW: It was my idea. I liked the name Frank because it means frank, honest. Being frank to the people. It also matched his Chinese name, Yee Fong, which means honor. Yee Fong, translated into English, means "honorable man."

Q: *You've been reluctant to talk about your family before this book, but I just wanted to take a minute to ask you about your family's move from Guangxi to Guangzhou.*
JW: My grandfather was a landlord in Guangxi. He owned a lot of land and fortune. He wanted my father to continue and take care of his business and become a great farmer.

But my father despised the fortune and he didn't care about money. He had his own idea. He wanted to be a school teacher. He taught Chinese culture and history. He was teaching high school when he was sixteen years old. So that's why he left home and went to Guangzhou.

In a couple years, he met my mother and they married. During World War II, he worked for a general doing a second secretary job. He was so patriotic. He had joined the war even though he was an intellectual.

Q: *OK, the next movie we need to talk about after* Plain Jane *is* . . .
JW: Let me go back a little bit. After *Plain Jane to the Rescue* . . . I made a movie called *The Sunset Warrior*. The movie was shot in Thailand; it was my first war movie. After I finished the movie, they didn't feel happy about it and they kept it on the shelf. They released it after I had success with *A Better Tomorrow* and they changed the name to *Heroes Shed No Tears*.

Q: *So this is your first war movie. What was this one about?*
JW: Actually, I just wanted to leave Golden Harvest. But with the contract, I still had two more years, so I couldn't go. I just wanted to make any movie for them to finish the contract. They gave me the script and it was pretty simple. There was a Chinese mercenary at the border of Thailand. Actually, these are real people in what we call "The Golden Triangle," which is in the middle of the Thailand, Vietnam and Cambodian borders. It was contemporary. And those mercenaries were fighting with the rebels, the communists. They were a huge army group, they had a lot of old-fashioned weapons.

There was a story about five of the mercenaries. They had a mission to capture a drug lord. The main character had a son, and he had to protect him. But he also had a job, he had to capture the drug lord and bring him to the authority. He had to fight with their gang. In the meantime, there was a war going on.

On the run, the American soldier and some foreign adventurer and a woman, these people all needed help. And he had to help his own son. At the end, a few of his colleagues were killed. He accomplished the mission, but he lost all of his good friends. It's a tragic story, and it was the first time I shot a war movie. The whole movie was focused on the father and son. It was a pretty simple script, so I had to make a lot of changes. I tried to make it more emotional. So, there were two things that were unforgettable. One, the film was shot in Thailand, since it was very low budget. We had to hire two French actors, male and female, who didn't speak good English. The Frenchman who played the American soldier was a pretty good actor. We had to hire three Korean actors, who were non-English speaking. We had to use a translator. There was only one actress who could speak good English. We had a

Japanese cameraman and DP [director of photography], who couldn't speak any English. They couldn't even say, "One, two, three. . . ."

And we used a Thai crew, which was great. We had about five different languages on set. When I communicated with my DP, it was only with body movement, hand signals to tell him the shot. It was funny. It was my first experience with people from different countries with different dialogue. Because we didn't have money, it was quite an experience.

Another memorable thing was, it was my first action movie with a heavy gun battle sequence. We were using all the prop guns from Thailand. And those people had been working on a lot of American films that were shot in Thailand, so they had a lot of good experience. So the first day, one of our shots was our stunt actor running through machine gun fire [hitting the ground]. The special effects group set up the charges in the ground. It took about four hours. They had to dig the hole, bury the dynamite and the cable. When the actor ran through it, the timing was wrong and I wanted to do it again.

I asked, "How much time to reset the whole thing?"

They said, "Another three hours."

But there was no more time. I said, "I don't have three hours, is there a faster way to do it?"

They said, "Oh yes, Mr. Woo. There is a much faster way, it will only take ten minutes."

I said, "How."

They said, "Using a real gun."

I was shocked. They did a demonstration for me. They set up two platforms on either side of the camera and put a mark on the ground for the actor running. They used their own people running. So my special effects guy was also the marksman. They used white chalk on the route that the guy was running. Two special effects guys standing on the platform, they were using M16s with real bullets and shooting right at the mark. When the guy is running through, they are firing right after the guy's heel—Pom! Pom! Pom! Pom!

The effect was so good and dust flew so high. After the guy ran through it, he was safe. He didn't get hurt. I was so happy. I said, "Oh, that's fast." And I loved the effects.

My stunt actor said, "OK, the Thai people can do it, we Chinese can also do it. Let's show some guts. Go ahead guys, do it." The guy got panicked, but he did it. He was really scared.

It was a really good effect. But from that day on, I told the guy to use real bullets for the background bullet hits for the entire movie. Most of the machine gun effects were using real bullets. Fortunately, no one got hurt.

Q: *Was that the last time you did that?*
JW: Yeah, the last time. I had so many good memories about that film. We were low budget. Me and three of my assistants, my assistant directors, we worked every night to come up with new ideas. I also had a very good experience working with the Thai people. The Thai people were very gentle and very professional. I was so amazed about that.

Q: *Why did the studio keep it on the shelf so long? What didn't they like about it?*
JW: The movie had some violent scenes. The style was very incomplete. Sometimes it was very emotional, sometimes it looked like a horror movie. They didn't know how people would feel about a war movie. At that time, people liked to watch their comedies.

It was a tragic story, you know. The actors weren't popular, which is why they put it on the shelf.

The other thing was, the original script was full of violence and sex. It also had a sex scene. But the sex scenes were a little too much for me—very obscene sex. There was a woman tortured by the bad army. There was a scene with a soldier putting heroin on the naked woman's body. While they are making love, they sweat, and the sweat mixed with the heroin and the guy sucked up into his nose. It was pretty sickening. He was licking heroin off her naked body. It was sick, so that's why I didn't shoot it.

That's why the studio wasn't satisfied with it. They wanted to have more comedy in this tragic story. They also hired somebody else to rewrite some of the scenes and reshoot one or two of the sex scenes.

Q: *Did you feel vindicated then, when it came out six years later?*
JW: I didn't watch it. And I didn't care much about it, because someone had changed some of my scenes.

Q: *You still have not watched it?*
JW: No.

Q: *Would you like to go back and edit it your way?*
JW: No. I wasn't satisfied with that movie. But [then again], I'm never satisfied with any of my movies.

Q: *So, let's jump to* The Time You Need a Friend.
JW: At that time, the reason I wanted to leave Golden Harvest and move to Cinema City was, they promised me, if I moved to their company, they would let me shoot what I really wanted to shoot. I always wanted to make a gangster movie. Like a very serious character-driven movie, which I couldn't do at Golden Harvest. So they promised me, after I gave them help, to help me make my dream come true.

But they didn't keep their promise. After I left Golden Harvest and signed up with them, all of the sudden they sent me to Taiwan to manage the company. I was shocked. They tried to move me away. When I was in Taiwan, in charge of the company office in Taiwan, I couldn't do anything. They just wanted me to continue making comedies. I was pretty upset, but I had to survive. I had to make a living. All I could do was make another comedy for them.

So they gave me a script called, *The Time You Need a Friend*. The idea was inspired by [Neil Simon's] *The Sunshine Boys*, although I didn't know that. At that time, those Taiwanese actors [we used] were very popular.

The movie was about two old comedians. They were friends and enemies, like an old couple. At the end, one of the old guys knows he's going to die, so he wanted to have one last show with his old friend. And the show was for a charity.

They were good friends, but somehow they didn't get along with each other, just like George Burns and Walter Matthau. But the movie didn't work, because maybe people weren't ready for that kind of story. People didn't buy it.

After that, I made another movie in Taiwan called *Run Tiger Run*. It was kind of a comic book, a cartoonish kind of story. Very over-the-top, cartoonish comedy starring Teddy Robin. *Run Tiger Run* was a fairy tale about a young poor kid. He was living in a very bad, poor neighborhood.

He dreams about [escaping]. And anyway, he finds out that he has a very rich grandpa—that he's a forgotten kid. And then, all of the sudden, he finds out that a rich uncle wants to find him, because he's inherited a huge fortune. He attracts some bad people. They try to kill this young kid, and take his fortune. And then there was this man, a wanderer played by Teddy Robin, who helped him—he saved his life. It was pretty much like a cartoon. It didn't work well. It was a disaster. I was very depressed at that time. I didn't want to stay in Taiwan any more.

After two and a half years working in Taiwan, I moved back to Hong Kong in 1985.

Q: *You had had successes and failures before; your career had been up and down. But what made this one hit you so hard?*
JW: After *Plain Jane to the Rescue*, none of my movies worked. None of my movies made any money. In the meantime, I was struggling, I was in pain—not able to do what I really wanted to do. In 1985, when I moved back to Hong Kong, those people at Cinema City said I should retire. They felt, some of the people felt, I was [out of touch]. They said, "Just go home and watch videotape, see what is going on in the outside world and learn from other people. Then just go make whatever is popular." It seemed I was [behind] the times. My kind of style didn't work.

Q: *When we first met, you told me that your anger was seeping into your comedies. Your comedies around this time weren't funny. Was that part of the problem?*
JW: Yes, I had so much anger about so many things. There was an unhappy message in most of my comedies. My comedies were about people's greed, a lot of condemnation of society. That's why my comedies were not like the others. I tried to make people cry and make people think. It didn't work.

Also, at that time, the kung fu comedy was very popular—Sammo Hung, Jackie Chan, that sort of thing. And the studio wanted to make movies like them, but I didn't want to. That's why they said I was [out of touch] and I couldn't fit into society anymore.

Q: *Out of your depth?*
JW: Yeah. They wanted me to start all over again. I said to them, "I don't know what happened. I'm pretty sure I'm a good director, I just

need a chance." I was extremely upset and frustrated. My good friend Tsui Hark realized that, and he talked to the studio. He was willing to take the responsibility to support me to make *A Better Tomorrow*. He knew that was the kind of movie I really wanted to make. And so, they gave him a medium budget and we worked out the story to make *A Better Tomorrow*. Tsui Hark was the producer, he helped me to package the whole movie, the actors, the style . . . and I came up with my own vision.

Q: *Now when this was happening, it was 1986?*
JW: No, it was filmed in 1985–1986 and it was released in the summer of 1986.

Q: *So this is happening, and Mr. Tsui comes and helps you.* A Better Tomorrow *was inspired by a Cantonese movie called* True Colors of a Hero. *Is that right?*
JW: Yeah, actually, it was the remake of that film. And actually the real English name is *The Story of a Discharged Prisoner*.

Q: *OK. So it was a remake, but what did you like about that film so much?*
JW: The film was made in 1967, directed by Lung Kong. He was one of the pioneers of Cantonese film. He was a great director at the time. He was the first one who used the handheld camera to shoot an entire movie. And at that time it was pretty rare. And he used half-documentary style and half-drama to make his story.

It also was about two brothers. The older brother used to be a gangster, and then he changed and he wanted to be out. He wanted to come out from that kind of society, from the underworld society, but those people didn't let him go. He struggled very hard.

He has a younger brother who misunderstands him. He never forgave him as a gangster. But he also learned from him and wanted to be the gang member. The older brother tried to help him, tried to bring him back, tried to pull him out of that kind of society.

There was a social worker played by a very famous actress, Ka Ling. Naturally, she was the real hero. The social worker tried many ways to help this older brother, because the whole world didn't understand him, didn't forgive him, even though he had changed, even though he had tried to find a way to get out of the underworld. But the people still saw him as a criminal and never forgave him. The woman was the only one helping him.

At the end of the film, the older brother tried to save his younger brother, and he had to fight. He had to go back to the gang to deal with the gang boss, and had to fight with them, because he wanted to save his own brother.

So the social worker is trying to get through all those things, and also helping him to regain a new life. We loved the story so much, and that movie also was a big hit at the time.

That movie was the big hit and also gave a new look to the Hong Kong Cantonese movie. We so much admired the director, and people loved the movie, and we wanted to remake a movie.

We changed the characters a little bit. The younger brother was a cop in my movie. It created more of a conflict between the two brothers. One is the right side; one is the wrong side. The social worker's character we changed to Chow Yun-Fat. Chow Yun-Fat is a good friend of the older brother's. He was a killer, but he has heart and the same kind of honor.

Q: *This is your first movie with Chow Yun-Fat?*
JW: Yeah, yeah, yeah.

Q: *What made you certain that he was going to be a big star?*
JW: I didn't know he would become a big star after that movie. The reason I wanted him was because I found he was a really good actor, even though he was just a popular TV star at the time. He also had done some movies, but they flopped. He got the name "box office poison." People liked him but people didn't appreciate him as a good actor.

When I read the newspaper, he was always helping poor kids, giving his money, helping his friends. He's a man with big honor. And I thought, "This kind of man is a true hero, and this man is my kind of hero." I also really liked his performances.

So I used him to play Mark, this character in *A Better Tomorrow*. Then I found that this guy was so elegant and also had great charisma. He reminded me of Alain Delon, and Steve McQueen, Ken Takakura—all my great idols, all in him. And I thought, while we are shooting, I just felt, "He's a great actor; he will be popular." But I didn't know he'd be *that* popular, you know? The movie worked so well. One of the reasons the movie became a big hit was because of him.

Q: *Sure. And that started the trend in Hong Kong with people wearing trench coats....*
JW: And sunglasses.

Q: *...and sunglasses.*
JW: And I'm not kidding, you know. All of a sudden, most of the sunglasses sold out in Hong Kong. Even though people couldn't buy the same kind, and they bought a similar kind.

Q: *And why do you think that movie was such a huge hit?*
JW: Beside the actors, I think that the story really moved a lot of the audience. They'd never seen a gangster movie that had a sense of great style. And also so emotional. Most of the drama looked so real, because it came from my heart—most of the dialogue was written by myself.

They were also moved by the character, Chow Yun-Fat's character. Everybody wanted to do the same thing, like him. Always, whatever he did, he did for his friend. That kind of honor and loyalty, that kind of higher dignity and spirit, for Asian people—they always admire those kinds of people. The way he sacrifices himself for a friend, that kind of a spirit.

The audience was also moved by the relationship between the two brothers. There's a lot of conflict, a lot of guilt and misunderstanding between the two brothers, and people felt sad about it.

Another thing is, the movie really had created a new kind of style in action, production design and cinematography. It was all very fresh for the audience. The action—they'd never seen a movie [where a character] uses two guns. The gun battle scene was so impressive.

On the other hand, the movie also had brought out the old-fashioned, the true value of the morality. Like in old times, people used to care so much about each other and took care of each other and had strong friendships or family to bond them together. Now, all those kinds of good things, it is all lost.

A lot of the old traditional things are lost. But when they watch the film, they find true values from the old time and the true value of a friendship.

Q: *So* A Better Tomorrow *came out and was a big hit. The sequel came next. Did you want to direct the sequel, did you think that was a movie that had to be made?*
JW: No, I just wanted to make the prequel, not a sequel. Because Chow Yun-Fat's character was dead in the first one. It didn't make sense to make a sequel. I wanted to make a prequel, so I came up with a story, which I used for *Bullet in the Head*.

I thought people would love to see how they started, how they became friends, and what kind of situation made them have that kind of life. How they all started in a slum and had been through so many things, so many disasters and adventures. How they got involved with the gang, and how they were forced to make the wrong choices. And then how they worked together and looked out for each other, became friends. So that was my idea. I had used some of my life story in that movie.

Q: *Right. I remember the whole drinking scene. . . .*
JW: Yeah. But somehow something else happened. One of my good friends, Dean Shek, he was one of the chairmen of the company Cinema City. He was so upset at that time. He was kind of a failure, and he wasn't popular anymore. He went to United States and wanted to retire.

So since we were good friends, Tsui Hark and I wanted to bring him back. We went to the United States to meet him and convince him and coach him and try to bring him back and then help him. So Tsui Hark came up with the idea and said he wanted to make a sequel about this guy, like how we were helping him and put it into the story. It changed all of my plans.

Tsui Hark came up with the idea that Mark had a twin brother in New York. He was so upset and [Dean Shek's character] brings him back to Hong Kong to get revenge.

But I wasn't happy with the whole concept of this story, but I wanted to make it for [Dean Shek]. But I wasn't really happy with the script. Then I came up with another idea. My idea was to focus on two younger brothers, Leslie Cheung and the young Chow Yun-Fat. They both had the same things in common. We shot a lot of scenes where they worked together, where they're talking to each other—but they all took it out because the movie was so long.

Q: *The first cut was three hours and forty minutes, is that right?*
JW: No, almost three hours. We were forced to cut it under two hours for the theatrical release.

Q: *The way that worked was: Tsui Hark took one part and you took one part, edited them separately and put them together, is that right?*
JW: Yeah, we only had a week to edit the whole film. [Laughs]

Q: *And what was your relationship with Tsui Hark? I got the sense that there's this deep friendship, but you don't always get along.*
JW: Well, we have a good friendship.

In 1981, after I helped Cinema City make a film, *Laughing Times*. They all believed in me, and so I was trying to make a deal with them. I introduced Tsui Hark to them. I said, "If you want me to work with you guys, you have to sign him first. Give him a movie." And then they said, "OK." They promised me. They also loved his work. I kept pushing them. At that time he already had made two movies, but they didn't work. They were flops.

Q: *One was called* The Butterfly Murders *in 1979 and the other is* We're Going to Eat You.
JW: Yeah, yeah, yeah, those are his two movies. The two of them didn't work, but he had been recognized as a very talented filmmaker. He had bad luck and was so upset at that time, so depressed. I always encouraged him and then I introduced him to Cinema City and I forced these guys to sign him, and I guaranteed to take full responsibility for Tsui Hark. They trusted me.

So after they signed him and let him make a movie called, *All the Wrong Clues for All the Right Solutions*. He made that movie very stylish, but when he was shooting the film, he was a little over budget.

The main studio, Golden Princess, was so nervous. They didn't know what to do and they asked me to take a look at some of the footage. When I looked at the footage, I found that it was very good; it was new. Then

I turned to all those executives and the chairman and I said, "I guarantee this movie's gonna make a lot of money. It's gonna be a big hit."

They all felt relaxed, and they said, "Oh, if John Woo said it's gonna be a big hit, it's gonna be a hit."

They trusted me, but actually I didn't know what the story was. But I took over full responsibility for it. So they gave [him] more money to invest in that movie. That movie he made was a big hit and it also won the best director from the Taiwan Golden Horse Film Festival.

I was so happy, I had tears in my eyes. I almost cried. People were shocked: "Tsui Hark got the award—why is John Woo more happy, more emotional than Tsui Hark?"

It was because I tried to get him a picture, I tried to help him for two years. And a lot of people didn't care much about him. And then after he made it, I was so emotional, and then we all hugged together.

At the time he became a big director, and I became down [on my luck]. We just switched positions. So that's why he wanted to pay me back and help me make *A Better Tomorrow*. Actually, *A Better Tomorrow* was based on our friendship.

Q: *Reading quotes from him, he has said that, as your producer, sometimes you were so independent that sometimes there was friction between the two of you. What's it like when you're such good friends with somebody to have to work with them and you're fighting?*

JW: Well, there's so many reasons [we fought]. Because I care so much about friendship and the movie. . . . When I'm making a movie, you know, I give it my heart. I only think about the movie and I don't care about anything else. I only focus on what I'm doing.

But for some of the filmmakers, besides creating their own movies, they are also involved with so many business and political things. Tsui Hark is such a brilliant filmmaker, you know, but sometimes he had to handle the whole company. He had to deal with the studio, deal with so many people, deal with so much pressure.

Sometimes, when we were talking about scenes, talking about our concept, he had a certain way to see the movie but I had my way of seeing the movie. So we had creative conflict.

After we made *A Better Tomorrow II*, I found that we had creative problems. Because like I said, I wasn't excited about the idea of the story of *A Better Tomorrow II*, and actually it was Tsui Hark's idea. In my version, I put my focus on the two brothers.

But after we had to cut the film, and a lot of my good moments were taken out. And I didn't feel happy about it. All of a sudden, all the focus turned to Dean Shek's character, which wasn't my wish. I found that creatively, we have different ways.

In my point of view he had changed a little bit. He was powerful; he had his own company. It was sometimes hard to talk to him; we really had so many different ways.

For the first movie, *A Better Tomorrow*. . . . When the movie has a huge success—it broke all the records—sometimes, it makes people change. Sometimes it changes people's lives, sometimes it changes people to have some other way of thinking.

And then after *A Better Tomorrow II*, I found we had quite a big gap between us. I was asked to make *A Better Tomorrow III*, and I refused, because I didn't want to do it anymore.

I wanted to do a movie, *The Killer*. But that movie, originally it was a story about two cops. And it didn't get approved, and I didn't get support from Tsui Hark. I couldn't make the film for a year, and I was so upset. Even though I was a big-time director, he still didn't let me make the movie.

In the meantime, they all wanted to use a big star like Chow Yun-Fat, but Chow Yun-Fat was so busy. He was doing two or three movies at the same time. And so I couldn't get him. I didn't get support, so I was so upset.

And then after that, we tried to see each other and Chow Yun-Fat asked me, "John, why are you so upset?"

I said, "I couldn't make this movie *The Killer*, because the studio said this movie couldn't be made without you."

But he was so busy, which I could understand. And my kind of character, I have never liked to ask people any favors, or to pay me back.

Chow Yun-Fat, he heard about this, and he knew I couldn't get support from Tsui Hark's company, because there was no star and a simple story. Chow Yun-Fat had talked to the studio, and he wanted to do it. So the movie could be made because of him.

Tsui Hark and I were working on a story. I wanted to make a movie tribute to Jean-Pierre Melville and Scorsese. Creatively, we had a lot of different thinking. Even though he came up with some good suggestions, I just made it in my own way. I had used a lot of slow motion, which was modern before, and made the film so stylish. And he suggested that I cut out all the slow motion. You are the first ones to know about this.

Of course, in his point of view, he thought that this film shouldn't use slow motion. But I said, "That's my style. I like it," because I liked Sam Peckinpah and Scorsese. He wanted me to take out all the slow motion, I didn't care about his opinion.

And that made me feel we should separate. But I still admire him, respect him. I found if we both work together on that one film, it's gonna be kind of a waste. If we separated, it would be good for both of us, and then the audience could watch two different kinds of movies.

Q: *Have you become better friends now that you don't work together?*
JW: Yeah, I think so. I found that I should make my movies in my own way.

Q: *John, there's a whole section on* The Killer, *so I don't want to spend much more time on it. Next up is,* Just Heroes.
JW: All right, *Just Heroes* was made . . . I forgot in which year.

Q: *It's says 1989 here. But you tell me.*
JW: Yeah, yeah, yeah. We wanted to make the movie to help our mentor, Chang Cheh. Chang Cheh was down [on his luck], and he was old, but he still wanted to continue making movies. But he was broke, had no money. He had never been backed by a studio or asked for anybody's help. He just waited, waited, waited to get some money to let him continue making films.

David Chiang [also known as John Chiang—ed.] and Danny Lee, we're good friends—they found out this situation. They wanted to help and also wanted to pay him back, because we all admire him, we learned so much from him. We wanted to make a movie and raise money just for him. So we all got together, all the actors who worked for him, because we were all his protégés. We made up a story called *Just Heroes*, and tried to make it like another version of *A Better Tomorrow*—that type of a film. We made it, as we got support from Golden Princess, and we all worked for free.

It did make some money, and all the money we gave to Chang Cheh. We wanted him to retire, because he was so old and sick. But after Chang Cheh got the money, he didn't listen to us, and he used that money to make another movie.

Q: *And what was the name of the movie?*
JW: I forgot. [Possibly *Hidden Hero*—ed.] The movie was made in China. He was a very strong character; he never liked to bother anyone, never liked to beg for money. So we gave it to him, and we wanted him to have good life, a better life—living better for the rest of the life, but he didn't care about that.

Q: *Well, that's understandable. If you're a director, all you want to do is direct.*
JW: Yeah, yeah, I always want to direct. But [Chang Cheh's] movie didn't work.

Q: *The next step was that you used your prequel idea from* A Better Tomorrow *to make* Bullet in the Head. *You were already popular, a big success, but did* Bullet in the Head *give you international success?*
JW: No, it was *The Killer* that got international success. *Bullet in the Head* was a failure in Hong Kong. After I left Tsui Hark, I had formed my own company called John Woo Film Productions, and that was my first and only film with the John Woo Film company. *Bullet in the Head* was shot in Thailand, and we spent a lot of money. It was a pretty big budget for a Hong Kong film. The first cut was two hours and forty-five minutes, so it was pretty long.

When we did the premiere for the film, for industry people, it was a pretty big premiere. We were using two big theaters, because of so many people. But the people didn't appreciate the movie, they just were stepping in and out during the show. There was a lot of talking. A lot of people didn't quite care for the movie. Some people even said, "Oh, what a bad movie." Then they talked to my boss. They said to him, "Why are you spending so much money to let John Woo make this kind of shit movie?"

I was pretty hurt. I was forced to cut the movie down to two hours. Two hours and ten minutes, something like that. There were so many versions even under two hours.

And it flopped. The movie was just right after the Tiananmen Square massacre. So when the people watched the film, they knew what kind of message was in the film—about people killing one another. They strongly related it to the Tiananmen massacre.

Q: *And it's about three friends who go and try to find their fame and fortune, and they end up in Vietnam, is that right?*
JW: Yeah, yeah, yeah.

Q: *For me, that is your darkest film. There's some ugly. . . .*
JW: The director's cut is much darker. Actually, that movie was inspired by Scorsese's *Mean Streets*.

But so the movie was a failure in Asia, but then after I moved to America, I found that there were a lot of people with so much interest in the film. I was shocked, and really appreciated that. The young people, they all mentioned about how much they liked *Bullet in the Head*. And also in Europe, the French people, the English and then Germany—they all liked it. I was really moved.

But in Hong Kong, it didn't work at all. People said a lot of bad things about that film. It's a completely different feeling. And then after a few years, I found that more people liked it. They released it on DVD in so many versions. In Hong Kong the movie was totally lost. But after it drew so much attention from the Western world, and from the DVD and video, it made all the money back. So I was really excited about it.

Q: *Tell me about* Once a Thief *in 1990.*
JW: That movie was shot without a script. The failure of *Bullet in the Head* was pretty tragic for me. I gave my heart to that film, and thought it had a pretty good message. Maybe the film was too dark for the audience. Even in the reviews, they felt I was a tragic person. But I wanted to let the people know that actually, I'm pretty optimistic. I wanted to make another commercial movie, to try to make the money back for my boss, Mr. Ng Sui-chan.

When the movie failed, I said to him, "I'm sorry, boss. The movie is a total loss, and I feel so sorry about that."

And then he comforted me. He said, "John, don't be sorry. Money means nothing, but I must say, this is the best movie you've ever made."

So I felt so appreciative of my boss, who was so understanding, even though he was about 40 million Hong Kong dollars in the hole. That was a lot of money at the time. He was a good boss, so I wanted to make another commercial movie to make the money back for him.

Chow Yun-Fat and I came up with the idea. I teamed up with Chow Yun-Fat, Leslie Cheung, Cheri Chung, and Terence Chang, as a producer. We had the idea to make a heist movie. It started in France. I tried to make a young, fresh comedy. It was a miracle. We shot the entire film without a script. We started from scratch and finished the movie in two months. We wrote and shot at the same time. We wanted to make the film for Chinese New Year. We had spent one month in Nice shooting the first half of the movie, and then we moved back to Hong Kong to shoot the second half of the movie.

From the script to shooting to post-production, it was two and a half months, just in time for the Chinese New Year release. That's why the style was incomplete. In the French part, was a tribute to the French New Wave movie, like *Jules et Jim*. The second half was an over-the-top comical action style. Whenever we figured out any good gag or action, we just shot it. But that movie was a hit. There were some good, fun moments. But the whole movie, it didn't make sense to me. I was happy the movie had made money, but I wasn't really excited about it.

Q: *The title of the film came from a Ralph Nelson film with Alain Delon?*
JW: Yeah, yeah.

Q: *There are some critics who've said that this is your Hitchcock movie, because all the guys dress well and they're suave and there's a robbery. . . . Was Hitchcock an influence for this one?*
JW: Yeah. Not only Hitchcock, but some of the classic movies in the 1960s with Cary Grant, Peter O'Toole, and Audrey Hepburn—all those sort of things.

John Woo's *A Better Tomorrow*

KAREN FANG / 2002

Q: *The journalism on* A Better Tomorrow *often describes the glamorously dressed characters as "Armani-clad." Were the clothes used in the movie in fact Armani clothes? If so, to your knowledge, did the popularity of the film spark a surge in local taste for Armani or Armani-style knock-offs, much as occurred for the Ray Ban sunglasses worn by Chow Yun-Fat in the film?*

JW: There is a story here. The producer, a good friend of mine, Tsui Hark, suggested that we make the whole movie very modern. Everything and everyone would be glamorous and charismatic. I wanted to build a specific image for Chow Yun-Fat's character. So I put all of my idols together: Alain Delon, Clint Eastwood, Steve McQueen, and Ken Takakura. Alain Delon was suave and always dressed in a long coat. Clint Eastwood, Steve McQueen, and Ken Takakura always wore those dark glasses. So we put Chow Yun-Fat in the long coat and the cool shades. The funny part is that Hong Kong always has tropical weather. No one wears long coats. I wanted my hero to wear soft material and look easy, elegant and smooth. I wanted the clothes to look good in slow motion. Anyway, the costumer recommended that we use Armani because they have that special style and feel to their clothes. When I am considering costumes, I think about the characters' style and image but also how the clothes will work with the action I am going to put them in. For example, in the beginning of *Face/Off*, Nic Cage is in a long silk garb. We chose this costume in part because the material looked great blowing behind him

---

We thank Hong Kong University Press for granting permission to reprint Karen Fang's interview with John Woo from *John Woo's A Better Tomorrow* (2004) by Karen Fang.

as he walked. When *A Better Tomorrow* was a big hit, it was the biggest in Hong Kong history. So all of the young people wanted to look like Chow Yun-Fat. After that, Ray Ban started selling out of those sunglasses. The young people started to wear those long coats. The gangsters even started wearing suits and ties with long coats. Before that they just looked like street gangsters.

Q: *You have appeared as a supporting character in a number of your Hong Kong films, ranging from* Hand of Death *[also called* Countdown in Kung Fu—*ed.] through* Hard Boiled. *Your appearances are unique in that, unlike the cameos of Hitchcock or the starring roles of Woody Allen, you seem to prefer a significant but not central mode of participation. In particular, you seem to favor a strongly moral identity and/or association with law enforcement, appearing as a scholar in* Hand of Death *and as a cop in* A Better Tomorrow *and* Hard Boiled. *What are your objectives and inspirations in these directorial appearances? Do you see yourself as enacting the kinds of directorial self-reference practiced by Hitchcock or Allen, or have there been other models for your appearances in your own movies?*

I am particularly interested in why you have cast yourself in the roles (cops and other moral characters) that you have, and whether you develop those characters with yourself in mind. In A Better Tomorrow, *for example, how would you describe the function of the Taiwanese inspector, as he contrasts with the romantic or tragic heroism of the Ti Lung and Chow Yun-Fat characters, the corrupt greediness of Waise Lee's character, and the relative incompetence of the local Hong Kong police? (Your presentation of the character is intriguing because Inspector Wu is ambiguous—both persecuting Ho but also expressing his respect for him—and because he often seems to be psychologically close to Ho and Mark, as he walks the hallway in the Taipei restaurant just as Mark did during the shoot-out.)*

JW: Sometimes I like to do cameos in my movies just for fun.

Sometimes it has meaning because of the role. I started out as an actor on stage in high school. I thought of myself as a character actor. I realized I had no chance of really being successful at it. I only do it in my own movies, I wouldn't have the guts to act in anything else. In *A Better Tomorrow*, when I was acting in a scene, Yun-Fat and Leslie directed me. I am not a good actor. I take too long, like thirty takes. I just can't get used to someone else calling "Action!"

In *A Better Tomorrow*, I did not intend to be in the movie. There was another actor who was cast in the part, but his performance was not suitable. My point was to use the inspector's point of view to show that morally things are not always black and white. I needed to prove this, I needed to find it out. Sometimes when you feel a person is bad, there is good there as well. This is a truth about human beings and a theme in all of my movies. I have always believed that good and evil are not black and white. They co-exist in people.

When I played Inspector Wu, at the end of the film he was completely wrong and he had to realize that. With this realization he became human. I always believe that if you want to catch a thief you have to think like him and act like him, first. Then you can make your judgment.

I like to appear in my films on the right side because I believe the good people always win. At the same time we have to understand each other and know the good and bad in all of us. I think that came from my Christian education.

While working on *Hard Boiled* I never intended to appear in it. Chow Yun-Fat is a very good friend of mine. On the last day of shooting he came to me with the idea that I do a cameo appearance. He wanted to create a scene between he and I that showed our true friendship to the audience. We made up dialogue and a character for me. Chow Yun-Fat wanted to show his respect so we made my character his mentor, someone who cared about him and gave him direction.

In *Hand of Death* I appear as a revolutionary because I deeply admired the revolutionaries. A lot of people sacrificed their lives out of love for their country. Their courage was a huge contribution. I always imagined that if I was born at that time I would be a revolutionary. I have always wanted to show my love for my country and people.

Q: *A recurring set piece in your films is a scene where villains masquerade as innocents or heroes, forcing the real heroes to pretend to be villains in order to stop them. For example, this occurs in the climax of* A Better Tomorrow *when Shing, wearing white, surrenders to the cops to gain their protection against Ho; in* Hard Boiled, *when Johnny Weng's henchmen wear police* uniforms, so that the undercover cop Tony has to put on a stolen uniform in order to pretend to be a gangster who has "arrested"—actually captured—Tequila; and in *Windtalkers* when Ben Yahzee uses his physical similarity to the Japanese to infiltrate their stronghold. I understand these scenes to imply the absurdity of the contemporary world, where things have gone so wrong that they are the opposite of what they are supposed to be, but is there anything more specific that you mean to suggest in these scenes? For instance, are you perhaps trying to make a specific point about corruption and the necessity to break the rules in order to stop those who have broken rules to worse effect?

JW: I always believe that people are born innocent. We all start out pure. Some people become evil because they are misled by society. They want to do something good but there are so many temptations, so much bad around them, so much greed that changes people. Unfortunately, when these people get trapped by the darker side of life there is often no way out. People who do bad things always have so many reasons why. Some have mental problems, some are abused and some just succumb to temptations. Before we judge those people we have to understand them first. We have to try to find a way to work with them. Try to show them a lighter side to change them. I always feel sad for those people. When I was a kid I lived in a very bad neighborhood. I had friends living on the dark side of the world. They were in gangs or using drugs. So often, they were abused by their parents. They were outsiders and they were despised. I saw them as friends and I tried help them to see a lighter side of life. Sometimes, I covered for them. And most of them changed but a few were lost and couldn't get out of that side. So things aren't black and white. There is good in these people and I would rather help them than judge them.

In *A Better Tomorrow*, Shing wears white. It was symbolic; originally he was an innocent man, then he got trapped by the dark side of life. He is a tragic character because those people can't help themselves. They think they are heroes in that dark society.

Everyone does things wrong. Nobody is perfect. For that reason, people in glass houses shouldn't throw stones. Even in that society, they have a human side. No one can judge right and wrong before we really understand the other side. I also learned from our history. In *A Better Tomorrow* I was expressing my feelings about missing the true spirit of the old time morals and ethics. The idea for *A Better Tomorrow* was inspired by the atmosphere in Hong Kong at the time. Tsui Hark and I saw that the youth were lost. They had no respect for their elders and no care for their families. Some people call me old-fashioned and I don't think that is all bad. I hold dear the old-fashioned values of honor, brotherhood, caring for your family, and respecting your elders. Tsui and I wanted to make a movie that would remind the youth of what they were missing. We wanted to remember those lost values and bring them back in style.

Q: *You have been quoted in other publications as being influenced by Arthur Penn. Please provide some of the titles of Penn's films that have influenced you, perhaps discussing in particular Penn's 1967 film* Bonnie and Clyde *(if it is, in fact, one of the films that influenced you).*
JW: I love Arthur Penn movies and I think he is one of the greatest masters of all time. He is the most influential filmmaker of the 1950s and '60s. *Bonnie and Clyde* gave me a lot of great influence. I was so stunned while I was watching that movie. He could take an ordinary gangster movie and make it poetic. He used strong film language to explore the stunning romanticism and beauty of life and death. In the end, the killing of Bonnie and Clyde: he builds it up with serenity, it is quiet sitting in that car and there is only a slight breeze stirring.

It seems like something is going to happen but he did not foreshadow anything. You see all the beauty of life. The characters are feeling the dream and all of a sudden the bird flies out of the bushes. Warren and Faye look at each other with that knowing smile. They feel the end but they also feel eternity. The duality of knowing they are going to die but also knowing that their love will live on afterward. That is the romance that makes me hold my breath. Then suddenly they get shot. It really contrasts the ugliness of the killing with the beauty that preceded it. Arthur Penn created a beautiful spiritual tableau. That scene, especially, opened my mind and inspired me for *A Better Tomorrow*.

The end scene in *A Better Tomorrow*—Chow Yun-Fat's death scene— I used the same feeling. Before he gets shot he is screaming at Leslie Cheung. Then he gets shot in the head and he is so still. He looks back with fear and regret. Then Chow Yun-Fat pushes Leslie away and takes all the bullets. That was inspired by *Bonnie and Clyde*.

Bonnie and Clyde in so many ways is the perfect movie to me. The directing, the script, the editing, the cinematography, and the costuming are all perfectly matched. Especially the editing holds the rhythm and makes it lyrical. I learned a lot about editing from this movie.

I think Arthur Penn is a poet and had a great humanity. I enjoy his other films, too. I like *Left Hand Gun*. *The Chase*, that's a great movie. *Little Big Man*.

Q: *The year 1967 seems to be an important time for you. It is the year of the Lung Kong film* (The Story of a Discharged Prisoner) *on which* A Better Tomorrow *is based; it is the year of Jean-Pierre Melville's* Le Samourai, *a film you have cited as one of your favorites; and it is the setting of* Bullet in the Head. *(It is also the year of* Bonnie and Clyde, *which I raise in the previous question.) For you, personally, in 1967 you would have been twenty or twenty-one years of age, and hence it might be pinpointed as a time of "coming of age"; historically, it was also a time of intense social upheaval, both in Hong Kong and throughout the world. Why, would you say, so much of your work has turned to 1967, both in terms of filmic references and cinematic subjects? What part of your memories of 1967 is more important to you—the cultural turbulence that you lived through or the cinematic achievements that impressed you?*

JW: One fueled the other. The cultural turbulence was a fuel for the cinematic achievements of others that spoke to me and both of these were fuel for my work. In the 1960s there were huge changes all over the world. It was a time of great progress. Everything was starting a new life. Fortunately, working and living in a free city (Hong Kong), we could accept influence from all over the world. In 1960-early '70s, I was deeply in love with the movies. Before this year I was in love with the classic American movies.

I loved watching Lung Kong and Chang Cheh movies. At that time Japanese movies were so strong and gave us a lot of artistic inspiration.

Then the French New Wave gave us the most influence. They gave a message of love to the intellectual groups. Stanley Kubrick, David Lean, Sam Peckinpah, Jean-Pierre Melville, François Truffaut, Jean-Luc Godard, [Michelangelo] Antonioni, Vittorio De Sica, [Bernardo] Bertolucci. The French New Wave were the first ones to take the camera out to the street to make movies. They made films as auteurs. They were against the studio system. They opened our minds and made us want to make movies like them. They created a new film language. I deeply like *Le Samourai*. Jean-Pierre Melville was the coolest filmmaker at that time. He made gangster movies so cool and stylish. He had a similar philosophy in filmmaking as we (the Chinese). I could so strongly relate to it. He helped me establish my style.

In the meantime I deeply admired Kurosawa movies. His movies have a great element of humanity. *Seven Samurai, Throne of Blood, High and Low*, and all of his films had so much artistic influence. They are so memorable. He also has fantastic technique in making these movies.

There were no film schools in Hong Kong (I was too poor to go anyway) so all we could do at that time was learn from watching movies and learn from books and watch the theater. It was great because the movies at that time gave us a lot of surprises and changed our concept of movies.

At that time, they were more concerned about the message than entertaining. It was more about the emotions between people. Aside from learning a new technique, I learned about how to get across a message of humanity. Even the Hollywood movies like *Lawrence of Arabia, 2001: A Space Odyssey, Spartacus*, and *Casablanca*. And the American New Wave, like Scorsese and Coppola, they were about human dignity. They gave me a lot of influence, I love those movies.

This is why my films are so concerned about people.

Q: *You've said that you created* Bullet in the Head *as your response to the Tiananmen Square massacre and the problems that tragedy foretold for Hong Kong after the 1997 handover. As you're no doubt aware, Western critics interested in your work frequently describe all of your Hong Kong crime films from the 1980s and early 1990s as being metaphors or allegories about Hong Kong's political situation. To what extent is this true of* A Better Tomorrow *(whose conversation between Ti Lung and Chow Yun-Fat, in which Mark says that the beauty of Hong Kong "will not last," is frequently cited . . .)?*
JW: Even though I have no interest in politics I have a great concern for what is going on in the country I live in. I love Hong Kong. There is so much freedom to accept things from all over the world and it is a good place to live. The harbor is beautiful. Hong Kong people work together to make Hong Kong successful. I just didn't want to see it change. I knew

there would be a time when Hong Kong would have to return to China. We can't change history. But I still hope all the beauty of Hong Kong will remain the same. That's why in my movies (even the early ones like *Plain Jane to the Rescue*) I try to make the point that no matter what happens, people need to stick together, to work it out, and keep the good about Hong Kong.

A Better Tomorrow was not a political statement, it was me trying to express my feelings about the inevitable and the dreams I have for Hong Kong. The outstanding feeling I want to express in *A Better Tomorrow* is about human dignity. No matter what happens, human dignity should not change. To preserve human dignity you have to be sure of yourself and true to the good in humanity. So at the end of the movie when Chow Yun-Fat sacrificed himself for Leslie, it served his code of honor. That is what we are here for.

Q: *Similarly, is it true—as is suggested in the press kit to the film—that* Hard Boiled *is set in 1997? If so, why is that setting not substantiated in film? (To my memory there are no direct and obvious allusions to the handover.)*

JW: Actually, *Hard Boiled* was not set in 1997. It was only slightly an allusion to the handover. My point was to show that at that time, the violence had gone too far in Hong Kong. The gangsters were ruthless with their gun smuggling and brutality. The police had a hard time dealing with them because they did not have the strength or the firepower. I hate to see so many innocent people hurt. There was so much confusion. At the same time Iraq invaded Kuwait. It made me feel so angry. There was so much injustice. So I wanted to make a new kind of hero with Chow Yun-Fat—like Dirty Harry, he takes it into his own hands to fight evil.

While shooting, automatically, I felt we were making an observation about 1997 without intending it. I was using the hospital as a metaphor for a small society. They were all taken hostage but they still stick together to survive. No matter what happens we have to stick together to defend ourselves and survive. When our hero is trying to save the baby, the baby represents new life, new hope. No matter what happens we always have hope and new life. We can't give up on that. We have to protect it. Even when the world is full of ugliness, there is always hope.

Q: *Another ambiguity in* Hard Boiled *is the mysterious ending (Tony's fate), which in previous interviews you've declined to comment on. Will you say why you want to keep this ending ambiguous? Does it have anything to do with the political metaphors in the film?*

JW: In my version of *Hard Boiled*, Tony Leung was dead. He sacrificed himself. It was a dark message and he was a dark character. But after I shot the ending, the crew and the actors were not happy. They were strongly asking me to keep him alive. Some of my assistants even cried. I could understand why. All that had happened in Beijing gave the people of Hong Kong a lot of sadness. It made them feel like the good person should stay alive. So we added another ending. Tony lives and it gives people hope. Also, it was good for Chow Yun-Fat's character, it was a great metaphor that he never lost his friend. It really touched my heart that people felt so strongly about this Tony's character.

It was not a political metaphor but it was influenced by what had happened and indicative of what people in Hong Kong were feeling at the time.

Q: *How much was your decision, in the early 1990s, to relocate to Hollywood a factor of your concerns about the political status of Hong Kong?*

JW: My move to Hollywood had nothing to do with the political atmosphere in Hong Kong. I never had any worry about the takeover. I never had a problem with Hong Kong and I don't have any fear about that. No matter what happens in Hong Kong everything will be OK there.

There were several reasons I wanted to come to Hollywood. I had been working in Hong Kong so many years and creatively I felt limited and needed to grow and change. It was an extremely commercial place. All the movies were commercial and entertaining. Action movies and comedies were mainstream and it was hard to do anything else. Artistic films did not have an audience and political topics you could not touch.

I really wanted to make a change in my filmmaking. I wanted to try something different. After a few of my movies like *A Better Tomorrow* and *The Killer* drew so much international attention, that started to convince me that my movies had international appeal. I wanted to prove my movies could be accessible to other cultures, not just Asian communities. I wanted to make a Western film and see how it worked. I wanted to prove to myself I could do it.

Q: *By contrast, how much of your decision to relocate to the States was a factor of your aspirations to work in Hollywood?*
JW: Before *The Killer* and *Bullet in the Head*, I never noticed how my movie was received by foreigners. After these movies drew so much attention from the Western world it was extremely surprising and exciting. That was so encouraging, I felt like people cared about my movies. Then all of a sudden there were forty scripts sent to me from Hollywood. I was so flattered. I had calls from New Line and Twentieth Century Fox. Oliver Stone flew to Paris to meet me while I was working there and he wanted to produce a movie for me. I was invited to direct a movie for Universal Studios (*Hard Target*) with producers Jim Jacks and Sam Raimi starring Jean-Claude Van Damme. That encouraged me to take a chance.

I have always dreamt of working in different places and different countries. I love to learn from different cultures and make friends all over the world. Only Hollywood could allow me to do that. The most important reason for me to come to Hollywood was that I wanted to learn something new, creatively, technically and personally. I can always learn more. I would like to try to make a European style film because I have gotten so much influence from the French New Wave. I would love to find a way to make a tribute to the French New Wave filmmakers by taking a small crew and one camera and going out into the street.

Q: *When did you first start to plan on moving to Hollywood?*
JW: I made the decision to move to Hollywood in 1992. Terence Chang and I decided to move here. We came here to meet with the William Morris Agency and they took us to meet the studios and film companies. We had twenty-one meetings in three days. There were a lot of people who had interest in my movies and my style. I felt comfortable right away. When we came to Hollywood I found the people in this country were very kind, polite and respectful. It is a very open country. They are all reaching out their hands to the new talent no matter where you are from. They wanted me to bring my style to their Western movies.

On *Hard Target*, I learned that Americans had a different working system in this country. It was all new to me. In Hong Kong, the director was on his own. We could write the script as we were shooting the movie. There were one or two meetings with the producers then the rest of the movie choices and decisions were up to the director. In America, there are so many more people involved in the process. There are endless meetings and negotiations. The movie stars have final approval on so many things.

In Hollywood, directors often have to fight for creative freedom.

Fortunately, with all these strange things happening, Terence Chang handled all of the political issues and let me concentrate on my work. All the producers were very helpful and tried very hard to protect me and my creative choices.

Although it was a painful growing experience, I learned a lot from the crew. They worked very hard. The actors were professional. I made a lot of friends. Everyone was together on getting the film done. The crew members were all very educated in filmmaking. I have learned so much from Hollywood. There are so many talented people here. Great writers and actors who have opened my mind. I have learned a lot from the technology too. On *Broken Arrow* I learned a lot about special effects.

Of course it is so tough to find scripts that fit my style. I am grateful to get the chance to make movies like *Face/Off* and *Windtalkers*. *M:I2* was such a fun movie to make.

Q: *I understand that in Hong Kong you are not thought of as an "action" director, as your best-known films do not feature the martial arts that in Hong Kong is associated with action and the crime films are, instead, admired for their heroic character development. In Hollywood, however, which categorizes all visually spectacular, physically and technologically explosive films as "action," you are thought to be one of the best—if not the best—of the current practitioners of the action genre. Do you feel comfortable with that label as an action director? Has Hollywood fulfilled your hopes and expectations, in terms of your ability to make the kind of movies you want to make?*

JW: I don't really feel comfortable when some people label me as an action director. But I don't really think it is an issue. As long as people take away some other message or entertainment from my movies, whatever they call me, I don't mind. Actually, I love human drama,

I also like strong characters and meaningful messages. That's what I'm interested in doing. I always wanted to make movies with noble themes about human values. No matter if you consider it action or drama as long as you take from it a noble message about brotherhood, loyalty, love, and honor, then I have shared with you the values that I hold dear.

Sometimes I love to make action movies for entertainment. I also like to make movies about love and peace or about people struggling for their ideals and justice. I would like to make a great drama with strong visuals, like *The Wild Bunch* or *Rebel Without a Cause* or *West Side Story*.

I am pretty satisfied with the opportunities I have had, but I am still working toward the next challenge. I still haven't made the movie I really want to make, the musical, the western, the truly internationally-themed movie. What I am looking for is a movie that embodies the great cultures of the East and the West. One that expresses the true spirit of these, brings them together and helps us to understand each other more. This is my dream. I have been making movies a long time and if I could make a movie to show true friendship between these cultures that would be great.

I am grateful to work in Hollywood, there are so many opportunities and great people. It is always a challenge but it has allowed me to work internationally. It gives me the chance to travel to different countries, meet other people and work.

Q: *In the past five years or so, American interest in Hong Kong film has been strong while, sadly, the Hong Kong film industry itself seems to be slowing down. Indeed, arguably it seems that Hollywood is cannibalizing Hong Kong, because recent American blockbusters like* The Matrix *and* Charlie's Angels *feature Hong Kong-style martial arts, enhanced by the special effects only Hollywood budgets can provide. In fact, both films used famed Hong Kong action choreographers. As one of the most prominent of the "Hong Kong transplants" in Hollywood, what are your thoughts on the imitation of Hong Kong style by Hollywood and the supposed creative slowdown in Hong Kong itself?*

JW: We are all learning and imitating each other. Hong Kong in the old days got a lot of influence from American movies, especially technique. We got a lot of inspiration from the West. We used Western technique to tell a Chinese story. We just combined elements to create a new cinematic language. Now it's the West that is borrowing back. It comes full circle. We are all in the same film family. It is a good thing, I think. The Hong Kong film business is pretty slow right now and getting to be a critical situation. Hong Kong film should start from zero and creatively invent new things to say and how to say it. That won't be hard for Hong Kong people. They are smart and strong. They work hard and they endure. They will be inspired again and it will bring back business. Hong Kong people learn pretty fast. Hong Kong made great action movies for so long. They had to change.

China has such an extraordinary history and now there are so many permanent changes happening there. So many great stories lie with those great people. Maybe Hong Kong will start with that for inspiration. For the Western world there is so much mystery and interest in China. So few Westerners have a chance to get to understand our culture. I think China should open up and share the stories of their great culture with the world, like a cultural exchange, to gain more friendship between us all and start a new movie market in the process.

Q: *You may be aware that the Western scholarly interest in your films often point out what is thought to be homoerotic tendencies, in the strong bonds between male characters in your films. For these critics this interpretation is supported by the romantic film grammar—of longing glances and embraces between male characters and the relative absence or insignificance of female characters. What is your reaction or response to this interpretation?*
JW: When I am done making a movie I feel like it is a painting that belongs to the viewer. They are allowed to feel what they feel and think what they think. I never intended it that way but it doesn't bother me that people have homoerotic feelings about my movies. The difference in perception is cultural. In my culture there is no hiding. If we need to cry, we cry. If you need to hug someone you do it whether they are your lover or your friend. I explore my own emotions while making my movies, so I'm glad that the audience explores their emotions while watching them.

In *A Better Tomorrow*, I wanted to represent my exceptional friendship with Tsui Hark in the film. Tsui Hark and I had seen each other through major highs and lows in our careers. We had similar minds and a great admiration for each other. There was a time when I was very popular in Hong Kong and Tsui Hark was yet undiscovered. I convinced an independent film company to produce a film with Tsui Hark because I admired his spirit and vision. His film was a great success and when he won a best director award for it, I was more excited for him than he was. He became very popular in Hong Kong. At the same time, my movies became box office poison and people who once believed in me were telling me to retire. I was broke and depressed. Tsui Hark was loyal to me then; he still had faith that I was a talented director. So he used his influence to help me make *A Better Tomorrow*. Then we broke box office records in Hong Kong. In *A Better Tomorrow*, I wanted to share with the audience my great appreciation for our friendship.

Perhaps another reason people perceive a homoerotic message in my films is because I like to stay in a moment. In America, the popular way of cutting films is quicker. They cut away from actors before the actor has completed the emotional journey. If I am moved by an emotional moment in the actor's performance, I want to stay in it. I keep the camera on them longer and wait to see what happens.

The Killer: Criterion Collection Commentary Track Interview Excerpts

DAVID CHUTE, MARK RANCE, ET AL./1994

[Editor's note: *The Killer* stars Chow Yun-Fat as Jeff, an assassin who gets double-crossed by his boss on a final hit—the proceeds of which were to restore the sight of Jennie, played by Sally Yeh, a singer he blinded. Danny Lee plays Inspector Li, whose destiny becomes entangled with Jeff's struggle to regain honor. *The Killer* remains famous for its final epic battle in church.]

DAVID CHUTE: *The killer—is he a good man, or is he a man who wants to be good?*
JOHN WOO: He wants to be good. That's why at the beginning, I put a church. In childhood, I always liked to sit in the church; I liked calm and peace and I liked to have time and a place for thinking to myself.

So, for the killer, he wanted to be good and he was fed up with killing and he's trying to stop, but the problem for the killer is that once you pick up a gun, it's hard to put it down. So, it's a matter of honor. So, he is also like me, sitting in a church and thinking, thinking of his destiny. . . . Friendship is the only thing he's got, so he tried to quit, and he's fed up with the killing already. But he'd like to do the last job for a friend. He believes in friends.

From the Criterion Collection's 1994 original commentary track interview from *The Killer* sessions, previously unpublished in this form. Reprinted by permission, www.criterionco.com.

DC: *Why does he go to the club?*
JW: Since he wounded [the singer], the killer feels guilty, and in a way he tries to help her and tries to repay [her for] what he did. So he always watches her silently . . . just trying to do something for the girl.

DC: *This is a very important scene.*
JW: Yeah, this scene, when the killer is looking at a picture of the way she was before. So when he looks at the picture and he realizes before the girl got blind she was so full of life and beauty, so when he looks at the picture, he feels more guilty about it . . . like he ruined her life. So, he feels more pain, because the killer has his own principles. He only kills the bad guy and never harms the good guy. Maybe the idea came from pictures all over the room and all over the living room, especially my wife, you know, she likes to put her picture in the bedroom. She wants me to look at her [all the] time.

DC: *There was something interesting that you said about the way Catholicism was portrayed in Scorsese's films, like* Mean Streets.
JW: I admire Martin Scorsese so much, and also am influenced by him so much—especially *Mean Streets*. I really love that movie. So, in his movie, they kept in the church, so it made me use the Catholic Church in my movie.

I learned from his powerful technique and also learned from his dramatic slow motion. Now, the way he uses the slow motion—he likes to use [slow] motion to capture some beautiful movement in the acting, or he likes to capture some expression from the actors. It makes it look so beautiful and dramatic, so I use it in my frame.

I also use slow motion on actors, not only on the action. The action is from Sam Peckinpah, and also the camera movement—my camera movement is also influenced by him. . . . I also learned from [François] Truffaut's movies. He was the first one who used freeze frame on film for an emotional touch. There is a scene of Jeanne Moreau, she turns and looks at Oscar Werner in [*Jules et Jim*], and he freezes . . . on her smile. It was an unforgettable technique to make scenes more romantic. I never forgot and I try to use [it] in my movies.

Even though I learned [filmmaking] by myself, I also learned film theory from all the masters. But usually I don't care about a theory, and

I don't care about the traditional way of making film. Usually, I will do whatever I want. And I do whatever I feel. When I do the editing, suddenly I feel—in this moment or this scene I would like to use the dissolve or overlap in an emotional way. But when the audience sees the dissolve in the film, [they think] it means flashback.

DC: ... *Some of the things that you're talking about are ways of taking what's inside the character and making it visible.*
JW: Usually, whatever I do, I never think about the audience. The first thing I think of is the character, the actor and myself—how we feel.

For example, when ... [Chow Yun-Fat's character] is betrayed by a friend. We usually talk before the shooting, and I ask him, "Did you have any similar experience, or do you have any friends just like that ... and how do you feel about that?" So usually he will figure out and pick up some memory about his same experience. So it makes his acting look very real and touching, because it was real. That's how I work with the actors.... So, usually when [Chow Yun-Fat and I] work together, we always put our input, our real feeling into the character. So, what I mean is that when you see Chow Yun-Fat, you see me. I always like to put myself into his character.

... *The Killer* [is about] trying to find out if there is something in common between people. Also, I was so fascinated by a Japanese movie in the '60s. I forgot the name, [Law Kar says it is a Teruo Ishii movie called *Dip Hueh Shuan Hung* in Cantonese—ed.] but the star was Ken Takakura and the movie was shot in Hong Kong and Macau, and was also about a killer who only killed the bad people—the killer has principles, and he only kills the bad guys, never kills a good guy. But since he took a job and goes to Hong Kong and was set up by the Hong Kong gang and the Japanese gang, the person who he killed was a good guy. So, he regrets that he was used by the gang. And in the meantime, there is a Japanese cop who tracks him down to Hong Kong and tries to arrest him.

And so, the killer tries to take the revenge, and find out who set him up to get revenge to the whole gang. When he was wandering in Macau, he met a Japanese girl, and she's a whore. The girl tries to go back to Japan but she is so sick with tuberculosis and her dream is to go back to Japan. So the killer helps her, and asks her to wait until he fights the gang. He asks the girl to wait for him in the dark. So Ken Takakura goes to fight the gang and he gets killed. The Japanese girl is still waiting in the dark and the hero never comes. This movie I love very much, and it gave me the spirit to make *The Killer*.

DC: *Did the book* Chronicle of an Assassin *that you read when you were younger have a direct influence on the movie?*
JW: How did you know? In general I like the story about the assassins. Especially in the ancient time of China, there were four very famous assassins. They have a great story, and it is the character of the killer. You can say that the character of *The Killer* and *A Better Tomorrow* are all based on the ancient Chinese assassin story. The movie, *The Last Hurrah for Chivalry*, was influenced by my master, Chang Cheh.
[Dragon boat scene]
JW: This is my favorite scene in the whole movie. I tried to use the dragon boat race as a metaphor for the cop and the killer. For every movie I make, I always like to make a classic or unforgettable scene. . . . And for *The Killer*, I also try to make a dramatic and powerful killing scene. I wanted to make the dragon boat scene a classic, like the final scene of *Day of the Jackal*, when the killer kills the French priest—just like that.

So this scene: we shot documentary [footage for] five months before we started shooting. And then we rebuilt the same set to do the real scene. We had a lot of footage. The editor had trouble cutting it, and he didn't know how to cut it and the editor was not used to cutting scenes with other shots, with other storyboards, and he got no idea how to cut this scene well. So I cut it for myself and used three weeks to cut the scene. For the idea for the dragon boat I wanted, I tried to use the dragon boat race to symbolize the killer and the cop—the competition between them is like a sport.

MARK RANCE: *What does the cop have in common with the killer?*
JW: Even though they're enemies, they respect the same thing from each other. For example, this cop has feeling—usually the cop has no feeling, [or] usually the cop doesn't express feeling, and the cop feels the same way toward the killer because the killer usually has no feeling. So they recognize this in each other. That's the idea for the scene.

DC: *Can you talk about how that was supposed to work in the movie . . . ?*
JW: The original idea for *The Killer* was a triangle love story. The killer and the cop both fall in love with the singer. For some scenes, for example, the killer was with the girl or the girl with the cop, and I wanted to shoot it at the same angle, and put them in the same position and almost use the same line and camera movements, the same cutting, just try to try to show them have the same feeling. . . . I love big close-ups.

DC: *Where does that come from? Some people say Sergio Leone.*
JW: No, no. It's maybe about my hobbies. No matter where I am, I love watching people's faces. Even walking on the street, I always love to watch the different faces. I want to know their feelings . . . I want to create an intimate relationship between the audience and the actors, and the big close-ups can show them their acting in more detail. It looks more like a sculpture—you can think and you can feel more from their faces.

DC: *We wanted very much to have you talk about violence, about how . . . much is too much?*
JW: I've never taken violence seriously in my films. All I'm concerned with is that when I'm making violent scenes, is that it has to be based on emotion, not based how to please the audience or try to make someone happy. The most important thing is to try to make me happy, because when I'm shooting the action scenes, I feel very excited, it's the most exciting moment in my work. So, I feel so much joy when I was shooting the action scenes. All I thought about was how to make the action look— this is a very silly thing—romantic and beautiful.

Usually, I don't think of how the audience feels. The most important thing is how I feel. Sometimes I use violence to send some message, because when I was a child, I saw so much violence, so many people get killed, especially in 1967. There were two big riots in Hong Kong. A lot of people got killed in front of my door.

So actually I hate violence. I'm a peace-lover, and I hate war. I hate to see people killing each other. I wonder if violence sends a message, that violence has got to stop. If it cannot stop, we need some kind of hero to stop it . . . the hero sacrifices his life for honor, chivalry, and sometimes for sympathy. It's a very Chinese tradition.

I'm not romanticizing the violence . . . I romanticize the hero. When I shoot a movie or decide anything, I usually don't think about the result. I just do whatever I feel. For example, when I shot *A Better Tomorrow*, I just wanted to put Alain Delon's image on Chow Yun-Fat, so I made Chow Yun-Fat wear the long coat with the sunglasses to look very '60s.

But somehow his character and the movie became so popular; everybody imitated him. The young audience imitated him, they learned to dress like him and also learned his behavior. I didn't realize that before. The people take the impression of my movie and turn to love the violence, and some people misunderstood. I tried not to glorify the Triad [Hong Kong mafia—ed.]. I really didn't intend that. When I make a gangster movie, it is just like making a Chinese swordplay [movie]. All I intended was to glorify the hero, the behavior of the hero, not the Triad society. I admit the filmmaker sometimes has to be concerned about the moral standard . . . but for me, I make the film as an artist, and just make the film.

DC: *I think this scene coming up is the most popular . . . [the killer and the cop point guns at one another in Woo's trademark style—ed.].*
JW: When I was a child, I was so fascinated with the cartoon—I love it very much, and this scene was actually inspired by *Spy vs. Spy*, the comic from *Mad* magazine. The white bird and the black bird are always against each other, but deep in their heart, they are still friendly, and the idea came from that.

Since I wanted to make the cop and the killer friends, I used the idea for the end of the scene, so when they pointed the guns at each other, the blind girl is in between them. It's the only scene I showed both men, the killer and the cop. They both love the girl and care for the girl, so when they use the guns to point at each other, they don't want to hurt the girl. So they pretend they are longtime friends . . . and they don't want the girl to have hard feelings. And just like *Spy vs. Spy*, they both have good hearts, even though they are against each other.

I always believe the people in the world can get along together, even though we are from different countries, different races. I'm sure everyone has something good in their hearts. Even though we are enemies, we can live and work together peacefully and appreciate each other.

This is always my dream, so that's why I like to use two extremely different characters and put them together to try to emphasize the nature in human beings, and also to try to make it funny. So this scene is not so serious.

MR: *An obvious question would be, why a gun battle in a church?*
JW: Good question. A lot of people wonder why I used a church for a gun battle scene, especially for the final fight. In the beginning, the killer is sitting in the church. I wanted to say that God is welcoming, no matter if it's a good man or a bad man, everyone is welcome. When a gun battle is in a church, I just use it to say the war in between people and evil, they always turn heaven to hell. It's just like *Apocalypse Now*.

When you see the statue of the Virgin Mary being blown up, it means the people ruined all the beauty, loveliness and holiness. To me, the Virgin Mary represents peace and love, the truth and beauty, and the love from God.... [When the Virgin Mary blows up], it makes me feel more sad. So that's why I used the church for the gun battle scene.

... Since I wanted to make it like the good against evil, I made the gun battle big, like a war was going on. Everything has been damaged and destroyed, including the truth....

MR: *Did it take a longer time to shoot this scene—was this scene bigger than all the other scenes?*
JW: Well, this scene, including the exterior and interior, took twenty-eight days to shoot. It's a different location, a different set. Between inside and outside it did take a long time to shoot the scene. Because everything is a new experiment—everything was a new experience for the stunt group, for the special effect group, and also for the camera group. Everybody, everybody was having a hard time, especially the stunt group.

DC: *Was there some disagreement about how this final scene should be shot?*
JW: That's interesting. The other reason I used the church was to represent the fate of human beings. I tried to use the church to represent a feeling of destiny. The killer, when he is shot, he is blinded. Even though he had a good heart, he still cannot avoid fate. So he lost everything,

even though he got love. When we were shooting this scene, Chow Yun-Fat had a suggestion. He said he and Jennie [actress Sally Yeh—ed.] should go out together and meet, touch each other and hold hands very tight, and then die. I didn't agree. I said, how about we make it more tragic, let both of them, crawl together and pass, and miss each other. It will make it more tragic, and more like they have been played by fate.

MR: *They've been tricked by fate?*
JW: Yeah, they have been tricked by fate. That's why they miss each other. And Chow Yun-Fat agreed, so we made the scene more sad and dramatic. . . . So the cop did the last favor for the killer. He killed the bad guy for him, but by the law, he turns into a criminal. He's also tricked by fate. So all he has is the memory of a good friend. That's why at the end, I put Chow Yun-Fat playing the harmonica as the end shot.

DC: *His friend is thinking about him?*
JW: Yeah, his friend is thinking about him. The original idea for the ending is after the killing, Jennie goes to the airport again, alone, to try to get aboard. When she is just waiting for help, Danny Lee suddenly appears, brings the money, and goes to the United States with her, then tries to help cure her eyes. It's more like a happy ending. But since I overscheduled too much, and Jennie's schedule was too short, we canceled the scene. . . . We put Chow Yun-Fat's shot as the end shot, and [it] also got [across] the other meaning of an unforgettable friendship.

MR: *So in the end, death wins over the criminal, and law wins over the cop.*
JW: It's a little pessimistic. That's the world we live in.

Hard Boiled: Criterion Collection Commentary Track Excerpts

JOHN WOO, TERENCE CHANG, AND DAVE KEHR/1994

[Editor's note: Woo's ultra-violent *Hard Boiled* matches Chow Yun-Fat, as disillusioned detective Tequila, with actor Tony Leung, who plays an undercover agent poised to take down the Hong Kong mob. The film culminates in an extended orgy of violence in a hospital, during which Tequila saves a baby.]

TERENCE CHANG: When we started making *Hard Boiled* [listed as *Hard-Boiled* on the on-screen video translation—ed.], we were shooting another script, which I was not crazy about. Tony Leung plays this psychopath who puts poison in baby's milk in supermarkets, and kills babies. But we had signed the actors and the crew and also the first scene, which took place in a teahouse—it's going to be demolished and we got five days to shoot that scene, the opening scene, so we went and shot that scene anyway. And then after we finished the scene, John just sat down and decided to change the script entirely, just keeping the first opening scene.

JOHN WOO: I also didn't like the idea. It could give a bad influence to the people. Maybe somebody would imitate or learn from the movie, so that's why I changed the whole idea to become an undercover story.

DAVE KEHR: Every once in a while—every once in a very great while—a director comes along who is so original and so startlingly new, that he

---

From the Criterion Collection's *Hard Boiled* commentary track, 1994. Reprinted by permission, www.criterionco.com.

seems to reinvent a genre and I think that's what John Woo has done with his films. He's somebody who really understands the medium and was born to make movies. I think in every shot in this film you see a cinematic sensibility working in a way that I'd say two or three other directors in the world possess.

TC: The Hong Kong audience is more accustomed to a stylized violence. It's not a violence that's meant to be taken literally. It's a violence that's known to be very choreographed, very colorful, very abstract. It's a tradition that goes back to Peking Opera and the martial arts films.

DK: I think the mistake that people make is assuming that there's only one kind of violence in movies, and that's very far from the truth. There are dozens and dozens of ways of filming violence and treating violence, and thinking about what it can mean in the context of the story. I think in John's films . . . violence becomes a way of these men relating to each other. It's able to express these very intense feelings that they wouldn't be able to express in any other way, certainly not verbally, certainly not physically, but through passionate violence. . . . John's films are this kind of celebration, a kind of breakthrough, in that they use this very stylized violence to achieve that.

[Woo plays a bartender, mentor to Tequila]
JW: In the original script, there was no bartender character. The bar scene was the last day of shooting. [Chow Yun-Fat] always wanted me to appear with him. We are very good friends, and he wanted to show our friendship on screen. So that's why we made up this character as his mentor. We only used one hour for my scene. We made up all the dialogue and all the story on the set, you know, just speaking something and he dubbed it afterward. . . .

When we were shooting the warehouse scenes the screenwriter, Barry Wong, died. And he had not finished the script. One night when we were shooting the warehouse scenes, my assistant came to me and said, "Barry has died." And when I first heard, I thought they said [Barry's] friend had died, so I didn't pay much attention because I was too concentrated on the work. But the next day they told me again that it was [Barry], and I was shocked, I couldn't speak a word the whole night. I was very sad. Barry was a good friend of mine. We had a friendship for over fifteen years, and even though we haven't been working together for over fifteen years, he was a true talent, which I really admired.

DK: *The Killer* came out first in America, although it certainly was not the first [Woo film] we saw at festivals. It was sold as a campy, fun, and excessive movie—an impression that wasn't helped much by the really amateurish subtitles it had in its first issue. I think it looked more like a novelty than it was—something exotic and crazy and goofy—in a world that had nothing to do with us.

I think it was shown at the Sundance Film Festival in 1992 at a midnight show. It was probably the first time a hip, professional audience had been exposed to Woo and the anticipation was very intense, largely because people like Quentin Tarantino had been talking it up and everyone was expecting something crazy, something wild to break up the excessively sober, excessively well-meaning [films] that tend to make up the Sundance Film Festival.

The audience came to laugh and hoot, and certainly during the first hour, they were laughing at the mistakes in grammar in the subtitles and the excessiveness of the sentimentality, but as the film progressed they become more and more quiet, more and more caught up in what they were seeing. I think that movie changed a lot of minds there. This was not a novelty. This was someone who had something to say, someone with a profound point of view, a director who was going to be around for years to come, not just the latest fashion in violence.

TC: Actually, 70 percent of [*Hard Boiled*] film was shot in one set. It's an abandoned Coca-Cola plant, and we turned it into a warehouse and a hospital, whatever, a morgue. The sets turn out to be very helpful. . . . There's no script, and we didn't know what he was going to do the next day. Different parts of the building turn into different sets. John likes to improvise. For his other films, even though there was a script, John would like to change things because he was inspired on the location to make things better.

JW: That's why I always go over-budget in every film.

TC: He likes to brag about it, but he stayed pretty much on budget for this film.

DK: There's very little doubt that John Woo is someone we could call an auteur, a director who expresses himself very immediately, very directly through his films.

TC: John's nickname in Hong Kong is "Headmaster." He was named by the crew when he was shooting *Bullet in the Head* because he's always very stern and serious. . . . He never smiled when he was making the film.

JW: Once in a while, they'd call me, "The Black-faced god." Maybe I was too serious.

TC: Some of the crew in Hong Kong are really very inexperienced, especially working on a film of this scale. And John had to teach them a lot during production.

JW: . . . I usually take a lot of good references from American films and ask the whole crew to watch and learn from them. I try to do it that way in every one of my movies and we learn from that experience. We're just learning [from] and influence each other. That's why they call me "Headmaster."

[The hospital shootout]
JW: When the hospital is under siege, it's like you're oppressed by a totalitarian government. People lose their freedom as well as their own nature. When the patients are getting killed, it's like innocent people getting killed in a war. I hate totalitarianism and ugly politics in general. I have no intentions to talk about politics in my films. I'm not interested politics, and there's no political system that's perfect . . . but subconsciously I can't help putting my own personal feelings toward politics into the film. For instance, I have very strong feelings toward [Britain's handover of Hong Kong to China in] 1997. The babies signify purity and hope. Even though the world is filled with ugliness, hatred, and crisis, I still think there's hope for the future. We should cherish and protect these new lives.

TC: There are gangsters everywhere, even in communist countries, but in Hong Kong, because we are in the film industry, we are very aware of the gangsters' presence in the film industry. For some reason, the gangsters in movies are very glamorous and they like to be involved with it and it's also very profitable for them.

I personally have had very few dealings with gangsters myself, except for when you're in production, they're always gangsters and hoodlums coming up to you and asking for protection money. And I remember, when you're shooting in the streets, you pay off one gang and they keep the other gangs away from you. But now, even when you're shooting at a private property, they'll still come to you. For instance, when we were shooting at that teahouse or at the hospital set, different gangs would come to you and ask for money and you just have to pay them off—all of them. I guess it's the popular actors that are most afraid of gangsters. The gangsters will go to them and sign movie deals. If they say no, then something might happen, not necessarily to them but maybe to the people who work for them or to the family or whatever.

JW: Generally I don't use a second unit in my films. Usually I like to do everything by my own hand, even a tiny close-up on a cigarette or a gun or the action done by a stuntman. . . .

But *Hard Boiled* is exceptional. Since we were way over budget and over time, I only used a second unit for some of the action sequences at the hospital. Every night, we had very long hours for shooting. We were shooting over eighteen or twenty-four hours a day, or nonstop shooting for four or five days. Since the hospital scene is a very big setup, we needed to do a lot of things at the same time. Like when I'm shooting the interior scene inside the hospital, we used the second unit to shoot other stuff outside of the hospital. Most of the time we had three units shooting at the same time. When I'm shooting Tequila and Tony Leung fighting the gang inside a room, my assistant director, Patrick Leung [is shooting the] scene where the policeman gets hit by the gunman and my brother is shooting the patients escaping scene . . . there's a war going on in the whole building. . . . I'm firing at the second unit crew and the second unit crew is firing at us. So we always got complaints from laborers and the police force.

I probably shot for more than thirty-five days nonstop at the hospital set. Everybody was extremely tired and exhausted. We didn't get much sleep. It was like shooting in hell—fighting in a war that never ends, and my producers were nagging me for going over budget. Creatively, I was also getting tired of doing shots of my heroes firing and getting reactions of gangsters getting shot. So, I decided to do something crazy, something totally new and exciting. Near the end of shooting of every movie, I usually went crazy and lost my senses, so I told my crew that I wanted to create a shot that lasted three or four minutes and have a lot of action going on. I discussed this with my actors and my crew and they were all excited about it. They looked upon this as a challenge to them, and the morale was suddenly very high. Aside from aesthetic reasons, I also wanted to create room for my crew to stretch their creative limits.

We would rehearse for one day, and have one and a half days to set up the script and special effects and explosive stuff. And we were using eleven monitors in every corner to see the whole thing, the actors and the stunt guy. So we are all hiding in a small room with the special effects guy and the stunt coordinator, so when our hero is firing and the special effects guy presses a button to blow up the effect, we got it matched perfectly. So we have eleven monitors in every corner. In rehearsal, we were using the Steadicam, but there was not enough room to use that equipment. It's so heavy and big. It's hard to put distance between the actors—they always crossed together—so at the end we just used the handheld camera, it's much more simple.

We took the whole shot three times, with the camera following the whole scene. It was antsy two times and we were way out of budget because we needed about $800,000 for one day, but . . . I tried to do it in separate shots because we didn't have the money. It's a difficult shot because the elevator door wasn't that good. Sometimes it wouldn't open, sometimes it was stuck, so we would have to do the whole thing again. I was so frustrated. But the whole crew—the actors, the stuntmen, the special effects people—asked me to do it again, and do it in one shot, because they thought it was a very good idea, we just needed to finish it. I couldn't really afford to re-shoot the entire shot, so I just re-shot the second half and the two halves were joined together by a dissolve. Guess where it is. The other reason is that Tony Leung got hurt on the first take. His eyes were hurt by the broken glass. He was almost blind, and he needed to rest for a few days. So when we did it again, I was so much more aware of people getting hurt. I tried to stop Chow Yun-Fat and Tony Leung from doing it, but they don't care.

DK: . . . this movie is kind of intimidating. It's too big for people. It's out of scale. Woo doesn't back off from his implications the way that a lot of American directors are smart enough to do. He doesn't play the audience's sense of embarrassment. He doesn't back down and give you a reason to laugh. There's very little irony or distance from the characters. He's right there with them. There's no distancing, self-deprecating jokes, the way Arnold Schwarzenegger will offer a wisecrack after he has just murdered somebody, which is a way of diminishing the horror of killing by telling the audience that it's OK, it's not serious, it's all just a joke. Woo doesn't ever really give you that—it's not a joke. It means something.

TC: There are three ratings categories in Hong Kong. It's equivalent to our NC-17, R and PG, we call ours Grade One, Grade Two and Grade Three, with Grade Three being equivalent to NC-17 or X. *Hard Boiled*, just by the violence, did not get a Grade Three rating, they only suggested that if John makes like four or five minor cuts, then the film would get an R or category two rating, which John did. The cuts are mostly bullets going into the body and stuff like that. The censors object mostly when a person gets shot and you have all these streams of blood spilling out of the body—that's what they don't like. Everybody knows that John's films are violent and it's not a big deal, and we like to joke about it on the set. In fact in the earlier, longer version, there's a line that was cut. It was in the library when Tony Leung killed that guy, and somebody said, "There's so much blood, this must be a John Woo movie," but that was cut.

[Bombs go off throughout the hospital]

TC: A dangerous stunt like this really takes a long time to set up, a lot of time to prepare. In *Hard Boiled*, John could literally have as much time as he wanted, so a lot of these amazing stunts are great. But in *Hard Target*, we had to keep looking at our watches all the time. I guess John is kind of lucky. I remember seeing the shot where Chow Yun-Fat is holding the baby and he is running away from the explosion. The first take, John didn't like that because the explosion is too far behind. So for the next take, he said, "Let me push the button," and before Chow Yun-Fat was ready, he pushed it and Chow was really scared and actually running for his life in that shot. But after, he runs up to DP [director of photography] and John and said, "How does it look? Does it look real?" He's really professional. And then he turns around and said, "That motherfucker."

JW: It's never a real baby in the gunshot scenes. I used a dummy. I only shot a close-up of the baby for twenty minutes. When I'm holding my baby, they usually pee on my pants, so that's where I got the inspiration for this scene.

TC: In the scene where the gangsters are trying to blow up the hospital, John rigged the hospital with so many explosives that the special effects guys were really alarmed. The first AD [assistant director—ed.] called me and said, "If John wants to use that much explosives, the whole building is going to come down and we're all going to get killed." But nobody dared to talk to John about it because he was always in a very foul mood. People were afraid of him. So I was in the office and I got the call and rushed to the set and tried to talk him out of it. Finally I did, so he ended up using just one quarter of the amount of explosives, and it was spectacular.

JW: Tony Leung's character was an undercover cop. There were only two solutions for him: death or go into hiding. And I called in the treatment that he should sacrifice himself to save everybody in the hospital. That kind of tragic ending was more consistent with my other films. However, after we shot the final shootout in the car park, my producers Terence and Linda [Kuk] and even Chow Yun-Fat and the whole crew, they all suggested that Tony should live. They all thought that it would create more hope and be positive. After all, life should not be so pessimistic. And after so many hours of filming, we were almost like a big family, and I really appreciated everyone's total involvement in the project, so I finally agreed with them and shot a little epilogue, where Tony Leung continues to chase after his dreams.

[Editor's note: Filmmaker Roger Avary also contributed to the original commentary track, but has been edited out in this truncated version for space.]

Star Director, With a Bullet: Hong Kong's John Woo Aims for Piece of U.S. Action

RICHARD CHRISTIANSEN / 1991

IN HONG KONG, where John Woo makes his movies, his 1986 film *A Better Tomorrow* caused a true sensation. A bloody tale of betrayal and revenge in the Hong Kong underworld, the picture was written and directed by Woo with a budget under $1 million and with a cast that meant nothing at the box office. Within a few weeks, however, *A Better Tomorrow* had broken every attendance record in Southeast Asia, and its leading man, Chow Yun-Fat, had become a star, the sunglasses and duster coat that he wore in the film were copied and worn by Hong Kong youths eager to imitate the cool disdain he displayed as the movie's doomed hero.

Woo has made four films since then, three of them even more violent than the original *A Better Tomorrow* and at least two of them, *The Killer* (1989) and *Bullet in the Head* (1990), surpassing the original film in craftsmanship and artistry.

For all his accomplishments, however, Woo is pretty much an unknown factor among Western moviegoers. His artfully made, intensely felt films are far superior to the standard buddy movies and car-chase spectaculars that provide fodder for American action fans, but so far, his pictures have been seen mostly on the film festival circuit and through an occasional limited commercial release.

The Hong Kong film festivals presented in the last two years by the Film Center of the School of the Art Institute of Chicago have helped

---

From the *Chicago Tribune*, 25 August 1991. © *Chicago Tribune*. Reprinted by permission.

give him a small but devoted following here. Beginning in late September, a similar screening of Hong Kong movies at the Film Forum in New York City (in a schedule devised by Barbara Scharres, director of the Film Center) may further increase his reputation and next spring Scharres hopes to bring Woo into Chicago for a personal appearance at another of the center's Hong Kong spectaculars.

A left-handed compliment to Woo's talent also has surfaced with plans for an American version of *The Killer*, starring Richard Gere and directed by Walter Hill (*Hard Times*, *48 Hours*).

Even more important, Woo himself is considering a leap into the American market. Aided by his friend and producer Terence Chang, he is negotiating to direct his first U.S. film. (Chang shrewdly arranged screenings of *The Killer* last year at several film festivals where critics and studio representatives were gathered, and as a result, Woo has been contacted and courted by several U.S. studios.)

For his possible move into the American system, Woo is going through stepped-up English lessons and is cautiously choosing his options in casting and scripts. His fans, meanwhile, are hoping that the unique sensibilities and sensitivity that he brings to his very personal films will not be diffused in the Hollywood system.

A movie director in Hong Kong since 1973, Woo made his early reputation through a string of musical, kung fu and comedy films. *A Better Tomorrow*, however, established themes that have dominated his movies ever since.

Chief among them is that of intense male bonding. Woo's heroes may be free-wheeling comrades from childhood or they may be opposing figures of law and crime who become fast friends under sudden mutual stress; but once their bond is formed, it is deep and to the death. The danger for this friendship comes chiefly from greed and lust for power, epitomized by cold-eyed corporate commerce, which will betray and victimize the individual hero.

The plot for *A Better Tomorrow* sets the pattern: Two buddies engaged in passing counterfeit money are spit out by the large criminal organization that had used their services. One friend—about to leave the game out of respect for his dying father and his younger brother, an aspiring policeman—is set up on his final job and is sent to jail; the other friend, a raffish and more impulsive character, is badly wounded in revenging his friend's betrayal and is reduced to being a stooge for the cowardly squealer who has now become a sleek mob boss. Pushed to a point both can no longer endure, the two friends finally unite in an explosive blood bath that pits the two individuals (and their small arsenal of firepower) against scores of mobsters.

Bullet in the Head puts the tale in a direct political context in the Vietnam War period, when the friendship of three Hong Kong men is brutally shattered by the lust for money that one of them acquires through dealing in drugs. Filled with scenes of almost unbearable inhumanity and climaxed by the most emotionally draining shoot-out of all Woo films, the movie was a rare commercial set-back for Woo, chopped up by exhibitors and spurned by action fans.

"I think it was too heavy, maybe too pessimistic for them," Woo says of *Bullet*. He next made the glossy, $4 million comedy-caper movie *Once a Thief*—to remind moviegoers, he says, "that I can still make people laugh."

For all its lighthearted action, however, *Once a Thief* still bears the undeniable imprint of Woo's powerful sentimentality and intense romanticism.

His films are wonders of craftsmanship in the way their action scenes are shot and assembled, but what elevates them beyond formula are the deep feelings that Woo invests in them.

His movies echo the styles and substance of many of the classic films directed by John Ford and Sam Peckinpah that Woo saw when he was still a youngster; but to the familiar characters and situations of the past, Woo adds an overwhelming personal commitment that refreshes and revivifies the old stories.

Born in Guangzhou (Canton), China, in 1946, Woo moved with his family to Hong Kong when he was three and developed an appetite for the movies when he was in high school. He started making his own films, in Super 8 and 16 mm, when he was nineteen, and in 1969, he joined the Cathay Organization as a production assistant. He worked at Golden Harvest studio early in his directing career and now makes movies under the banner of his own organization, Milestone Pictures.

The Hong Kong film industry is a loose, scattershot business, without any large studio facility to speak of, that nonetheless turns out an immense amount of product for its public. It does not have the advanced facilities of a Hollywood studio (Woo and Chang both complain of the lack of up-to-date sound recording techniques), but it does allow for a very personal kind of filmmaking to exist—the kind that Woo points to in the works of directors Akira Kurosawa, Stanley Kubrick and Martin Scorsese (also a Woo admirer).

Woo has been able to flourish in this hectic Hong Kong environment, and in the process he has helped make the careers of several actors.

Chow Yun-Fat, Chang says, with a laugh, was "famous for being box-office poison" before Woo cast him in *A Better Tomorrow*, but his dynamic, explosive presence in that film made him a truly famous star. Since then, he has made three more movies with Woo and is working in the director's current film in progress, a cop versus killer picture that Woo lightly describes as "Dirty Harry in Hong Kong."

A married man with three children, the soft-spoken Woo does not seem at all the type to create the super-violent scenes that have marked his pictures. He takes about three to five months to write the film script, alone or in collaboration with another writer, and then spends about sixty-five to eighty days actually shooting the film.

His most sensational shoot-out sequences are punctuated by long slow-motion shots, reminiscent of Peckinpah in *The Wild Bunch*, where bodies fly and blood spurts at an incredible pace. A studious fan has logged sixty deaths—by pistol, automatic weapons and grenades—in the last few minutes of *A Better Tomorrow II*, but Woo laughingly dismisses this as inaccurate. "There must be over one hundred," he insists, with a smile.

He uses the television technique of shooting individual scenes with two or three cameras placed at various angles, and then puts the shots together in the editing room. Amazingly, considering the complexity of his editing, he does not use a storyboard to plot the sequence. "It's up here," he says, tapping his head, "and my actors and crew know what I want."

For big, complicated, one-chance-only scenes, where buildings blow up and whole battalions of gangsters are mowed down, Woo will increase his cameras to four or five, sometimes greeting his actors with surprise explosions.

One of the choice bits in *A Better Tomorrow II* for example, finds Chow Yun-Fat walking away from an exploding building with an extremely startled look on his face. "The surprise was real," Woo says. "He didn't know it was coming."

For his films, Woo draws partly on his own life, partly on the films he has seen and partly on the events and issues he notes in Hong Kong. The early part of *Bullet in the Head*, which deals with the friendship of the film's central trio of buddies, is partly autobiographical; the later half, which takes the men into the jungles of Vietnam in scenes of excruciating pain and betrayal, are entirely fiction, Woo says, but were born out of his own concern for the desperation he sees lurking beneath the race for money and power in Hong Kong.

Once a Thief, which takes place partly on the French Riviera, pairs Chow Yun-Fat with Leslie Cheung, the innocent younger brother of *A Better Tomorrow*, in a tale of two art thieves in love with the same beautiful woman. But despite the movie's sunny setting and comedic touches, Woo can't escape from the dark themes that are always on his mind. The two men and the woman, it happens, have been friends from childhood, when they were trained in thievery by a Fagan-like monster, and the chief plot element in their story has them besting their former master in a daring duel of free-spirited individuals versus powerful mob forces.

These themes are likely to appear in John Woo films, no matter where he makes them. As Chang says, "When John makes a movie, the feelings he has about friendship, romanticism and love are everything. He doesn't care what the audience expects or what his exhibitors demand; he just wants to make the movie that he feels so deeply."

The Hard Road to *Hard Target*

BARBARA SCHARRES / 1992

IN THE PRODUCTION SCREENING ROOM in a hotel in New Orleans the lights go down and the *Hard Target* dailies begin. Actors Lance Henriksen, Arnold Vosloo and their henchmen are making an entrance in slow motion. Shot wide, from low, extreme angles, the men, whose hair and long duster coats ripple from the touch of some mythic breeze, advance across the screen—fearsome, harshly elongated, threatening yet mysteriously noble. Several shots come on in succession, and although this is unedited footage, it already works with a poetic logic through the flow of the camera movement and the intricately devised multiple points of view. Time has ceased to have a meaning in the ordinary twenty-four frames per second progression of storytelling, and is expanding and contracting to reflect a mind's eye vision.

Bad guys have never looked quite like this, at least not in American movies, and their disturbing power is not the power of guns, although they wield them. Yips and hoots of appreciation in the crowded room give away to a concentrated silence. These tired crew members, as if they had not just spent the past twelve hours crafting shots such as these, fall under the spell of the images as an audience. John Woo, the director responsible for the flamboyant work on the screen, sits unobtrusively in the back, watching intently with Russell Carpenter, the director of photography.

The next day, in a vast warehouse where the film's finale is being shot, fog billows from machines spotted among the dozens of tattered

---

A version of this article originally appeared in *American Cinematographer*, September 1993. Reprinted by permission.

Mardi Gras floats. The assistant director shouts "Fire in the hole," crew members reach for their earplugs, and Jean-Claude Van Damme lunges backwards in a crouching position across the open floor with a gun blazing in each hand, his shoulders propelling a heavy painter's utility cart behind him for cover. Flames rise ominously from burning oil drums, and sparks shower from explosions. Dolly tracks criss-cross the set on three sides like a private railway manned by camera operators in plastic face shields, each hunched for protection behind a sheet of Lexan bracketed to the matte box. The shot takes just a few seconds and then an army of technicians rush forward to cut the gas lines to the fires and to tend to the star, the guns and the cameras.

Hard Target is in its forty-seventh day, and laying what by now amounts to miles of dolly track is down to a science for this crew, as is rigging the inordinate number of squibs, fires and explosives required. The abundance of equipment and the routine efficiency of people on the set are just about the last things out of the ordinary on this $19.5 million Alphaville Renaissance production. But for Woo, directing his twenty-second feature, but his first in the U.S., these very conditions are a daily reminder that he's a long way from Hong Kong.

In a break between shots, Carpenter tells of watching Woo's *Hard Boiled* and *The Killer* before taking the job: "When I first met John Woo, I knew nothing of his work and, of course, wanted to see his films. Looking through the eyes of my own cultural chauvinism, I expected a Hong Kong film to be somewhat 'rinky-dinky' and chintzy—but instead came away impressed with the technical acuity, flair and polish of John's films—and what's more, impressed that his films operate on many levels that American action films don't. There were several levels of story, and the acting was excellent. I saw that John was a formidable filmmaker."

But Woo, whose complexly choreographed action is legendary in Asia, says, "The results that you see were usually accomplished under very difficult circumstances. There are some good technical people working in Hong Kong, but they are in the minority. Unlike in the States, where every department on a film is very accomplished and they have a lot of support to give a director, in Hong Kong this is the reverse—the director has to support them." He describes working in the U.S. as, "A dream come true; the crew members here are more professional, better trained, more precise in what they are doing. No matter how difficult a shot is, they will use any means to get it done."

"And," he says with approval, "they are full of energy, very aggressive." Asked if he is a perfectionist, Woo replies, "I like to work with professionals."

Flash back exactly two years, and Woo is in Hong Kong at work on his action comedy *Once a Thief.* While the stunt coordinator gives last minute instructions to the nervous young stunt double who is about to perform an aerial back-flip with an unwieldy gilt-framed painting in his outstretched arms, the small crew replenishes the heavy fog that rises in the cavernous room in preparation for the shot. That is, they carry in smoking buckets of water over dry ice. Even the film's star, Chow Yun-Fat, idol of millions and one of the highest paid actors in Asia, is pressed into service.

There is little to separate the mega-star and the flunky on this set, certainly not dressing rooms or special privileges. Co-star Leslie Cheung, a top-of-the-charts pop singer/actor, is sprawled in the only chair on the premises waiting for his next shot, while producer Terence Chang, partner with Woo in the production company Milestone Pictures, sits on the floor checking production stills. Woo is providing some of the muscle to push the camera on the dolly in a dry run for the shot. Outside there are no trailers or trucks, no honey wagon or caterer. There is no director's chair because Woo never has the chance to sit down, and if at times he appears to be patiently marshalling a group of students on a field trip, it's because few on his crew would appear to be much over twenty-one. Only the director of photography and the stunt coordinator have the look of seasoned veterans, and the hard-working crew's willingness to perform multiple jobs under Woo's direction is also a function of the fact that few have experience in anything specific.

Despite production circumstances that might in North America be the hallmark of the leanest of independent films, and budgets that typically range between $500,000 and $4 million U.S., many Hong Kong films of recent years have jolted an international audience with their creativity, energy, and indeed, technical excellence. Through the '80s, films like Woo's *A Better Tomorrow* and *The Killer,* as well as Jackie Chan's *Police Story,* Tsui Hark's *Peking Opera Blues* and Ching Siu-Tung's

A Chinese Ghost Story, screened at Western film festivals to enthusiastic response. The wildly eclectic nature of Hong Kong's many popular genres, the speed and kineticism of the action, and especially in Woo's work, the full-blown emotionalism of the stories, won fans that included prominent film critics in the U.S. and Europe. Seemingly influenced in part by Western genres and themes, which are developed in ways that could only describe the hybrid nature of Hong Kong itself, to Western eyes these films looked like nothing else on earth.

A kind of golden age of local production which began in the early '80s, spearheaded by directors including Woo, made Hong Kong one of the few places on earth where the audience came to demand its own indigenous cinema over American imports, and still does. Director/screenwriter Mabel Cheung, whose most recent film *Now You See Love, Now You Don't* was produced by Milestone, describes the situation with, "In the '80s, people bet on box office figures like it was a horse race."

The film industry, the world's third largest after India and the U.S., produces well over one hundred features per year. While a high percentage of the films are distributed throughout Asia theatrically and on video and laserdisc in markets including Taiwan, Japan, Korea, Thailand and Singapore, this is a cinema that is driven primarily by the tastes of a voraciously film-going hometown audience. In tune with the city's here-today-gone-tomorrow culture, and shaped by what is possibly the world's most stringent capitalist work ethic, the films are extravagantly escapist, modeled on Hong Kong's prevailing whims, fears and fantasies.

But the boom of the '80s, when film industry and audience seemed ecstatically in sync, was from the start booby-trapped by history. In 1984, Britain sealed a fateful agreement with the Peoples Republic of China to restore the island of Hong Kong, once ceded "in perpetuity," and the adjacent Kowloon peninsula, leased for ninety-nine years, to the jurisdiction of China on June 30, 1997. An exodus from Hong Kong ensued, and in time filmmakers saw the most educated, sophisticated and affluent portion of their audience leaving for Canada, Britain and the U.S., while new immigrants, mostly from rural areas, arrived. Mabel Cheung says, "Once I was making films for my friends. Now Hong Kong is full of people from the mainland and all over Asia."

While production companies and studios had long been considering their options outside of Hong Kong, including Singapore, offering attractive tax breaks to the film industry, Taiwan, Toronto or Vancouver, fears about the future were crystallized into a worst-case scenario by the Tiananmen Square massacre on June 4, 1989, and filmmakers felt the impact acutely. Woo says, "People used to believe that nothing would happen in 1997, but that changed with the massacre. It really changed people's point of view. They didn't want to go to the cinema, they wanted to stay home and save money. There was a sharp decline in box office." Terence Chang, presently co-producer of *Hard Target*, concurs: "The massacre changed everything, because it reminded people that 1997 could bring something like that or worse."

Speculating on what 1997 might mean for filmmakers, Woo says, "When the time comes, I don't think the government will abruptly change the way things are, but somehow they will impose a system of very tight controls on freedom of expression, creative freedom. I want to say whatever I want to say and do whatever I want to do with my films. I don't like to compromise. I don't want to serve a government I don't believe in."

An otherwise forgettable film had the line, "Hong Kong's on borrowed time—we all need to make a quick killing." The ordinary difficulties of producing films in Hong Kong were increased after the massacre at every level for directors like Woo, the result of the drain of talent and capital and a high turnover in the labor force. He says, "A lot of people just want to make a fast buck and get out. A very good cameraman could be working on two or three films at the same time. Actors are the worst—they are usually working on three or four films simultaneously. Each day they only give you a certain number of hours, maybe three to five hours, then they go to another movie. This makes you very upset, very depressed."

The quest for a pre-1997 fast buck brought a new set of players to the film business, from real estate developers seeking some glamour to go with their cash, to underworld kingpins laundering money. A common pattern of extortion developed whereby a criminal organization threatens a big name star and/or his manager with death or disfigurement unless he agrees to sign a contract for a film at a very small fee. Directors and technicians are "hired" in the same manner. The resulting film, made on a shoestring, does huge box office due to its stellar cast and low overhead.

The problem was so extreme that in February of 1992, virtually the entire film industry, including stars, made a dramatic march through the streets to police headquarters demanding protection from organized crime. Further down in Hong Kong's criminal hierarchy, smalltime hoodlums became considerably bolder in their own extortion techniques. Where once any production might have expected to pay small amounts of protection money to a local street gang when shooting outdoors, now gangs demand payment even for working indoors in their territory. Terence Chang relates that while Woo was shooting the extended opening sequence of *Hard Boiled* on location in a rented tea house, the production was shaken down for protection payments by as many as six different rival gangs daily, who threatened to smash equipment or hurt technicians and actors.

Ironically the screen lore and mythology of the Hong Kong gangster has been defined by none other than John Woo in films including *A Better Tomorrow* (1986), *A Better Tomorrow II* (1987), *The Killer* (1989), *Bullet in the Head* (1990), and *Hard Boiled* (1992). *A Better Tomorrow* became one of the smash hits of the '80s; it single-handedly launched a genre, and went on to influence the look and content of action filmmaking throughout Asia. Woo's gangsters are men whose law is dictated by the heart rather than the police. The violence and pyrotechnics in his films serve as astonishing metaphors for the raging emotions of his heroes.

Woo, surprisingly enough, is a man who has played by the rules, and his quietly observant demeanor does not at first give a hint of his passionately held ideals or the intensity of the drive that led him to excel in making extravagantly action-oriented films. After attending Matteo Ricci College, with experience in theater, 8 mm experimental filmmaking, and writing, he began his career in 1969 in the traditional manner, by taking an entry level job at a major film company. Working first as a production assistant at the Cathay Organization, in 1971 he moved to Shaw Brothers, where he became assistant director to the prolific martial arts director Chang Cheh. In 1973, he directed his first feature at the age of twenty-six, the independently produced *The Young Dragons*, at a time when it was still usual for aspiring directors to serve an apprenticeship until well into their 40s. The film was picked up by Golden Harvest for distribution, and Woo was signed to a contract as a director.

For the next several years Woo directed in a variety of genres that included martial arts films and even a Cantonese opera. His *Countdown in Kung Fu*, 1975, gave future stars Jackie Chan and Sammo Hung their first leading roles. He was pigeonholed by his success at directing comedies such as *Money Crazy* (1977) and *Plain Jane to the Rescue* (1982), and quit Golden Harvest in 1983 to get off the comedy treadmill. He joined the relatively new Cinema City, and ended up exiled to Taiwan, disillusioned and angry, to direct two low budget comedies that even today he is reluctant to discuss.

Returning to Hong Kong in 1985 with the hope of starting over, Woo was regarded by some of his industry colleagues as completely washed up. Finally, at Tsui Hark's small Film Workshop Company, he was able to put together *A Better Tomorrow*, the kind of film he had long dreamed of making. The story of male bonding and brotherhood in Hong Kong's underworld starred the boyish Leslie Cheung, hoping to make a breakthrough as a serious actor, Ti Lung, a former Shaw Brothers martial arts star considered past his prime, and Chow Yun-Fat, a television and film actor whom stardom had so far eluded. The film was made on only $800,000, and was released by Cinema City.

It was clear that *A Better Tomorrow* broke the mold of the Hong Kong action film. When Chow Yun-Fat slow-motion-danced into a nightclub with long coattails swirling about his legs, to gun down a roomful of gangsters amid slow-flying dishes and blood-splattered walls, a wooden matchstick rotating pensively in the corner of his mouth and the expression of a cunning young tiger on his face, a star was born. But it was not simply the audaciousness of the action in a genre notorious for its visceral thrills that made the film resonate, but its emotional landscape. To die with honor, to sacrifice one's life in harrowing combat for an ideal or a friend were the ultimate values, recalling the code of honor of the swordsman, but entirely transposed into a contemporary world. It was no accident that Woo, who admits that the film had great personal meaning at a turning point in his life, cast himself as the police inspector on the edge of the story who watches Chow's character come back from near-defeat to avenge his best friend before dying gloriously, shredded by his enemy's bullets.

Woo's camera was everywhere at once, moving in on his actors' innermost thoughts, but traveling frequently with a momentum that seemed to express a force of life larger than his characters' world, yet encompassed them. Rather than the minimal and straightforward storytelling that the audience expected in an action film, *A Better Tomorrow* gave them time fragmented in the realm of myth, tragedy-drenched in romanticism, and emotions expressed in velocity, earth-shaking explosions, and spurting blood shed as the ultimate sacrifice. It was action with a soul, and the Hong Kong audience clamored for more.

In 1990, *The Killer* was purchased by Circle Releasing to become the first Hong Kong film to receive a mainstream theatrical release in North America, and Woo already had a growing cult following in the West due to the exposure his films had received at festivals. Admirers of his work included Martin Scorsese, whom he credits as an influence, Walter Hill and Oliver Stone. Simultaneously, he had reached another turning point in his career. In an interview that year at the Toronto Festival of Festivals he expressed frustration with Hong Kong's changed market—"It's getting more difficult for me to work in Hong Kong. The films being produced are getting more and more simple. The audience just wants a few laughs and some emotional release. They don't want to watch films that make them think. It's meaningless to work in that kind of environment." Asked whether he would someday make a film in English, he laughingly replied "Never," although he related with the next breath that he was entertaining offers from the U.S., Canada, France, and even South Africa.

Screenwriter Chuck Pfarrer, whose previous films have included *Navy SEALs* and *Darkman*, relates with relish that Woo chose his script for *Hard Target* from among the more than fifty American scripts he was offered because "he liked the story." After weeks with the *Hard Target* production as a co-producer, Pfarrer expresses his enthusiastic admiration for Woo in colorful similes. "Action movies are like Detroit automobiles," he explains. "They used to be really good, then they got to be clunkers. And this one is going to be a Maseratti Bora, and no one's going to know what to do. Just watch his smoke—watch this."

Set on the seedy side of New Orleans, *Hard Target* is a contemporary treatment of the theme of Richard Connell's short story "The Most Dangerous Game," in which men hunt men for sport. While numbers of homeless men of the city disappear without a trace, a young lawyer,

Natasha (Yancy Butler), searches for one of the missing, her father. Cornered and robbed by some opportunistic loiterers in a rough neighborhood, she is saved by Chance Boudreaux (Van Damme), an unemployed merchant seaman. On the verge of homelessness himself, Chance agrees to help her in her search for her father in return for the $200 he needs to renew his union card to get a ship. Together they begin to discover the horror of the fate of all the missing men, tracked to the death like animals by wealthy hunters who have paid for the thrill.

The story of course offers the opportunity for a maximum amount of action, as Boudreaux turns the tables on the hunters and brings them down, but it also has the heart and emotion that both Pfarrer and Russell Carpenter acknowledge as essential to a Woo film. Carpenter says, "What's unique, I think, to John, is that in the middle of an action sequence you'll find a moment or two that's very emotional, where something is actually revealed about a character. Just in the middle of all this mayhem he'll find a way to tell you something new about a character. That's one of the reasons he uses the emotion. He's very gifted in terms of being able to put the camera in the emotional center of an action sequence." Of Woo himself, Carpenter says, "He's a real poet, a man of passion, but his passion is very calm. To me, to see a man who's so quiet and peaceful making these films that are full of action and mayhem—it's really something to find that in the same package, the same person."

As the cold rain and mist outside the Mardi Gras warehouse mingle with movie set fog in the beams of the big Xenon lights shining through the second story windows, Carpenter nods at the maze of dolly tracks around him: "This will be new for an American film, for action scenes to be approached in this way. I won't say it's a Chinese way, I'll just say it's a John Woo way. This is a first for me, running multiple dollies, usually at each other. It's like the meeting of the Union Pacific and Central Pacific railroads. John works the most exciting sense of movement into his films, and he knows that a camera movement does not have to be big to create visual excitement. Very often, a small, slow dolly movement of only a foot or so can create much visual excitement if used in the right context. Of course, with John Woo, you can bet that a rocket-fast, one-hundred-foot dolly around an exploding building isn't far behind."

Adapting to the "John Woo way" has generated its own lore on the *Hard Target* set, where the dolly has been nicknamed "the Woo-woo Choo-choo," and every camera crew member has a favorite "dueling dolly" story to tell. Key grip Lloyd Moriarty says: "We've surely laid more dolly tracks than any other movie. I'd say we've laid at least five miles this time." There's a gleeful satisfaction in the way he ticks off the challenges of the past few weeks, which have included "multiple dolly moves, three cameras on three dollies, minimum moves anywhere from sixteen up to one hundred foot and that's consistently, all day long. In fact, I don't think we've run one single camera at any point in this movie, and this is around day fifty, but this is a very unusual movie. For all of us it's very exciting."

Carpenter says, "Because of the sheer amount of pyrotechnics and the complexity of many of the stunts, multiple camera coverage was a must on this film. But this is not just a matter of randomly setting several cameras with various lenses on the action. First of all, John likes to surround the action with his cameras, with many angles, many of them very wide. Often we might have a camera low with a very wide 10 mm lens. On the opposite side of the action might be another camera, hidden from view, with a lens that is almost as wide. Also, scattered here and there, there might be four or five other cameras, manned and unmanned, on a variety of different focal lengths and running at different speeds. Now, to top it all off, as many as two or even three cameras may be on dollies, somehow miraculously missing getting into each other's field of view. We called our Primo 21 mm lens, traditionally viewed as a wide angle lens, John's 'telephoto' because of his penchant for working on wider focal lengths.

"On some shows I've been on," he continues, "we just set cameras out to set cameras out, hoping—we hope this camera will get a good piece of something, or that camera will. Well, John knows that each camera is going to contribute a bit of energy to the whole, and that when all that energy from those cameras comes together it's like nuclear fission. The scene explodes with an energy that's twenty-five times more than what those five cameras contributed. I'm convinced that he has all these sequences edited in his head before he comes to the set. There aren't many people you can say that about. There are some very fine directors, but not many who have such an intuitive grasp of where they're going with a scene."

While Jean-Claude Van Damme, the macho jokester of *Double Impact* and *Lionheart*, is alive and high-kicking during more casual moments on the set, in front of the cameras it's clear that he has a whole new persona. Woo's emphasis on body language and gesture capitalizes on Van Damme's physical grace, and his frequent use of slow motion gives the actor a surprising seriousness and dramatic presence that appears to be light years beyond his previous work. "I think Jean-Claude Van Damme is going to come off as a different sort of character than he's been," says Carpenter, "he's a real hero in this film."

Given the constant use of wide-angle lenses and multiple cameras, lighting posed some special difficulties for Carpenter. He says, "A lot of times on American productions, if you shoot multiple cameras they're kept rather close together. John doesn't do me any favors when he puts his cameras out there. Sometimes I'll just start weeping and say, 'Please don't put the camera there.' And I'll tell him the reasons I can't do it, but usually I'll be able to find a way to give him the shot that he wants. My problem, especially on the large interiors, was to find a way to light the scenes with some depth and interest for a variety of widely varying angles. And if two of those lenses happen to be very wide 10 mm or 14 mm lenses that covered an interior floor to ceiling—well, it was time for the Nuprin."

Describing how he worked to create visual excitement with the lighting in the frequent situations that did not allow for fine modeling with light, he says, "Sometimes I might find some lighting motif, like light penetrating the scene from a window, that would inherently be interesting because of a strong contrast range or the way the light bounced up when it hit the floor. In that lucky instance, I might be able to let the exposure range of the Kodak film stock carry the scene and may be able to place several cameras with interesting results. More often, though, I'd have to make the decision to light for one or two angles predominantly, and then try to mold the light so that some of the other angles were not too flatly lit."

While crew members joked about being ready to walk through fire for Woo, some actually did. As Carpenter tells the story, "Michael St. Hilaire, our operator, and Michael Gfelner, our focus puller, donned full length fire suits to film a hand-held shot of Lance Henriksen walking through a burning warehouse with his clothes on fire, all the while delivering a good three-quarters page of dialogue. What's more incredible is that Lance wanted to do a second take." Like most aspects of *Hard Target*, it was what first assistant director Dennis Maguire describes as "bigger than life." "At times I worry," he says, "Are we going too far over the top for American audiences?"

According to Carpenter, some of his greatest technical challenges involved working with locations that presented unique problems. "Tales from the crypt," is how he refers to his recollection of filming at night in one of New Orleans's above-ground cemeteries in the historic Garden District: "John wanted a long Steadicam shot of a hunter's point of view as he chased his 'hard target,' Willie Carpenter, through a labyrinth of crypts and grave markers. Because of tight scheduling, I did not have enough time to cable, set and hide from the Steadicam the many lights one might necessarily need for this one shot. Instead, I used a Mini Musco light set at three-quarters backlight to the majority of the action. This one source bounced off the white walls of the crypts, which the camera did not see, and provided a 'fill' light of just a few footcandles, but just enough to make the shot utilizing Kodak 5296 stock and high speed lenses. Randy Nolen was able to run several hundred yards at high speed and not worry about seeing lighting units or cable runs. For other scenes in the cemetery, we flew a twenty-by-twenty Gryfllon from a Condor and bounced a couple of 12 k HMI units into it for a nice soft but directional night source."

Another location that involved ingenious solutions in order to get a shot from the angle Woo wanted was a hospital operating theater just off the morgue. Says Carpenter, "The object of the shot was to follow actress Kasi Lemmons down the very steep amphitheater steps, and then down a rung ladder to the operating theater at the bottom. Conventional means of getting the shot, and even Steadicam, were out of the question because of the terrain. Even a hot head on a python arm or Louma crane was not going to work because of a low ceiling. Finally key grip Lloyd Moriarty settled on the Lenny Arm by Chapman, a variation of the Louma. Because the arm is assembled by fitting smaller lengths together in whatever proportions the key grip desires, the instrument can be tailored to the surrounding space. We were able to make the shot with three-quarters of an inch to spare."

Moriarty and his crew also take the credit for devising the camera shields, which were in use almost constantly. During pre-production Woo had shown him photos of shields rigged up by his crew in Hong Kong, and it was up to Moriarty to find a similar solution to protect the operators from explosions and powder burns from an estimated thirty-five thousand rounds of ammunition, while still allowing the cameras the necessary mobility. The problem was magnified by the fact that even though the guns were firing blanks they were usually full loads with much gunfire at close range, according to the production weapons expert, Robert "Rock" Galotti.

Moriarty says, "On most camera protector shields we use one-fourth inch Lexan in front, but then you can't move the camera around. We took a one-eighth inch sheet of Lexan because it's the lightest, but being so durable it still withstands powder burns and projectiles, compared with Plexiglas, which will just shatter in front of you. We came up with the idea to put brackets on the matte box of the Panavision camera and attach the shield to that. A four-by-four foot sheet of Lexan would cover an operator and assistant and still be able to go on a 60-foot dolly move through explosions and everything."

In Hong Kong, Woo's colleagues often told of occasions when he became so excited while directing action scenes that he would inadvertently step into the range of one of the cameras. As the story goes, the sight of Woo enthusiastically gesturing for more bullets, more blood, more motion, in front of his own camera was not an unusual one. In New Orleans, the crew's impressions of working with the director more often involved references to his calmness and concentration in the midst of frantic activity. Carpenter describes a significant experience early in the production, the same occasion on which he discovered Woo's sense of humor: "One day I was out on an exterior location on a bridge, and we hadn't quite set up the shot. So he came up to me and said, 'Russ, I don't see you doing anything.' Immediately I tensed up. And he says, 'I want you to get to work right away.' And I said, 'OK, what can I do?' He takes me over to the bridge as the sun is coming up and says, 'Admire that sunrise.'"

Riding the dolly and looking through the camera on one of the final practice runs for a shot, Woo looks serenely happy, like a man who really is achieving a dream. Expressing satisfaction with the professional progress *Hard Target* represents for him, he says, "I'm not reinventing myself, rather, I've moved a great step forward. First, I'm working with more professional people. Secondly, I'm using more advanced equipment, which allows me to further my creativity, so I think I've improved. I feel much happier than in Hong Kong. Here, I think I can work like other American directors, with more freedom to create. I hope other filmmakers have the same opportunity to work here, because Hong Kong has good talent, good filmmakers. But I must say, it won't be easy."

ACTION! Woo Said It!

MARK CARO / 1993

NEW ORLEANS—The Hong Kong director famous for gunning people down by the dozens and blowing them up by the megaton sat pensively on the set—a chilly, damp warehouse stuffed with Mardi Gras floats, many of which already had been torched or torn apart by gunfire. Members of the crew quietly asked him questions, and small-framed John Woo murmured back in accordance with his apparent credo: Speak softly, detonate loudly.

This particular shot involved the double for the movie's hero, played by Jean-Claude Van Damme, applying an airborne kick to the chest of the villain's double. Upon impact the villain, aided by hidden ropes, would fly several yards backward through the air and crash into a big pile of boxes, with his landing cuing a flock of pigeons to take off.

The director barked the one word on which he raises his voice—"Action!"—and the shot came off, with the birds lending a strangely majestic touch to an otherwise violent scene. In other words, typical John Woo.

It seems fitting that the city of gumbo would be the setting for Hong Kong's most accomplished action director to make his Hollywood film debut—entitled *Hard Target*—with the "Muscles from Brussels" as his star.

Woo, forty-seven, had plenty of reason to move his family from his homeland to Los Angeles, not the least of them being Hong Kong's precarious political situation. But the artistic pull was just as great. Woo is an avid student of Hollywood films, and his works have a way of taking American movie conventions and infusing them with so

From the *Chicago Tribune*, 7 February 1993. © *Chicago Tribune*. Reprinted by permission.

much conviction that the result can overwhelm or even baffle the more jaded moviegoer.

The Killer (1989), Woo's one movie to receive significant American distribution, has a whopper of an old-fashioned gangster-film plot: A hit man accidentally causes a female singer to be blinded, so he decides to take one more job in order to pay for her cornea-replacement operation. In the meantime a cop pursuing the killer ends up bonding with him upon realizing that the two of them share a sense of honor all too rare in this cruel world.

The combination of such high melodrama and a breathtaking amount of shoot-'em-up carnage prompted the movie's American distributor to promote it as camp—and many audience members concurred. But Woo was serious, crafting a male-bonding extravaganza that puts Hollywood buddy movies to shame in terms of action and sheer emotion.

Woo earned much clout and freedom in Hong Kong but lacked the tools in his paint box to rival his American counterparts. The move to Los Angeles would be his chance to draw upon Hollywood's bountiful resources, just as the great American filmmakers have done.

"It's like dreams can come true," Woo said after a tiring day of filming. "No matter how difficult or complicated a shot, I still can do it. The people here, they have more respect for the movie. In Hong Kong I usually have a very good crew, but most of them, they just come to work for money."

But if money isn't as big a factor for the American crew members, the studio is another matter. Hollywood film companies aren't in business to make dreams come true except when the dream is compatible with being a guaranteed profit-maker. Studios don't just hand over the reins to a director and say, "Make a masterpiece," especially if the director is an outsider from another hemisphere.

So *Hard Target*, tentatively scheduled to open in July, is not John Woo's dream project. It's his chance to show Hollywood that he can be a good citizen and make the kind of movie they'd like him to make.

"This is a very, very commercial project," said co-producer and longtime associate Terence Chang. "We know it's going to make money; it will recoup with just the foreign market. The combination of Jean-Claude and John Woo is a good one. He chose this because it's a safe project."

The story is a variation on *The Most Dangerous Game*: As a police strike renders New Orleans lawless, wealthy mercenaries come to town to stalk homeless men on hunts set up by an evil schemer, played by the intense, sharply lined Lance Henriksen. A drifter named Chance (Van Damme) busts up the game.

Van Damme was already "attached" to the script when Woo decided to get on board. The director said he'd received numerous offers from the Hollywood studios, "but most of the scripts were about martial arts and kung fu, and *Hard Target* was a little different. At least it has some meaning. It talks about men hunting men, talks about homeless people."

But Woo also admitted that the story may not have the depth that his fans may be used to.

"The studio (Universal) said that the American audience doesn't like the story too complicated. For an action movie, the audience will like a more simple story."

He added that when he received this edict, "I was a little upset. But for a first experience, I think to do the simple story is good for me. It's much easier for me."

And then there's the touchy matter of ratings.

Unlike many American action films, *The Killer* contains no scenes of sadistic cruelty or gross splatter shots designed to shock, yet the ratings board slapped it with an NC-17 anyway, apparently for the sheer accumulation of violence. (In fact, Blockbuster Video insisted that an R-rated version be cut for the chain to carry, so *The Killer* that now sits upon Blockbuster's shelves replaces epic shootouts with mere skirmishes.)

Neither the studio nor director wants *Hard Target* to be stuck with the NC-17 stigma, so Woo said he has to "tone it down a little."

The translation: Fewer people get offed in the new movie than in the opening scene of his previous thriller, *Hard Boiled*.

"Roughly thirty," Chang offered as a body-count estimate.

Woo shook his head with a scowl. "No, no, no, no—around twenty."

On the flip side, Woo and Chang said the studio did press for the director to insert a sex scene. Woo—as well as leading actress Yancy Butler—resisted, and the studio finally "realized that it's not necessary," Woo said.

Another difference between *Hard Target* and previous Woo movies is that the director has tended to cast a soulful, introspective leading man—often Chow Yun-Fat and/or Tony Leung—as his own stand-in on screen. From the footage that was screenable last month, the villainous Henriksen shares some of that quality, but Van Damme is, well, Van Damme.

The director's and star's styles could hardly be less similar on the set. Woo says few words while everyone leans in to listen. Van Damme is a chatterbox, talking through his and everyone else's directions ("He comes out, and I go kick, kick, kick, kick, boom, boom!") and frequently exhorting the crew, "Let's go, guys!" Could Van Damme be Woo's alter ego?

"It's different," Woo acknowledged.

For his part Van Damme said he was just trying to help out with what he saw as Woo's communication difficulties.

"It's just his English," Van Damme said. "I was having the same feelings that he has. That's why I talked to the other actors, to make them understand what John Woo wants. And then I say, 'John Woo, am I right or wrong?' and he says, 'You're right.'"

So the question is how much of a John Woo picture will *Hard Target* be? "The story is less John Woo, but the visual aspects are very John Woo," Woo said.

Others on the set said the director certainly is leaving his mark. Writer/co-producer Chuck Pfarrer said when Woo signed on, "the body count went up. When this first started, it was just two guys at the beginning and six guys at the end. But you're not going to have a John Woo movie with just eight killings."

"It's downright, full-out John Woo," said Henriksen, who added that he took his role because he was such a big fan of previous Woo works. "Those movies to me were so creative, so balletic, and had this incredible philosophy in them. The violence was only a container for the philosophy."

On *Hard Target*, Henriksen added, "We have an agreement: My character has a certain dignity. All of his bad guys, if you notice, have great dignity, and I won't surrender my dignity at all. He's allowed me and the other characters to flesh out their insides, and he's captured it on film."

Dramatics aside, the real sparks have come from the pairing of Woo's outsized approach with a capable crew and a full bag of tricks. A stroll around the warehouse revealed various experiments taking place. In one corner, weapons expert Robert "Rock" Gallotti was firing an arrow from a specially designed rifle into a Plexiglass sheet to make sure the material would act as a durable camera shield.

Elsewhere someone playing a hunter was being "squibbed"—that is, wired with blood pouches that would explode upon his being shot. Back in one of the trailers sat a full-size, red-goop-filled replica of Henriksen. Several days later—sorry to ruin a key plot element, folks—it would be blown up.

Parked outside the warehouse were remnants of earlier carnage: a beaten-up Lincoln Town Car with a bloody, mashed windshield and a dribbling can of aerosol cheese on the dash; a motorcycle mounted by the charred remains of a leather-clad headless guy; a New Orleans police car dotted with painted-on bullet holes.

"He wants the explosions bigger, he wants the fires bigger, he wants the reactions bigger," Gallotti said, adding that in most movies if a bullet enters a barrel, "usually you get a hole in the barrel. John wants the barrel flying fifteen-twenty feet in the air with fire coming out of it."

Gallotti recalled Woo's disappointment the first time a gun was fired. "The first shotgun blast, he wanted it bigger," Gallotti said. "I just thought, 'He's nuts. This is big, what does he need bigger for?'

"I fired it up again, and he said, 'This is OK. I want it bigger.' So I doubled it and shot it, and all I could see was him smiling. Everybody said they needed to change their underwear."

Key grip Lloyd Moriarty said Woo and the crew have been involved in a kind of can-you-top-this game, with the director providing daily new challenges and the technical folks refusing to be stumped. Aside from a showy head-on collision between a motorcycle and pickup truck, many of the tricks have involved multiple cameras filming at different speeds moving on multiple tracks all aimed at the same shot.

As for Woo's sometimes halting English, crewmembers said they quickly learned to read each other.

"Sometimes I will use something to make them understand," Woo said, "such as if I take a long track shot from here to there, I just tell them, 'Now this is a Martin Scorsese shot.' When I shoot the action in slow motion, I say, 'Sam Peckinpah slow motion.' Some typical visual shot, I say, 'Now comes the John Woo shot. Big close up on the eyes. . . .'"

Something must be getting through because the crew had nothing but bouquets to throw at Woo, typically calling him "the nicest director I've ever worked with."

"I'm not asking for power or that kind of thing," Woo said. "I'm just asking to make a good work. When I find out everybody is trying their best to work for the movie, I so much appreciate it."

As the allotted number of days for shooting in the warehouse ran down, tensions occasionally surfaced. At one point, after a jiggled camera forced a take to be reshot, Van Damme proclaimed, "My movies must be done on time!"

Later the action star would say, "John Woo for his debut in America, they should have given him more time, more money. But no matter what, it's going to look fantastic."

Woo said the budget—which Van Damme estimated at about $20 million (though the studio is mum on the numbers)—is "much better than Hong Kong, much bigger. But I think half of the budget is spent somewhere else that I don't know."

As end-of-the-day fatigue crept in, Woo complained of "so many politics, so many games, so many personalities. It makes me feel upset and so frustrated for quite a long time. In Hong Kong I don't need to worry about economic things because me and Terence, we produce our own films, and nobody gives us that kind of pressure. So I'm very unhappy."

Even at this low point, is Woo still happy to be a Hollywood filmmaker? "Yeah, I still say I am. In Hong Kong the creativity usually has limits. All you can do is an action movie or comedy. Here I can fulfill my dream."

The Woo Dynasty Comes to Hollywood

TED ELRICK/1995

JOHN WOO (born Wu Yu-Sheng) exploded into film history books with his masterful direction of Hong Kong action pictures. His best known films, *The Killer, Bullet in the Head* and *Hard Boiled*, are populated by characters struggling with questions of loyalty and honor. They are punctuated by elaborately choreographed, violent and over-the-top action sequences. Film festivals, art houses, videotapes and laserdiscs brought his work to a legion of new fans. Numerous contemporary filmmakers praise his work and several have been heavily influenced by his bravura style. Woo's second American film, Twentieth-Century Fox's *Broken Arrow*—a Pentagon code term for a lost nuclear weapon—stars John Travolta, Christian Slater and Samantha Mathis and opens in December. *The DGA Magazine* spoke with the director about his background, his films, his trademark and the differences between directing in Hong Kong and for U.S. studios.

TED ELRICK: *How did the* Broken Arrow *project come to you?*
JW: Before *Broken Arrow* the studio had offered me another project called *Tears of the Sun*. We had been working on that project for eight months. But the star we wanted had a schedule problem and I didn't want to wait, I wanted to get back to work. They had another script, *Broken Arrow*. I read it and loved it very much. I thought it would be a challenge because I've never shot any visual or optical special effects before. That interested me. Everybody knows that I'm good with an

---

From *DGA Magazine*, 20.5 (1995). Reprinted by permission.

action sequence, but I also like to show something about human nature. And this script had pretty good characters. It's by Graham Yost, who wrote *Speed*.

Q: *It has been a while between your last film,* Hard Target, *and* Broken Arrow. *Was it difficult finding the right project?*
JW: Yes. I have to struggle with myself. I know there's a lot of fans and critics who are looking for something from me, they are looking for my style. So I kept looking for the right script that fit into my style.

Q: *Whose decision was it to use John Travolta and Christian Slater?*
JW: Let me put it this way: the studio gave me full freedom to choose the actors. But they also had a lot of great suggestions. John Travolta— the studio liked him a lot. But it was my suggestion to have him play the bad guy. I think John, by his great performance, will make the usual character unusual. He's got great eyes, he's so elegant and intelligent. In all of the action movies the bad guy is so typical. You can see he's a psycho and a maniac. I think John brings a new kind of elegance to that character. I want everybody to see that the most dangerous enemy is not from outside, but from inside—the people who are very close to you. The enemy can be your neighbor and you'll never notice what he's thinking because he looks so normal. So I wanted John Travolta because of his eyes, and he always smiles.

Q: *Isn't that what made Henry Fonda work so well in* Once Upon. . . .
JW: . . . *a Time in the West,* yeah. And nobody had tried that before. So the studio agreed with John Travolta playing the bad guy. And then I suggested we use Christian Slater—I wanted to change his image and make him look like the good boy from the neighborhood. So we made him clean cut, healthy and a charming good-looking young boy. We tried to build a new kind of character—a young man who really cares about the others, who will take responsibility. A lot of young people don't take responsibility for their country, their family, for anything. I tried to give the young audience a character to follow. The young people, all over the world, seem to be lost. Maybe I'm a little bit old-fashioned, but I think we need to give something to the young people. They really need something right now.

Q: *And Samantha Mathis?*
JW: Usually in an action movie, the actress only knows how to scream and yell and run scared. I liked Samantha Mathis because she looked different. I think she stands for a strong character, always independent. Not a scared girl who needs protection. I usually put the actors' photos together, to see how they fit. And when I put their pictures together it looked like a golden boy [Slater] and golden girl. That's how we cast.

Q: *You have said you never used storyboards on your Hong Kong films. Has that changed with doing American films?*
JW: Yes. For the American film there is a question of budget. So the storyboard really helps budget-wise, and also helps to communicate with everybody.

Q: *On* Hard Boiled, *you had thirty-five days to shoot that last action sequence in the hospital. Could that ever happen in the States?*
JW: No, never. I must say, in Hong Kong we are much more simple. My partner Terence Chang and I had full control of the production. We had one meeting with the financing company. We just let them know how much of a budget we would need, how many days we would need and what the story was about. That was it. Very simple. We would never have interference from anyone. And the studio was not allowed to see any footage. We only gave them the answer print. All we wanted was to get a good movie. We had no games and no politics. That's the big difference. In Hong Kong, I work like a painter. We have a script but we have a "competition" lifestyle—not in competition with the other movies, in competition with myself. For instance, [in *Hard Boiled*] we have the teahouse sequence. The next scene, I've got to go a little bit over the teahouse. I have to keep thinking. If you have planned everything before, or have done the storyboard, it doesn't have the same interest for me.

Q: *So how did you work out those action sequences in Hong Kong?*
JW: Usually, since I have the control, before we shoot the scene I tell everybody roughly what we need. "OK, for this scene I need about twenty stuntmen, five bad guys. The story's about [leading man] Chow Yun-Fat and his partner; they're doing some undercover stuff in the teahouse. Somehow they have an ambush and they have a fight from

the first floor going down to the lobby." That's it. Most of the action is done by my instinct while I'm there; everything is all in my mind. When I go to the set, I put myself into the character. If I'm him, ambushed by twenty guys and there are a lot of people there, what would I do? I shut down everything and make everybody quiet. Then I do the whole scene by myself. If I have two guys on my right side and one guy on my back, I imagine that I shoot the two guys then turn, spinning in the air to shoot the guy behind me. And I will imagine those kinds of actions so that it looks more like a ballet. I want to keep the beauty of the body movement, so I say, how about adding another guy on the ceiling? So the hero spins in the air and also shoots the guy above him. That guy falls and then there's two more guys in the hallway and I grab another gun and shoot them. When I shot that scene with the banister, I said, the two bad guys are shooting like crazy in the lobby, and our hero slides down the banister and shoots them. I said, "I think it's going to be fantastic." I go to the stunt coordinator and say, "This is the climax of the scene. From this point, let's figure out how to build up the emotion and motivation to get here." We usually have a lot of time to do that. There was no point to having a storyboard. Just like a painter, I paint how I feel.

Q: *How do you translate that painterly approach to American filmmaking?*
JW: It's difficult. I think only the independent companies can do it easily. It's hard to do in the big studio. I understand, because they have more concern about the budget and time. Also, for our Hong Kong movies, the market is so limited—really Asia only. My movies and Jackie Chan's movies do a little better because we have more of a market. But American movies have a worldwide market. They have reason to be concerned about the rating and the different kinds of audiences. I found out that the larger the budget is, the less time you have.

Q: *What were your Hong Kong budgets in American dollars?*
JW: *Hard Boiled* was $4.5 million and shooting days were 123. *Bullet in the Head* was $3.5 million and 110 days.

Q: *What was the budget and shooting schedule on* Broken Arrow?
JW: $50 million and ninety days. A lot of the stuff will be shot by special effects, but that's a different schedule.

Q: *Bullet in the Head was a very personal film for you. . . .*
JW: Yes. The first half of that was based on my biography. I had the same kind of friends and I also grew up in the slums. There was a lot of gang fighting and I also got beat up by the gangs because I didn't want to join. I was never in a gang. So I had to struggle very hard. We also had a lot of dreams about a better world. What we did have were valuable friendships. I think that the old times are much better than nowadays. The people cared more about each other and looked up to each other more. There were more ideals. The new generation seems to be lost. For the second half of the film, I was influenced by the Tiananmen Square massacre in Beijing in 1989. I was very sad, very upset and felt ashamed for our country. It was so inhuman to kill the students. And so I put the pain into the movie, I changed the whole second half of the script—the scenes when they first arrive in Vietnam and they see students demonstrating. When I shot the movie, I almost went crazy because I shot the film with pain. I kept thinking of the tragedy. The original idea for the story didn't have the Vietnam part. I just used it as the future Hong Kong.

Q: *Do you fear that happening in 1997 when Hong Kong becomes part of China?*
JW: No, but I see that something good will be lost. When the time comes, I think there will be chaos, and people will find it hard to trust each other because of the political situation, like in a war.

Q: *I've read that* The Wild Bunch *is one of your favorite films. It has strong loyalty undercurrents like your Hong Kong films. And the Bunch know they're going to die, yet they go back to attempt to rescue their partner.*
JW: Yes, the romanticism. Let's talk about *The Wild Bunch*. I like the last moment, before they die. It reminds me of the same moment before Jesus died. He was sacrificing himself. The movie made me feel the same way.

Q: *You've said you don't set out to make political statements in your films. But you do make moral statements.*
JW: I like old-fashioned, traditional moral standards. People don't seem to realize what honor and loyalty are. I am fond of Chinese history.

There are a lot of famous stories about honor and loyalty. I was so moved reading about the revolution in China. Sun Yat-sen led the revolution [against China's Manchu rulers in 1911]. A lot of people sacrificed themselves, dying for their country. It always moved me, and I always wished I could be one of them. I always try to do something for somebody or for my country. The other thing is that I am a Christian. I am influenced so much by the church and the Bible. When my family moved from China to Hong Kong, we had nothing. We were homeless for years, we lived in the street and we had a very rough time because my father was sick with tuberculosis for ten years. I couldn't go to school until I was nine years old because we were so poor. Then we got help from the church. An American family sent money through the church for my school fee. I am so grateful to the church and the American family for their help. So this kind of a favor I always remember. This kind of feeling I always try to put in my films and give to my hero. When I was in high school I wanted to be a minister. I wanted to give something back to the people. So my heroes are always helping people who need it.

Q: *How did you discover film?*
JW: When I was eleven, even though we were poor, my mother was a fan of the movies from the west. She used to bring me to the theater. At that time, a parent could bring a child into the theater for free. I was fascinated by the musicals, I think they influenced me the most. *Seven Brides for Seven Brothers* and *Singin' in the Rain* are my favorites. Also a lot of Fred Astaire. Because we were poor, I always thought we were living in hell. I had fantasy and only the musical could fulfill my fantasy. I always thought that there must be a better world for us out there where people care for and love each other. That's why I was so fond of the musicals. Gene Kelly was so beautiful. I used to take a piece of glass and use a Chinese brush to draw some images on the glass—a cowboy, Bugs Bunny or some Chinese legend hero. I would cover myself with a blanket to make it as dark as a theatre. Then I would use a flashlight and shine it through the glass to project the image on the wall. I would move the glass or torch a little bit, back and forth or up and down to make a movie. I loved movies and I wanted to be a filmmaker some day.

Q: *Do you rehearse with actors?*
JW: No, I usually put myself in the character's [place]. When you see John Travolta, Chow Yun-Fat or Tony Leung, I put my feelings into them. Before we start shooting, we talk about the character. In Hong Kong, I usually write my own script and I know the actors very well. When I've written the script and the actors do exactly what I write, it's no fun. After I've written the script it seems I've seen the movie already. So when I get to the set I usually say to the actors, "OK you're free. For the scene, the whole theme is this one line—it's about your character, you're tough. All I need is this line." Then I'll ask the actors, "In your real life, did anything happen to you that made you feel like the line?" And I'll let them think. [If it's a good response,] I'll say, "That's a great story. Can you put that feeling into the scene, make up the lines? All I need is the last line." There's no way to get that in rehearsals.

Q: *In the U.S., you've had two films presented in the Voyager Company's Criterion Collection laserdisc editions—*The Killer *and* Hard Boiled*—on which you've also participated in the audio commentary. How do you feel about these packages?*
JW: Very honored. After I finish a film I don't want to see it again. I just want to put it there and let the people enjoy it, love it or hate it. Whatever kind of feeling they get from the picture is their own. If I find people appreciate my work, I feel like I've gained a friend. If I find somebody gets something from my movie, or even hates it but lets me know why they hate it, I feel very happy because this business is a lonely business. When I saw the Criterion Collection, I thought it was great because it would let more people understand what the films were about. It's a great opportunity to have more friends. *The Killer* was not as popular in Hong Kong as it was in the Western world. So when I got here and saw the Criterion Collection selected *The Killer*, I was very happy because *The Killer* and *Bullet in the Head* are my two favorite movies. So that's why I felt honored because at last I found some people who really like them.

Look Woo's Talking

MAUREEN "MO" RYAN / 1995

JOHN WOO IS RESISTING the urge to dance.

The soft-spoken Asian director, whose hard-charging Hong Kong action movies (*The Killer, Hard Boiled*) make the average Stallone vehicle look like a six-year-old's tricycle, is trying to explain how he comes up with the bullet-and-blood ballets that have become his calling card.

"When I was a kid, I was fascinated by cartoons and by musicals—especially musicals. I'm crazy about them," he muses. "So I've got a very strong feeling for the rhythm and the beauty of body movement. When I'm deciding how to do an action sequence, I'm creating a dance scene."

Those who've seen Woo's films know exactly what the director means when he speaks of the exquisite appeal of well-choreographed mayhem. His deft touch with destruction makes it easy to understand why Twentieth-Century Fox trusted the director with the $70 million actioner *Broken Arrow*, which stars John Travolta and Christian Slater as dueling Stealth bomber pilots.

In hiring Woo, whose Asian films are revered touchstones for auteurs like Quentin Tarantino and Robert Rodriguez, Fox may have been trying to re-create the success of the studio's 1994 breakout hit, *Speed*. *Broken Arrow*'s script is by Graham Yost, one of *Speed*'s writers, and several of *Speed*'s key players, from the stunt coordinator to the film editor, signed on to work with Woo.

Perhaps producer Mark Gordon, who was also on the team that helped speed Keanu Reeves to success, thought that hiring the Hong Kong native

---

A version of this article first appeared in *Cinescape* magazine, December 1995, volume 2 number 3. © Mania Entertainment. Reprinted by permission.

would work the same box-office magic that hiring Dutch director Jan de Bont did for *Speed*.

Whatever their reasons for hiring him, Woo is glad to have a second shot at directing an American film (his first was the 1992 Jean-Claude Van Damme head-kicker *Hard Target*).

"I've gotten great support from Twentieth-Century Fox," Woo says. "I also have a lot more pressure—the studio has pretty high hopes for this project, so I've got to make it good."

But unlike *Speed*, which starred the up-and-coming—and relatively inexpensive—Keanu Reeves and Sandra Bullock, *Broken Arrow* boasts two high-profile Hollywood talents, John Travolta and Christian Slater. The genial Travolta, who garnered an Academy Award nomination for his turn in *Pulp Fiction*, plays the villainous B-3 pilot Vic Deakins, who holds an American city hostage with a purloined nuclear weapon.

"I think John is going to really surprise the audience. He's a really likable bad guy, which is a hard thing to do," enthuses Woo. "John really has a very special gift, especially with his eyes. He can look so charming, but sometimes when he's staring at you, he can have the eyes of Satan. I didn't want this guy to be the typical bad guy. I wanted to make the audience feel like he could be anyone—your neighbor, your colleague, your friend."

Slater, who turned down a starring role in Sylvester Stallone's *Assassins* to work with Woo, plays straight-arrow pilot Riley Hale, who, along with park ranger Terry Carmichael (Samantha Mathis), wages an epic battle with Deakins through the arid landscape of the Southwest to retrieve the stolen nuke.

"Most of the action sequences were filmed on location—in the desert, on cliffs, at the Grand Canyon, on trains and in helicopters," Woo says. "It was really tough to shoot. We shot most of the final fight scene on a moving train. It was tough for the actors, for the camera people and for the stunt crew. Filming a chase scene with a helicopter, we didn't use stunt doubles—it was Samantha and Christian, and the helicopter was flying very low, just about three feet above their heads. So if one mistake had been made, Christian and Samantha would both have been in trouble."

Despite the demanding nature of his role, Slater was game for the challenges the film presented. "We worked very well together and sometimes [Christian] gave pretty good input, not only on the action, but he also came up with new lines that made scenes work better," Woo says. And like the other actors in the film, Slater did most of his own stunts himself, which no doubt caused the film's producers the occasional moment of panic.

"Stealth bombers to helicopters to trains to Humvees to boats—you name it, we rode it," says former football star Howie Long, who plays Sgt. Kelly, Deakins's partner in crime. "At one point I had just gotten knocked off one ladder [on a moving train], and had fallen on to the other ladder, and I was hanging with my legs dangling underneath the train. I had a strap on my waist that you can't see, but that was just as insurance. Hanging by one arm and dangling and pulling my weight back up—that was a bit of a rush."

Woo, modest to a fault, says he can't pick his favorite action sequence in the film, and instead saves his praise for his gung-ho cast: "The performers are all so great. The thing that will most excite the audience is watching them."

But being on a John Woo set, despite the familial atmosphere, certainly isn't for the faint of heart.

"When I'm shooting, I sometimes get crazy," Woo says with a sheepish chuckle. "For the last sequence in *Hard Boiled*, we had more than fifteen bombs going off everywhere, and we had seven cameras set up in different positions. So we had all the explosions going off one by one, and the actors running through the explosions. When I saw that the explosions looked so great and the fire looked so great, I pushed the cameraman and said, 'Pick up the damn camera and go into the fire!' The explosions were still going off, so I pushed another cameraman to take his camera off the dolly and run into another explosion. They got pretty good shots for me," Woo laughs, noting that his cameramen emerged from the shoot unscathed. "When I'm shooting, sometimes it feels like a drug. Of course, I never take drugs, but the feeling is . . ." he stops, temporarily at a loss for words. "Anyway, I'm just very into [making] movies."

Woo, whose given name is Wu Yu-Sheng, nurtured that love for movies in his native Hong Kong, where he was born into a poverty-stricken family in 1946. "When I was in high school, I dreamed of being a filmmaker, but my family was so poor they couldn't afford for me to go to college," he remembers.

Even if he had had the money to go to college, Hong Kong didn't have a film school at that time, so "all we could do was learn from the movies. In the '60s, and '70s, we had a lot of opportunities to see the great movies from everywhere, from France and Italy and the States. I also used to go to every library and every bookstore to steal the film books. I was so poor, I couldn't help it—I needed to study [them]. I stole the film books, art books, philosophy books, and that's how I learned film theory."

After getting his first movie-related job as a script supervisor, Woo worked his way to the top of the Hong Kong film industry. At first, he directed comedies, then in the mid-'80s, he segued into the ultra-action flicks for which he is best known.

No one who's seen his 1989 actioner *The Killer* could ever forget the evocative candle-lit church, filled with fluttering doves, in which the film's key showdowns take place, or the imaginative sequence in which two rivals at the home of a blind woman nearly kill each other while pretending, for their host's sake, to have a sedate cup of tea. Stylish flourishes that are equal parts French New Wave and John Wayne epic made the director a god to an entire generation of Hollywood directors, many of whom have both put blazing guns in each hand of their actors in key scenes—a signature Woo touch.

For Woo, the reverence in which he is held by American directors is part of a long cycle by which the film industry renews itself. "I think it's like a circle—in the 1960s and '70s, I was so influenced by Western directors, by Sam Peckinpah, Martin Scorsese, Jean-Pierre Melville, Stanley Kubrick, François Truffaut, Arthur Penn. Now having those young [filmmakers] like my movies completes the circle."

And coming to America to make movies completes a cycle that, for Woo, began with reverence for all things American—from Peckinpah to musicals. Like the film masters he learned from, Woo hopes with *Broken Arrow* not just to give audiences a hell of a ride, but to provoke an emotional reaction as well.

"At the beginning of *Broken Arrow*, the two pilots are friends, then they turn on each other. It's a theme of tragic friendship," he says. "Some people see me as an action director, but action is not the only thing in my movies. I always like to show something about human nature—something deep inside the heart."

Honor, Loyalty, and Chivalry

MICHAEL SINGER / 1997

MICHAEL SINGER: *The cover story in* Asiaweek . . . *said that your decision to come to the United States had as much to do with family as it had to do with business. Is that true?*
JOHN WOO: Yeah, it's true. Because there's so many reasons, and one of the reasons is that first of all, my wife is a citizen and two of my kids were born here. But before, I was just only interested working in Hong Kong and I had never dreamed to come to Hollywood.

Hong Kong is a place that will drive you crazy. It's very, very competitive, a lot of pressure and people don't respect other people's privacy. There's so much competition and the pace is so fast. You have to work faster and smarter than the others or else the others will beat you down.

So, I mean, the Hong Kong people trained me to work harder. And of course, it's very unhealthy. So that's why I went to work seven days a week and spent most of the time in the office and in the studio. I never had enough time for my children. When I got home, they had already gone to school. When I started work they were sleeping. My children and my wife felt very insecure. They didn't get real love from me and I was so crazy about work. So my family was thrown apart. My children hated me because they didn't really know about me [and thought] I didn't care much about them. My family is the most important thing in my life, so I realized that, since

---

A version of this interview appeared in *A Cut Above: 50 Film Directors Talk About Their Craft*, Lone Eagle Publishing/IFILM (www.ifilm.com), 1997. Used by permission.

I got the opportunity to work here, why not just build a whole family here?

The people here are much more normal. It is also a lot of pressure to work here but I think it's a normal pressure, and people have to work hard and do a good job. But the people here are more respectful. . . . I could have my own privacy and have more time. Because people don't work on the weekend, I can spend more time with my family and my children, and then we can talk more and reunite. Now we have more of an understanding. For a few years it worked pretty well. I got back my family, and my children are very happy now. In Hong Kong they were small, but now they're growing up. I just felt like I needed to do my job for the family. Now, I realized that I didn't give them the right direction, and give them love and give them some guidelines and give them some support and encouragement. And that's what they needed.

Even though I feel I have failed here, I still don't want to go back to Hong Kong because I can't stand that kind of lifestyle anymore. Even though I love the place and I love the people there, the lifestyle is still crazy.

Q: *I got a small taste of it. In 1986, I visited there and had some friends in the movie business, and even the few days that I spent around film sets and clubs and restaurants where people from the movie business were hanging out, it was insane.*

A: Yeah, the people are social, so there's a lot of social parties and things. I never liked that. It always took away your time. I was pretty low key in Hong Kong. Every big city is like a cruel world. If you fail just one time then you're finished and no one will care about you, you won't get any phone calls, you won't get any people you know knocking on your door. That's why people there got to work like hell.

But in this country, it's different. In this country even though you fail, one or couple times, you still can keep your reputation. You still can [make your own] decisions. The people still respect you. They are concerned about your work, not if you're a winner or not, even though you're a loser, but the people understand the reason and you still can have another chance. But in Hong Kong, no way, if you fail. . . .

Q: *You're out.*
A: You're out, especially in the film business. For example, for the star and actress, if you're over thirty, they almost have to retire, because when you're over thirty, you're old.

Q: *I met Chow Yun-Fat, in 1986, on the set of one of his films. I met him, Sammo Hung, and lots of other people. Even then, Chow was expressing some fears to me about his future in Hong Kong. He was saying things like, "Well I don't know, I'm getting older, maybe I'm not going to be on hold this way, maybe I'll go to America someday." I thought that was a great idea. And now both of you of course are having great success. When you came here, as you just said, you weren't even sure what your fate would be.*
A: Yeah, I just wanted to learn and experience because I always liked challenges. Even though I don't speak the same language, I still like to take challenges. I like to learn from the people. That's why I came here. And I always believed, all of mankind, we all are pretty much the same. We have a similar style of work, we have similar kind of feeling, and we have a similar kind of thinking. And I also believe we have a lot of things in common as well, no matter where we come from, I do believe we all have the same kind of beliefs, the same kind of ability, the same kind of goodness, and the same kind of dream. We also have same kind of morality, we just do it in different ways. But basically, we all believe one thing. That is what I call international.

That's what I like to discover in my films, so that's why I like to work here. I also see myself as a bridge. I feel I've got the responsibilities to bring the good things from the East, from our country, and then to discover the real things from the West, the real good things from the West, then put them all together, put them into one film and then try to look for the harmony. That lets us get to know each other more. There's a lot of people who say my kind of movies are international. That's what I'm doing now. For the first time, for the first American movie, I couldn't do that because I thought I knew enough about this country but actually did not. In *Hard Target*, I intended to make it a little bit more like a Hong Kong film or more in my style and just do what I do. But it didn't work well. The movie looks only at one side, and pretty much like a Hong Kong movie.

That's why I had to spend a couple years off after that. I took the time to learn more. I watched TV every day, kept in touch with other people and saw how they talk, how they feel. I found out what the real culture is. Then I had more compassion for the society. I tried to reach people's hearts and see what everybody's thinking. I even tried to find out what the good things and bad things are about here—what the real problems were. Then, I tried to figure out a way to put the two things together in one film. *Face/Off* gave me a great opportunity to combine [this sensibility] into a good film.

Q: *And it was. Your fans considered* Face/Off *to be the most like your best Hong Kong films, even though your style expanded even further, on the grandest scale of all. But all of the themes that we've enjoyed in your Hong Kong films, we saw, some of the visual motifs, we saw in* Face/Off. *But you seemed to take it to the next level, and so in a way a lot of us thought that that was much more of a pure John Woo than* Hard Target *or even* Broken Arrow. *And so the most pure John Woo film became the most successful, which we thought was a confirmation of what's best in your filmmaking. A lot of people were afraid that working in the States would homogenize your work that you would have to do it their way instead of your way, but you've escaped that potential trap, which is wonderful.*

A: [Laughs] The other thing that I was really surprised and shocked to realize was that I had so many fans in this country. I didn't know about that. Before I came here I went to one or two film festivals to meet some people and I knew some people were interested in my work but I didn't know I had so many fans here. That really encouraged me. When I saw all these fans, they were so much concerned about me and they all cared about me and were all happy to see me come to work here. That gave me a great responsibility.

I tried to keep my own style, and not let people down, especially the critics. All the critics and the journalists and writers here gave me full support. I was *totally* surprised. When I was stuck in a small place, I never cared or knew much about the outside world, and I didn't know how the people felt about me. I just concentrated on making my films. I'm movie-crazy.

Q: *You were so busy, you were working all the time.*
A: And all of a sudden I saw everybody as my friend and, in the meantime, I saw the movie as a bridge for myself. Every movie I made, I wanted to send my regards and send my message and my feelings to a friend. It seemed like it is a very good communication method to your friends. That made me feel no matter where I was, I have to be myself, keep my own style, keep my own character. I knew that people cared for the film. That's very encouraging, and I'm really grateful to all the fans.

And the other thing is that I am also very surprised that I've gotten so much support from the film society here. Of course, all the studios are really open for talent, and they're so open to me. I've got so many opportunities. I also heard from a producer, who said it's very strange that there's no one in the business who is jealous of me. And also there's not any competition in the kingdom. Everybody seems to be very excited about me to come here. And everybody wants to see me succeed.

Q: *That's true, and you did.*
A: And no one wanted to see me fail. So I was so moved, I'm so moved.

Q: *That's absolutely true.*
A: I'm so grateful about that. Because people love my movies and also like me as a person, so I feel so lucky. [Laughs] That's really encouraging and it just gives me a new life. Having worked in Hong Kong for more than twenty-five years, I think I've done enough. Hong Kong is so limited; all you can do is action and comedy or some little drama, and that's all. It's hard to try anything new, or anything political, it's very sensitive.

So when I felt myself beginning to go down, I had to try something new, something very human. I like real drama. I like to try some more new thing to express myself, to express how I feel about the whole thing. That's why I feel so lucky when I have done enough in one place and suddenly I have another chance. And also I have so much great support, I just started a new life.

Q: *So you can see yourself moving away a little bit from action films, here.*
A: Yeah.

Q: *And is this what you hope to do, not necessarily permanently, but to work in other genres besides action films?*
A: Oh yeah.

Q: *Will you ever go back to comedy, because a lot of your early films were comedy, and humor is an important element of your action films anyways?*
A: Yeah, I'd like to try. I like comedy. One of my next projects is a light comedy, of course with some action but not as much as before. I'd also like to make a musical. That's my biggest dream. When I was a kid I was so crazy about musical, and I must say, I was influenced from musicals. As you can see, I'm using the musical theory in the action scenes.

Q: *Right, right, and the choreography and the action, I mean, that's like dancing.*
A: And the camera.

Q: *And the camera movement, it's all choreography.*
A: The camera movement and everything, it's pretty much like a musical, with rhythm, you know. I love musicals. I found the real beauty in musicals when I was a kid. I was raised in a slum. It was awful, more awful than here nowadays. We just felt like we lived in hell. We were living in a very bad neighborhood, with drug dealers, gangsters, and gamblers around. Almost everyday I had to deal with a gang.

Q: *Which neighborhood was that in Hong Kong?*
A: Kowloon Side. There's an area called Shek Kip Mei. There was a lot of crime in the old times, in the 1950s and '60s. I used to get beat up by the gangs, so I had to fight very hard. I struggled very hard to survive. I also portrayed myself as strong. I had to fight back. Everyday I lived in paranoia, in panic and insecurity, and I tried to figure out how to survive. So I always dreamed of flying away from hell, going to another place, a place where there's no crime, no hatred, no violence, where people only trust each other and love each other, and everybody's so beautiful.

And I found my dream in two places. One is the church. The church saved me. The church gave me good guidelines. Whenever I got beat up or I felt upset or lonely, or even did something wrong, I would go to the church, to my confession, and I would feel safe inside.

The other thing is the movies. I found my dream in musicals. Musicals are so beautiful. The world of the musical is so beautiful and people are very charming, elegant and they're so happy. The people are so full of love and colorful, and so peaceful. The singing is so lovely, as lovely as angels sing. I watched a lot of musicals and tried to relax. I was so crazy about musicals. The first couple musicals I saw were *Singin' in the Rain*, *The Wizard of Oz*, and *Seven Brides for Seven Brothers*. And I watched them a lot. In the '60s my favorite musical was a French movie called *The Umbrellas of Cherbourg* and *The Young Girls of Rochefort*.

Q: *Yes, the two Jacques Demy films.*
A: Yes, Jacques Demy films. His musicals are much more beautiful and more romantic. From his movies I learned about love, I learned about romanticism. That's why I'm always dreaming of making a musical. My other problem is that I never know how to use the proper language to express myself. Especially when I was a kid, I was so shy—so shy that I didn't know how to deal with the people. I even had a problem with my own language. Even now, when I'm directing a Hong Kong film, it's still hard to express how I feel.

That's why I like action, why I like to use action to demonstrate the ideas I have, to let the people know what I like. When I was a kid, I loved dancing, and I loved singing. I tried to use body language to express myself. So that's why when I became a film director. In my earlier Hong Kong films, I liked to choreograph the action myself, because I didn't know how to describe it. Let's say if one of the guys punches me on the right side, and then I duck on the left and then spin around and kick him in the stomach, kind of, I did all of the action myself. That's why I love visual things. I love to use them, it trained me to be a visual storyteller, more than a verbal storyteller. Sometimes my films are pretty much like a painting. The painting tells more of a story and more of a feeling—that's why I'm so concerned about camera work.

Q: *And of course now I know why we see why churches play such an important role in your films.*
A: Yes. I'm Christian. I have a very strong relationship with the church. My parents were Christian, too. Without the church and my parents, I might have become some other person.

In old times it was tough, it was so tough for every young kid in Hong Kong. In the '50s most of the people—90 percent of the people—were poor. They were all refugees who came from China with nothing. Everybody was stuck in a prison, and we had to struggle very hard. There were only two ways to go, one is being bad and one is being good. My parents were very strict, very tough on me. They also had to educate me to become a decent person. They taught me a lot of Chinese culture and things. And since our family was so poor, we were homeless for a couple years, living on the street. Right before I almost joined a street gang, the church helped me.

The church helped our family. Also there was an American family that sent money through a church to support my school fees. That's how I got an education. My family couldn't pay for me to go to school until I was nine years old and in a church. The American family sent money every month for us to help me go to school. They supported me for six years, and also supported my younger sister and younger brother. They were so nice to me.

Q: *You must relate pretty strongly to one of my favorite 1930s Warner Bros. gangster movies,* Angels with Dirty Faces. *It's almost like that story.*
A: Oh, yeah?

Q: *Well, two best friends are both very young, tough kids. A priest played by Pat O'Brien always is trying to. . . .*
A: Yes, yes, yes.

Q: *One gets caught as a child, the other doesn't. Jimmy Cagney becomes a hardened criminal, a killer, and like a god to these dead-end kids. The other one is Pat O'Brien, who becomes a priest. It was my favorite movie as a kid.*
A: I remember the movie.

So I was so grateful to the church and I'm so grateful to the American family. Then I had to work hard and I made it. That's why when I was in high school my first dream wasn't to be a filmmaker. I wanted to be a minister. I wanted to pay back society, and I just wanted to help others who needed help. And I was such an admirer of the Bible and Jesus, I wanted to send the great messages to the people, to the other young people. I also respect all kinds of religions. That's why in my movies, there's so many religious things.

Q: *Yes, very deep spiritual elements. What turned you away from the idea of becoming a minister and onto the path of becoming a filmmaker, because that's a pretty big switch right there?*
A: Yeah, there were two things. When I was young, it was hard enough to get a chance to go to school. And then I also had a gift of art, but I didn't know what it was. I knew I was good at drawing, painting, music, dancing, and writing, I didn't know why. As I say, I was shy, and it was hard to communicate with the other people. I felt that I needed to use an art to express myself.

So I learned everything when I was a kid. I learned thinking, I learned music, but none of them would work, because in the old times the school was so tough, since our school was run by the rules from church, it was very tough. The other thing about the Hong Kong education is what we call "stuffing duck": If you're going to sell the duck at a good price, you have to stuff a lot of things into the stomach, to make it look fat, so the people will buy it. The Hong Kong education is just like that. You got to stuff a lot of things into your brain, so everybody is pressured with a lot of competition.

I didn't like it. I liked art, so my parents were a little disappointed with me, because they were afraid I couldn't get any job. But, I needed to discover myself. I was so fond of movies, but I never dreamed of being a filmmaker because it was really hard to get a chance. If you were related to the film society, you will never get a chance in Hong Kong.

In the old time, European, American, and Japanese films were very popular. They were the mainstream films in Hong Kong, and the great thing about Hong Kong was you could see everything from every country. And then, the French New Wave hit in the early '60s, and I saw a lot of the French New Wave films, like films by François Truffaut, Jean-Luc Godard, Jacques Demy, and Jean-Pierre Melville. It was so amazing. The movies were so new. They all started from a dream and were on a very small scale, but they're brilliant films. The movies are so honest, so original, full of intelligence and new elements, just like Hitchcock films.

I realized that movies are a perfect tool for me to express my feelings. The movie is a party, the movie has everything, it can be a painting, a poem, a storyteller. Also the movie can be very spiritual and very intellectual. The movie is what we call an Eighth Art in Hong Kong.

Q: *Yes, the Seven Lively Arts, and the seven arts, and film.*
A: Yes. So many different elements go into a film. That made me make the decision to start using film to express myself. That was when I was in high school. But before that I intended to go to missionary school but they didn't accept me. They said that I was too artistic and they didn't think I could concentrate on the mission. They suggested that I become an artist rather than a minister. They thought I was too crazy about art.

Q: *Were you disappointed?*
A: I was a little disappointed because my father wanted me to be a minister. Because I loved my father so much, I listened to him. He was my god. He passed away when I was sixteen.

In the '60s, the people in Hong Kong were still poor. There was a lot of disaster, a lot of people suffering, a lot of people were poor and frightened. I just wanted to help those people. I like social work because I was so compassionate to society, and I always liked to help do something for the others. So that's why I desired to be a minister. But since my teacher and other people know me pretty well—better than I know myself—they also suggested that I go into art.

Q: *They knew you could help people in a different way?*
A: Maybe, I don't know. [Laughs] I was really in love with movies. And after high school, my mother couldn't afford me anymore, since my father passed away; my mother took care of the family . . . alone. She worked on a construction site to raise the family . . . So I had to work. She really couldn't afford for me to go to the film school. And there were no film schools in Hong Kong, so if you really want to study film, you go to the United States or even Europe. But there was no way; it was like a dream.

But I still didn't give up movies. I learned by watching movies. I watched every classic and art film in the art house. And the other big thing in the old time was most of the art films were in the public theater, so you could watch them very easily.

I stole the film books from the library and the bookstore. I stole the film books, art books, philosophy books. That's how I finished my college education. [Laughs] I knew stealing was a crime, but I couldn't help it, I had no choice, I needed to learn, and I had no money. And I couldn't find work. So I had to steal the film books to learn. Of course, the people nowadays do the same. I don't encourage people to do that, it's not a good thing, but in old times most of the people did the same thing.

Then I started gathering with a group of young people who also followed movies. We made an experimental film together. In the beginning, I was just crazy about movies, and I had never dreamed to be a film director. I just wanted to be part of the movies.

Q: *Any way at all?*
A: Yeah, I just wanted to work in the film business. In the old times, all the film directors were pretty old. They had to be old enough and have enough experience to direct a movie. So the average age of the director was forty-five to sixty-five. And in the old time, the Hong Kong film system was very political. The director had so much power, he was like a warlord. And if you didn't relate to film society, you'd never get any chances. That's why I was only thinking of being an actor or a cinema photographer. That was enough for me.

Then, me and the other young people found out that Hong Kong movies were so bad in the old time. Most of the Hong Kong films copied American movies; they even stole the music and story. Then, we learned from the French New Wave. If you want to make Hong Kong movies look different you got to do it by yourself, just like the French New Wave, and the American New Wave—like Scorsese and those people. Just like them you have to take over and do something by yourself. So that made me decide to be a film director. When you become a director, you can make your dream, simple as that.

And, in the meantime, I got lucky. When I was twenty-six years old, I got support from a friend who suddenly made a lot of money on the stock market. He gave us a little amount of money to form an independent company to make my first film.

Q: *When do you feel that you really came into your own? When did you feel that you were finally clicking? What's the first film that you made that you really, really liked?*
A: I must say, my movie called *Princess Chang Ping*, which I made in 1975. That movie made me feel like I was a real filmmaker. I love that movie so much. Before that, I wasn't sure of myself. I knew I had made a movie, but my movie wasn't that great. It was like practicing the skill, the technique, you know, a working experience.

But *Princess Chang Ping*, the movie gave me a very strong feeling. It was the first time in a few ways that I really controlled everything and made a movie as my own personality.

And then after that, I made several comedies. And even though they made a lot of money, I still didn't feel strong about the movie. My comedy was silly, it wasn't like a movie at all. The studio was only interested in me making a comedy because my kind of comedy made money, you know. But that wasn't my desire. That wasn't my favorite type of film. And then in 1985, when I made *A Better Tomorrow*, I felt very strong.

Q: *And that was also really the film that truly brought you over here.*
A: No, not that one. It was the *The Killer*. I mean the people started to pay attention to my films with *A Better Tomorrow* sure, but I didn't know that.

It's so funny, there's so many stories about *A Better Tomorrow*. But not too many people expected that movie to be a hit. When my partners and I started on the project, there wasn't enough confidence about that movie. They just saw it as just another gangster film.

And before I made that movie I failed for quite a few years, and people didn't like my movies, and some people even said I should retire, that I should go home and stop working for a couple years and just watch videotape and learn how to make movies. Oh shit, I was so sad, because I was so sure of myself. I knew I was a good director, and I'd never let the people look down on me. So I put the feeling into the film. Remember there's a dialogue when Chow Yun-Fat says, "I've failed for three years. If I get a chance I will get back." I will get back to fame from my own hand.

Q: *That's a very personal statement.*
A: Yeah, very similar statement. So after the movie had huge success—the movie broke all the records—everybody was so shocked and surprised. And since the movie was a big hit, all of a sudden I got back everything—I got back all the friends, reputation and money. It also caused a lot of jealousy. So many people were jealous of me, and some people who had criticized me before didn't feel comfortable.

So when my movie got so much attention overseas, the people working in the studio didn't let me know about it. They just said, "OK, well the foreigners didn't like the movie much, is it OK?" And well I said, "No." They never showed me any clips, any press clippings or any reviews from overseas, so I didn't know anything. And some people tried to cover that and, well, I didn't care. I just wanted to keep making my movies. Some film festivals were very interested in me. They wanted to invite me to the film festival but [the studio] didn't let me know.

And some people even said I didn't direct the film, that somebody else directed the film. Some people even said the producer directed the film, not John Woo. I was so mad. That's typical Hong Kong.

Then I left that company and made another film, *The Killer*, which I did all on my own, and I tried to prove myself one more time that that's my work, my movie. And I didn't care about the producer, I didn't care about anyone, I just made my own film. And that movie got so much more attention than *A Better Tomorrow* did in the Western world.

And then the film festival people, like the Canadian David Overbey, came to me and directly asked me to go to the film festival and . . . Terence Chang, who is a great friend. He was the one who felt sorry for me. He knew some people in the company were jealous of me and didn't let me know anything and try to cover something. So he brought my film to every film festival—Cannes, Canada, Toronto, Italy, Sundance—to let the people know about my work and to introduce me to the whole world. I still feel lucky and extremely grateful to have my partner.

Q: *And now the two of you are conquering America.*
A: Well we started, and we are always grateful to the people here, to have this moment and this opportunity to work here. And mainly it's all because of him. Terence made the path for me. He did all the hard work.

Q: *You do a little of it too. And you of course now, you're blazing the path for the other Hong Kong filmmakers who are coming here.*
A: Yeah, not only for the Hong Kong filmmakers, I also want to help anybody who has a gift for making movies but has no chance. That's one of the reasons we had to form the company—we just wanted to help others produce and direct a movie. We have met so many young talented filmmakers. If we can find the right project for the right person, we would like to help. Even though it's not a big help, at least it's a little help.

It's not easy for everyone in Hollywood, and since we have the opportunity, we like to pay back society. That's why I like to use some film students. We couldn't help everybody, but at least we can help some of them—that's our wish. And I think Hollywood itself also needs to change. We find that most of the Hollywood films are pretty poor, pretty empty. They hardly accept the new and young talent. I just feel we can provide some opportunity for a young filmmaker, let them do whatever they want, let them express themselves, show their talent to make American films look different. So beside the Hong Kong directors, we also like to pay attention to the others. There's so many talented people in this country and they all need a chance.

Q: *So in a way you fulfilled both dreams. You became a director, a filmmaker and you're also sort of a missionary too.*
A: I know how to be grateful. I'm not the kind looking for a great fortune. I'm not crazy about fame and money. I know how to appreciate. If somebody can do me a favor, I will pay back double or triple.

I like America, I like this country because I've got so much help from the people here. So like I said, when I was a kid, I've got support from the American family and my father was sick with tuberculosis. He stayed in a hospital for ten years and the hospital was run by the church. And this American nurse who had a very kind heart took care of my father for ten years. When my father got sick and his life was falling apart, she carried my father to the emergency room and saved his life.

And when I was a kid, my English teacher was American, and she suggested that I use a Christian name because it was hard to read our Chinese name. So she made me choose John as my Christian name.

I always try to pay them back, since I couldn't keep in contact with them. It was a long time ago, but I got help from them, I learned from them, and I try to do it the same way, same as they did for me. I also like to help others. It's something about our culture. In ancient China, the people are a lot more spiritual and they have a code about honor, loyalty, and chivalry. Something about chivalry, if you got help from the others, you got to pay back double to the others and help out, and always grateful and appreciate what you've got. And people like helping each other, that's our spirit. People can sacrifice themselves for the others. That's what we learned.

And that's what my movies are about. So now since I've got so much from here, I've had so many opportunities. I've got my work, I've got my family, I've made several successful films, I think it's time to do something to pay back. I can be very selfish. I can keep making my own films, and I can make a fortune, but that's what I'm not looking for. I'm looking for an even bigger family. I like everybody to share their spirits from each other and then learn from each other. I just feel we are not living alone. We have a lot of concern, and a lot of people care about each other. In the movie business, everybody should help each other, care for each other.

Wooing Hollywood

AMY WU / 1997

HONG KONG—In person, director John Woo is the antithesis of his movies: quiet, calm, cool, and down to earth, with an ear-to-ear smile that makes him look like a laughing Buddha. There are no sudden outbursts, no violent movements. During a recent tribute to Mr. Woo, aired on TV here, the director stood in front of an audience filled with Hong Kong celebrities—many of whom have worked with him at one time or another—and for several seconds he was speechless. "Still haven't changed much, huh?" joked host James Wong.

That's not really true. Nearly five years after leaving Hong Kong for Hollywood, much has changed for Mr. Woo, now fifty-one. He has traded in his T-shirts and sneakers for dark navy suits and paisley ties, he speaks fluent, if less than perfect, English, and he's pursued round the world by the paparazzi. But such changes are only to be expected when the breakthrough film of your career, *Face/Off*, has just grossed more than $100 million.

Terence Chang, producer of *Face/Off*, says it was "like fate" that Mr. Woo would direct the blockbuster film. But he wasn't the first choice. Only after a couple of directors dropped out and the project was shopped to several studios did writers Mike Werb and Michael Colleary stumble onto a late-night showing of Mr. Woo's *The Killer* and discover the perfect man for the job. And while Mr. Woo, resting in his suite at the Island Shangri-la hotel here, now can't talk enough about how he finally found his dream team—the right studio (Paramount), right support, right actors, and the right amount of creative freedom—it

---

From the *Wall Street Journal*, 6 August 1997. Reprinted by permission.

wasn't until offer No. 3, after the shooting of last year's *Broken Arrow*, that Mr. Woo accepted.

The new director immediately began to mold and shape the movie, dropping its science-fiction setting if not its science-fiction premise, adding a human element, and insisting on John Travolta and Nicolas Cage for the leading roles, rather than the two stars who were originally envisioned—Arnold Schwarzenegger and Sylvester Stallone. "It became my kind of movie. I had a say in any change on the set," he says.

The Hong Kong director didn't have any trouble with the bizarre premise of the movie, in which a detective and a psychotic criminal literally switch faces. "It suits my style, and suits my philosophy in life," he says. "My theory is there are no really good guys or bad guys in this world, so good and bad is always like a mirror. I always believe that all the very good guys have some kind of warts, so that's reflected in the characters."

Mr. Woo has said that *Face/Off* is his first film that is truly "made in America." "I felt so comfortable, so calm and cool, much more calm than the Hong Kong films because I knew everything would work," he says. He talks about the filming as if it were a vacation instead of a production: "The actors did whatever I said; it was a totally controlled performance." But he also has plenty of stories about the confusion caused by the switched identities of the characters. "I would mess up their names, and call Nic, 'John' and John, 'Nic.' Even the crew messed up their names," Mr. Woo says, the smile spreading over his face again.

The two leading men were eager to perform in one of Mr. Woo's legendary action scenes. "When I designed something for [Nicolas Cage] he just felt like dancing," he says. "Cage always wants to do the same thing as Chow Yun-Fat," (one of Mr. Woo's favorite Hong Kong action stars). During one shooting Mr. Cage emerged looking dapper, put on a small mustache, and asked, "John, do I look like Chow Yun-Fat?"

"I love action films, but I don't want to be known as [just] an action director," Mr. Woo says. That's a major reason he moved to Hollywood from Hong Kong, where he was offered only action and comedy pictures. "It's not very important where you come from," he repeatedly says of the American film industry. "They're very open and fair as long as you have talent." Mr. Woo is now giving a hand to fellow Hong Kong directors, such as Ringo Lam and Kirk Wong, who are new to Hollywood. He and Mr. Chang are executive producers for Mr. Wong's new project, *The Big Hit*, which is shooting in Toronto.

Mr. Woo says he is trying to move beyond his signature explosions and stunts to focus on story and symbolism. There's even an antiviolence message in *Face/Off*, he claims. The evidence? The scene in which a young boy sits and listens to the Olivia Newton-John version of "Over the Rainbow" as an extremely violent shoot-out occurs. "I really hate to see people killing each other," the director says.

Judy Garland's version of the song was Mr. Woo's favorite as a child, and the first musical he saw was *The Wizard of Oz*. "I was raised in a slum. The place where I lived had a lot of gangs, drug dealers. I felt I lived in hell," he says. "I always dreamed I could fly away from hell— no hatred, no violence, people only care for each other." Now the inspiration for his action sequences comes from comic books, which he devours, and his imagination. He says he doesn't watch many movies because he wants all of his material to be original; he was once accused of plagiarizing a James Bond film.

The success of *Face/Off* is already opening many doors. Mr. Woo is filming a comedy, *King's Ransom*, starring Chow Yun-Fat, but Michael Douglas is offering him a psychological drama, and a few weeks ago Warren Beatty suggested a film about China and America. He's also working on a new movie starring Tom Cruise as a missionary in China. Since the film isn't political, Mr. Woo is hopeful he'll get permission to shoot in Shanghai, even though he's now a Hollywood director who hones his English at endless Tinseltown meetings. He says he's also learned an important filmmaking credo that may or may not help him in Shanghai: "American heroes can't cry, and can't die."

Number One with a Bullet

ANNE THOMPSON / 2000

TOM CRUISE, his face dipped below a baseball cap, disappears into the rabbit warren of the Preston Sturges building on the Paramount studio lot. Inside, narrow hallways are lined with giant garbage cans overflowing with long strips of 35 mm color film; in rows of cubicles, editors stare intently at Avid computer bays. Into the hall pops a beaming John Woo, wearing his characteristic black turtleneck and black jeans and looking tan and serene amid all this madness. His assistant closes his office door behind her. It is quiet.

Woo, fifty-four, sits down at his Spartan desk with a pack of cigarettes at his elbow (since coming to America in 1992, he has repeatedly tried to quit). For the next hour and a half, he doesn't touch them. Woo is the leading wedge of the Hong Kong cinema new wave in Hollywood. Filmmakers from Stanley Tong, Kirk Wong, and Peter Chan to stars like Chow Yun-Fat, Sammo Hung, Jackie Chan, Jet Li, and Michelle Yeoh have followed his lead in reinvigorating the pace and lexicon of American movies. Directors Quentin Tarantino, Robert Rodriguez, James Cameron, and the Wachowski Brothers owe much of their best action moves to Woo's groundbreaking, two-fisted, slow-mo pyrotechnics. After all, his kung fu is the best.

But it hasn't been an easy transition for Woo and his producing partner, Terence Chang (who also manages Chow and Yeoh). Jean-Claude Van Damme did his best work in Woo's first action effort in the States, 1993's *Hard Target*. But the clunky New Orleans policier (which was

---

From *Premiere*, 1 June 2000, vol. 13, no. 10. With reporting by David Chute and Alex Lewin. Reprinted by permission.

taken away from him in the editing room) was a far cry from Woo's passionately violent Hong Kong gangster melodramas starring Chow Yun-Fat, including 1986's *A Better Tomorrow* and its 1987 sequel, 1989's *The Killer*, and 1992's *Hard Boiled*, Woo's last and arguably greatest Hong Kong film. Woo admits to killing well over eighty people in *Hard Boiled*, which may be why his Hollywood films do seem a tad watered down.

But Woo, who emigrated with his family from Guangzhou Province, China in 1949 to the slums of Hong Kong when he was four, has nerves of steel, and like many who are lured by Hollywood, is driven to succeed. After seven years, he has ascended to A-list multimillionaire status, and has mastered the rules of the Hollywood game even if that means occasionally deferring to a major star. Woo helped build the stardom of John Travolta in 1995's *Broken Arrow* (which the studio also re-edited) and 1997's *Face/Off*, which also boosted Nic Cage's career. *Face/Off* was Woo's most satisfying major studio experience.

Like his best Hong Kong films, *Face/Off* blended emotionally complex characters with percussive action. But his twenty-seventh feature film, *Mission: Impossible 2*, starring Cruise, Ving Rhames, and Anthony Hopkins, has been arduous, to say the least. Cruise, fresh from a fifteen-month sojourn on Stanley Kubrick's *Eyes Wide Shut*, exercised full control as producer of this sequel. The production went over-schedule and over-budget (from $80 to over $100 million) on-location in Sydney, Australia, and Moab, Utah, pushing the release date back from Christmas 1999 to Memorial Day 2000; overages will be taken out of both Cruise's and Woo's back-end shares of the gross.

While Cruise encouraged Woo to reinvent *Mission* in his own style, by all accounts Cruise ran the show. And famed editor/fixer Stuart Baird helped the *M:I-2* team make it to the finish line. "We're running out of time," says Chang. "It's a very happy collaboration between the original two editors and Stuart. John and Tom both have final cut." Woo and Chang are already scouting locations for Woo's second film with Cage, *Windtalkers*, a $100-million World War II spy-code movie which starts filming in Hawaii this August. They recently escaped from an inhospitable deal at Sony (they were brought in by ex-Columbia President Chris Lee) to a more welcome home at MGM. After that, Woo insists, he wants to take on something completely different: a musical or a western.

PREMIERE: *When you shoot your leading men, from Chow Yun-Fat to Tom Cruise, you make them glow. You give them a powerful aura.*
JOHN WOO: I love my actors. I always relate to my hero. I shoot everyone with love. I see the actor as one of my friends, my children, my family. If you really love somebody you know how to take good care of them. And I think all actors have some kind of beauty: sometimes in action, sometimes in acting, sometimes from the face, sometimes from the heart. My job is to bring out their great quality on the screen. So, when I shoot Tom, his face is structured like a Greek sculpture: when I look at him, I need to find out what is his best angle, how to use the camera to best capture his great action. Every actor gets a different treatment. Because I care. When I shoot Chow Yun-Fat, I know his specialty: Chow Yun-Fat's eyes are very charming, very dramatic, so I focus always on his eyes.

Q: *And John Travolta?*
A: John Travolta is such a pleasant man, he's happy, he has so much self-confidence, and he's relaxed. When I look at him, I see a dancer. I'm thinking, he doesn't have much movement, but my camera moves, so I use a lot of camera movement to capture his joyful character.

Q: *What is Tom Cruise's special quality?*
A: Tom always likes to challenge himself, he always wants to do something different, loves action. I was shocked when he told me he never fired a gun in all of his movies. He wanted to do it [in *M:I-2*], not in a violent way, in an elegant way.

Q: *Does he use two guns, one in each hand, like Chow Yun-Fat?*
A: Oh yes. I gave him two guns. He's very clever, he did 95 percent of the action by himself, even the fistfights, because we both so much love Bruce Lee. I said, "Tom, do you want to do some physical action?" "Yeah!" So I designed some Bruce Lee kicks, and Tom was amazing. In some of the shots, he jumps and flips in the air, lands on the ground and kicks the guy all in one shot. So the stunt man planned to do it for the second time. But Tom, he flipped very beautifully, with energy, all in one take.

Q: *Did he ever get hurt?*
A: He knows what he's doing. He knows how much he can do. We have a very good stunt coordinator; everybody protects him.

Q: *Which action sequence was more dangerous for Cruise, the cliffhanging or the motorcycles?*
A: The cliff. That really worried me. The scene is the introduction of Ethan Hunt. He's enjoying a little rock climbing vacation, he's enjoying nature, he's climbing up a cliff, he almost reaches the top, sees a ledge coming out from the wall, one spot, he jumps to the ledge, when he jumps he was two thousand feet high off the ground. We shot in Moab, Utah. The cliff was a straight wall. There was a safety cable for the stunt double to try to jump to one spot. There's nothing underneath, no protection, we were suggesting that we use for the jump the stunt double, who is trained for it, knows how to do it. And Tom was insisting that he do it by himself. I was sweating. "Tom, this is crazy. For this jump, the camera was set up for the stunt double, you'll see his back!" And Tom says, "No, I don't want to cheat the audience." He's like a child, "John, don't worry, I'll be safe. It's safe." I appreciate it, but it's not worth taking the risk. But he has so much confidence, and we have such a fine stunt crew, and everybody made sure the cable was safe. But I was still worried, scared. OK, I like him as a good friend, I don't want to see him get hurt. He did the jump, just with a little safety cable, and he did it seven times. Sometimes because of the camera angle, or where he landed, he wanted to do it perfectly. And he was perfect.

Q: *How many cameras did you use?*
A: Five cameras. And also on the high-speed motorcycle, with the motorcycle speeding around 360 degrees, shooting the gun, he looks so much like ballet, so beautiful. And in the fistfight at the end of the movie, he looks very strong and powerful.

Q: *How do you use camera speeds to manipulate time? How do you know when a shot should be fast, slow, extended, compressed? And as you usually storyboard your complex action sequences, you must know how you're going to structure the sequence in advance, like 3-D chess?*

A: Yes. When I'm working on a scene I have the whole scene in my mind: the action, the tempo. When I'm shooting, I know exactly what I need for every shot, every set-up, and also about the speed of the camera, which angles use double speed, which ones use slow motion. I also listen to music, the music tells me the time.

Q: *So each of the five different cameras is set up for a different speed?*
A: There's the shot in *Mission* when Tom leaps up in the air to kick Dougray Scott's chest. When he leaps and jumps, twists his body upside down and kicks, I put a Steadicam at a low angle to see him jump up into the air high. And I put one camera top shot from on high, looking down to see Tom flip in the air in slow motion, so the camera on high looking down will see his face. And I put a low angle camera over Dougray Scott to see Tom jump and kick on his chest, another camera at normal speed to shoot Tom running very fast, and a camera pans with him as he jumps and kicks. Another camera angle is a close-up on Dougray Scott's chest as he kicks his chest. So we cover every angle. But when we put it all together, no matter what all the angles, we will see our hero's face: in the air, upside down, I have a tough time seeing his face, but before he turns, I have a low angle to cover his face; another at the start of the jump, and I have an over-the-shoulder camera angle to see Tom kick the guy's face.

Q: *So you know how the rhythm of it is going to go, before you do it: when you're going to cut from the fast shot to the slow shot?*
A: Yes. I know that. Also how many frames I need. Sometimes with a car chase or explosions, we use nine, ten cameras. I usually shoot every angle at every speed to get whatever we get, then work on editing it together to get the real timing of the action in the cutting room. Sometimes it depends on the actors. Some actors are good in slow motion, some not. Some you want to see them fast like Jackie Chan (pow, pow, pow, pow!). That's his real character. He's just like a tiger. (Pow, pow, pow, pow!) That's the action. There's no reason to use slow motion. For Chow, Cruise, Travolta, or Cage, they're actors, they're like dancers, their moves are so elegant, the only way to show them in an elegant way on screen is in slow motion. Each different actor has a different speed. Some actors are good for 120 frames in slow motion; some

are good at ninety-six frames, some for sixty frames. Normal speed is twenty-four frames per second, so 120 frames is the slowest.

Q: *Do you give each actor his own slow-motion signature?*
A: Yes. Cruise is 120 frames, because his action is so beautiful. Cage, sometimes sixty, sometimes ninety-six. He's like a ballet dancer. His figure is so slim and strong. When he moves, you just slow down a little bit. Travolta is ninety-six. Chow Yun-Fat, also 120, he's good at any speed.

Q: *You also slow things down in dramatic scenes: as if to say, look at this, remember this?*
A: It's tricky. Sometimes I want to capture an unforgettable moment, so I use slow motion to shoot the expression. Sometimes American actors play their expressions too subtle and fast; it's not long enough for me. If I find that great moment, it's the most valuable: I want to hold it longer. So I usually set up two cameras, one at normal speed, one slightly slow motion, 60 frames, and I won't let the actor know.

Q: *Did you do this to Tom Cruise on* M:I-2?
A: Everyone. Do I want that moment more dramatic? Then I will use a little piece of slow motion. The first *Mission: Impossible* was a Brian De Palma movie, an impersonal, twisting '60s-style international spy thriller.

Q: *How did you come to take on the sequel?*
A: I was on the set making *Blackjack*, a TV pilot, in Toronto, when I got a call from Tom Cruise. I was pretty surprised. He says, "OK, I'm very interested in meeting you, I really like your work." [Cruise's producing partner] Paula Wagner calls me twice; he wants to meet me in London, he's shooting *Eyes Wide Shut*. Then I fly to London and meet Tom, at his house, and he asks me to do *M:I-2*. I was a little surprised: "I'm interested, but I don't know how to do it. I have never liked the computer; I was never good at the special effects thing. It was so great, the first one." I had never done a sequel aside from *A Better Tomorrow*. [Not entirely true; *Plain Jane to the Rescue* was a sequel—ed.] I don't like to do sequels—how do you follow the same style? I have my own style. He says he likes my style, he loves *Face/Off* and *The Killer*, he wants every episode to have a different director and a different style: De Palma,

Woo, next one someone else different from James Bond. He keeps talking about which scenes he likes in the [script]. I say, "Great. In the first one, your character, he was a little too cold: I want to see you smile, I want to see you charming, I want to see you in tears. If you make a better story, with more of a [lead] character, more humanity, more romance, then I'll take it." He says, "You got it." From there I and a series of writers [Wesley Strick, William Goldman, Michael Tolkin, and Robert Towne among them] made many changes in the script. It's about Ethan Hunt saving the world from a lethal virus. They changed the whole story to fit my style. I really appreciate that. And after Tom finished shooting we met again back in Los Angeles and he gave me the new concept, it was about good and evil, two men in love with the same girl. "Oh," I said, "fantastic."

We both had the same thought: We wanted to make a very classic, romantic spy movie. Tom always wanted to do a real hero who really cares about what he believes and what he loves. So the story is not only save the world, but also save the girl. Thandie Newton's not like a piece of furniture, it's a very romantic role. And we came up with some ideas to change the image of Tom. He has long hair; he looks so charming, more real. We threw the story back and forth. Robert Towne became involved: he's great at dialogue; he's a great storyteller. They worked on the script, and I worked on my storyboards, creating the action. Why all the delays in getting started? Because this is a pretty complicated story, it took quite a long time to develop the script.

Q: *There were some production problems shooting in winter in Sydney, Australia. You had a lot of rain.*
A: It kept raining every day. We had bad luck: whenever we went on location, it rained. Sometimes we only got one or two shots a day, sometimes we got nothing. So it was pretty bad.

Q: *Did the Australian crews have a different work ethic?*
A: Yeah (laughs). At the beginning there was a little conflict, it took some time to solve all the work-rule problems with the unions, but later on when we were getting to know each other, they learned very fast. They worked very hard. The problem was with the second unit, not my unit, they were setting up the cameras, sometimes when they had too

many cameras, they were seeing each other (laughs). Not very well planned. That was one thing. And the other thing was the shooting schedule was always very tight. Always not enough time.

Q: *So you replaced Australian cinematographer Andrew Lesnie for being too slow?*
A: It was the first time he was shooting with an anamorphic [wide-angle] lens. So he took a lot of time to test and prepare. He's good at working with Super 35 mm. We couldn't afford to take that much time to do the tests. I'm fighting time. I like to work with the same old crew, they know my style; I don't need to tell them what to do. They find interesting angles for me.

Q: *How badly did Dougray Scott get hurt?*
A: He fell off a motorcycle; he had never done a big action movie before, and when he sees Tom do anything by himself, he also wants to try. He was driving the motorcycle and coming very fast and he needed to stop but he went too fast and he couldn't and he fell off the bike and almost broke his neck. He got hurt on his back and his ribs. It took a month and a half of rest and we continued shooting.

Q: *Were you hoping to persuade the studio to let you make an R-rated picture?*
A: We all agreed before we started shooting to make a PG-13 movie. The action is the same; it's just a different treatment. We don't do the over-violent kind of thing.

Q: *Your first American movie, 1993's* Hard Target, *starring Jean-Claude Van Damme, was a far more bare-bones action flick than the more ambitious films you had been making in Hong Kong. How did it feel for you to have to simplify and adapt your mature style to such a radical degree?*
A: The movie I like to make is very rich and full of passion. We did try to do *Hard Target* that way but somehow it didn't work well. I felt the story was very straightforward, always one dimension, all about action. In the beginning it was a little confused, because they wanted my style but they were afraid to make an action film too dramatic: "too much emotion." It was hard to convince everybody. It took time to let people get to know my work.

My second movie *Broken Arrow* was closer to my style. My usual characters are between good and evil, they have different dimensions. They're not only good guys and bad guys. *Broken Arrow* worked pretty well. *Face/Off* was the movie that showed Hollywood what John Woo could do. Right before I finished *Broken Arrow*, Michael Douglas and Steve Reuther, they're great producers, they came to me to do *Face/Off*. It was originally a sci-fi movie: great special effects, very futuristic. And when they offered the project to me, I told them: "I'm not good at special effects, I know nothing about computers. I like to see a movie about human beings. I hate to shoot a scene in front of a blue or green-screen background. I like to see a tear of pain and the joy of life." But it was a great concept.

After *Broken Arrow* I was making a TV pilot, in Vancouver, where Michael, Steve, [Paramount production chief] John Goldwyn, and the writers flew to meet me, in the hotel meeting room. They wanted to tell me about the new concept, but after sixteen hours of shooting I was so tired, and during the meeting I didn't say a word for three hours. After the meeting I said to Michael two words: "Trust me." And he said, "Yes, I know, I have a good nose." That's it. They didn't know what I felt about a thing. But he knew that I could make a different movie. [Paramount chairman] Sherry Lansing was very supportive; they gave me no notes—I was so surprised—they left me to work with the writer, they were hands off.

I wanted to take out 90 percent of the sci-fi things and change the movie to be more contemporary, with more focus on the friendship and the family, and the good and evil character exchange, the two people taking each other's lives. It was so easy. We had great actors, Travolta and Cage: they helped me a lot. We tried to make everything real and touching, to make these two characters more convincing for the audience, so they had to do everything alike and look alike and talk alike. So before we started shooting we spent about two weeks with the two guys learning and imitating each other.

During shooting, I try some experiments: after I finish each scene, I edit them right away so I let them watch each other's work. I let John watch Nic's scene and Nic watch John's scene and follow what they're doing and follow the character, because they're playing each other. I like the instincts of the actor, and I never try to limit their performance.

Q: *How did you help the actors adapt to your larger-than-life style?*
A: On the second day of shooting, when Nic goes back to his house to see his wife, he tries to convince her he's her real husband, and he talks about, "Do you remember ten years ago you went to see the dentist and the doctor took the wrong tooth?" So on the first take he's very subtle, he just tells the story. Then I suggest, "When you do the scene and talk about that moment, maybe you cry. I want to see your tears." Nic says, "Oh, can I do that?" I say, "Yeah!" He tries two versions, one with tears and one without. And when I see the footage, the one with tears was much stronger. And from that day he's relaxed and more free. After the operation when Cage loses his face, he looks in the mirror and takes off the bandage and reveals his face. In the script he's so angry, he gets up and smashes the mirror.

But I say, "Let's forget about the script. I'd like to see how you really feel about it, in your face, I want to see your pain." I told everybody, "Quiet, and give him a moment to build up emotion."

Q: *How long did Cage have to think about it?*
A: Just a few minutes. Then I set up three cameras at different camera angles in case something happened. I was expecting something more than the script, expecting something from the self. He came down after a while and he said, "John, can I say, 'Fuck you'?" He did the whole scene, he's angry, in pain, he smashes the mirror, and all of a sudden he turns, he's yelling at the doctor, yelling at everybody, "Fuck you, fuck you!" He blamed the whole world for making the face change. It was completely unexpected. I was moved, shocked, I almost cried. When he did that extra part, he just went crazy, the camera had to follow all of a sudden, but unfortunately none of the cameras captured that part. We had to do it again. This kind of thing we all create on the set.

John, Nic, Joan Allen, and I, we all stick together, we work as a team, as a family, and everybody feels free to do anything.

Q: *How did the studio react to the movie? Did you have the same kind of problems getting an R that you did on* Hard Target *and* Broken Arrow?
A: There were no problems. We didn't cut anything: we just made the opening scene, when John's son got killed, a little more subtle. The studio had never seen an action movie packed with so much emotion and

humanity. But they didn't know how the audience would react to it, because it was so new. Then after the test screening, everybody relaxed, we had the highest scores they ever had, the audience was so moved by the story, they had a lot of fun with the characters. That movie was the highlight of my career.

Q: *So after this great experience—*Face/Off *grossed $545 million worldwide—you were in great demand. Yet it still took a long time to come up with your next movie. You shot some TV pilots, an award-winning Nike commercial. The studio development process can be frustrating; it's a long haul to get to a shooting script. You never made the Vietnam vet ghost adventure* Shadow War, *or* Tears of the Sun, *a contemporary reworking of* The Treasure of the Sierra Madre.

A: Yeah, that was a long time, but I must say, after *Broken Arrow* and *Face/Off*, that things got a lot easier. People know me, know more about my work.

Q: *When you were at the height of your Hong Kong directing career, from* A Better Tomorrow *onward, Chow Yun-Fat became your movie alter ego, the Robert De Niro to your Martin Scorsese. Yet your two careers in Hollywood have taken parallel tracks, and you haven't worked together. Tarantino was going to write something for you and Chow, but never did. What ever happened to* King's Ransom, *a heist caper that you were developing for Chow?*

A: The character changed. We're still working on a script. It's a very delightful Cary Grant kind of movie, young, with a lot of romance and energy.

Q: *Does it bother you to see how American directors are using Chow in movies like* The Replacement Killers?

A: I don't think they know Chow Yun-Fat well. He's not only good at action but he's also a great actor, they don't know how to appreciate his performance, they should give him more drama. The movies nowadays miss a lot of very good things, story, charm, and character. I think the problem was the script: it was one dimension. But his next movie *The Corruptor* was brilliant, and *Anna and the King*, charming.

Q: *How did you feel watching him presenting an Oscar?*
A: I'm always happy to see him. He's changed a lot. He looked so calm, elegant, self-confident, more charming than before. More class. I see that a lot of people like him a lot. I wish I could work with him again.

Q: *I heard that Andrew Lloyd Webber approached you for* The Phantom of the Opera.
A: It was John Travolta, a few years ago John really had a great passion about *The Phantom of the Opera*—he knew I was crazy about musicals—and he thought my kind of technique would make a different kind of musical. I flew to San Francisco to watch the play and I fell in love with it. Somehow the project didn't work out. I really want to do it.

Q: *And Goldie Hawn approached you to direct* Chicago?
A: She wanted me to do *Chicago*. At that moment I had already taken *Mission*. I hadn't seen the play. But when I was making *Mission* I went to see the play in Sydney. I loved it. I didn't know it was a Bob Fosse musical; I admire Bob Fosse. I so regret I didn't take it.

Q: *One memorable trademark of your films is the frequent use of doves, from* The Killer *and* Hard Boiled *onward. What do the doves mean to you?*
A: I love doves. I am a Christian. Doves represent the purity of love, all kinds of beauty. They're spiritual. Also the dove is a messenger between people and God. When I was in high school I used to draw posters for the church, they had topics like Jesus dying, whatever, but I used to draw a picture of a dove. When I shot *The Killer*, these two men, the killer and the cop, they work in different ways, but their souls are pure, because they do the right thing. In the church scene, I want to bring them together. When they get shot, when they die, I want to use some symbolism as a metaphor of the heart. I came up with doves, they're white, I intercut the doves with what they're feeling, "Are they being shot? Are they being hurt?" When they die, I cut to the dove flying, it seems to be the soul, rescued and safe, and also pure of heart. So the dove becomes one of my habits: I used it in *Hard Boiled, Face/Off*, and this one too—at the end of the movie.

Q: *After the car chase? The fistfight?*
A: I cannot tell you.

From *The Actor's Encyclopedia of Casting Directors*

KAREN KONDAZIAN/2000

IT IS ALWAYS A TEMPTATION for critics to draw parallels between an artist's life and the work he creates. With John Woo, it's almost irresistible. Raised in Hong Kong in the 1950s, having fled communist South China with his family, Woo grew up around gangland violence comparable to 1920s Chicago, as communists and nationalists fought for control of the burgeoning metropolis and the easy money to be made there. Woo's escape from the streets was the Alliance Franchise, which showed foreign films like *The Wizard of Oz*, a movie the director fell in love with along with many other of the great American musicals. It is not surprising, then, that Woo's greatest action films—*The Killer, Hard Boiled, Bullet in the Head, Face/Off*—are a combination of bullets and ballet, violent in the extreme, but choreographed beautifully and often set to lyrical music.

It was laughter, not lacerations, which first earned Woo his reputation as a director. His late 1970s comedies, most notably the Asian box-office explosion *The Pilferer's Progress* [also called *Money Crazy*—ed.], set Woo up as the Hong Kong comedy king. However, Woo felt limited by the genre and with the backing of producer Tsui Hark and the talent of a young actor named Chow Yun-Fat, Woo made the gangster epic, *A Better Tomorrow* which went on to break all box-office records and invented, or rather re-invented, the Hong Kong action film.

From *The Actor's Encyclopedia of Casting Directors*, Lone Eagle Publishing/IFILM (www.ifilm.com), 2000. Reprinted by permission.

Unlike the reigning trends in the genre at the time, defined by the successful Shaw Brothers, for whom the director once worked, Woo preferred the gun to the hand or the foot. Audiences seemed to prefer it, too. The string of successes that followed *A Better Tomorrow* revealed some definite thematic trends in the director's work. Woo's heroes were marked by their extreme self-sacrifice, and the ensuing trend which swept through Hong Kong filmmaking was dubbed the "heroic bloodshed" craze. Again, it might be too easy to point to Woo's Lutheran upbringing—he once considered the ministry as a young man—as the root of all the selfless blood sacrifice imagery in his films. But in many ways, it's a valid connection, and one Woo himself has admitted to.

Despite his success in China, Woo, like Jackie Chan (who, coincidentally, served as fight choreographer for Woo's first film, *The Young Dragons*) and Woo's alter ego Chow Yun-Fat, found some difficulty locating the right U.S. project to introduce his artistry to Americans. *Hard Target* was a hard learning experience for Woo, who found that the directors in the States are often at the mercy of producers. Next up was *Broken Arrow*, a traditional American action film. While devoid of Woo's poetry in movement, it was a big hit and demonstrated to Hollywood that Woo could be left on his own and still come across with the goods. And that's exactly what he did with *Face/Off*, a truly bloody and beautiful John Woo classic and an American box office hit. Woo is now at the top of his game in the States, and is currently in production on the Tom Cruise film, *Mission: Impossible 2*.

Sitting with Woo in his office on the Sony Studios lot was not the experience I'd expected. All of his action work hadn't prepared me for the warm, gentle man I spoke to. We talked of filmmaking, acting, and the love it takes to be an artist.

Q: *Did you ever want to be an actor?*
A: I started as an actor when I was in high school. I did about ten or eleven plays, both acting and directing. When I was a kid I was so shy. I couldn't speak well; it was hard to express myself in words. So I started doing plays to try to overcome the weakness and to train myself not to be shy. I wanted to try to find a way to communicate with people. It also helped me to learn a lot more about life and about people. Being an actor can really help with self-confidence.

Q: *Why didn't you continue acting?*
A: I had so many things that I wanted to say. I wanted to be a painter, a musician, a poet, a choreographer. I had so many roads. So only doing performance was not enough. I wanted to use many ways to express myself. I was so much stronger as a painter and I realized that I had a good visual sense. I realized I could use a camera to tell a story and it was worth more to me. I could get more magic. Plus, the actors were tall, handsome, and charming—I didn't have any of that; I just have a common look. So I gave it up. I think great actors also have to be really focused and always concentrating on their characters. I couldn't do that. I do too much thinking. Being an actor, you have to live with a character and it's hard to notice anything else. Being a director is much more broad. You can go anywhere, see the world and other people, observe other lives.

Q: *[Federico] Fellini once said, "Even if I set out to make a film about a filet of sole, it would be about me." Is that true for you?*
A: Yes, it is. I always put myself into the movie and use actors to represent me. For example, in *A Better Tomorrow* the main character is part of a gang. I used that as a metaphor for how I struggle, how I see family and friendship, and to send a message of honor, loyalty, and chivalry. The movie was also how man cannot be without dignity. Before I made that film, I was a failure for quite a few years. My movies didn't work anymore and I was looked down on by quite a few people. It was quite discouraging. Some people even thought I should retire. I was sad and hurt for a year. But I still had a very strong drive and I told myself that I was a good director and I wouldn't give up. So I put this experience into the film and used it to speak for me. In the story, it's a fight against evil. And I showed that I had my own dignity; I wouldn't give up. It worked very well because all of the feelings came from my heart and the audience got it. They were touched by the story and it was a huge hit in all of Asia. It changed my life.

Q: *Is there a difference between directing American actors and Chinese actors?*
A: Well, in general, Chinese actors can be very stagy. Some of the actors trained on stage and some on television. There are no real acting training schools in Hong Kong. Another group has been trained in the

Peking Opera. They're trained in singing, acting, dancing, action, and fighting. Sometimes those actors can be a little bit too big for film. Some of the great Chinese actors also learn from American movies. Some of their idols are Paul Newman, Al Pacino, Robert De Niro, Steve McQueen, and Marlon Brando. Chinese actors have been really influenced by them. By imitating the American performers, they'd find techniques for themselves and create their own methods. They know their stories, how they started, how they worked, their acting philosophy. For example, when they find out that Robert De Niro worked as a taxi driver to study for *Taxi Driver*, that makes them understand what a real actor is. That wasn't from school or from any acting class. They were learning from life. That gave them heart and a lot of improvement.

I learned the Western way. I believe in and love actors. They are the soul of the movies. I always like to work with a real person. There are two kinds of actors. One is an entertainer who can put on a really good show and try to amuse the audience. Another kind of actor is believable and has a great heart, like Brando or Newman. They came from the heart. That's what I mean by real people. I never know how to demonstrate or teach actors what to do. I wouldn't dare to teach them; the actor is the artist. I usually give them a lot of freedom. I want them to put themselves into the character.

Q: *Do you let them improvise?*
A: I let them improvise and I let them change dialogue.

Q: *Do you rehearse much?*
A: I don't think much of rehearsing on a set. I like happenings, surprise and instincts. The most important thing is for actors to trust their own instincts and believe in what they are doing. The great actors have great instincts. But some actors, especially American actors, care too much about acting. They work too hard. I think you can work too much and then it's not natural. That's why I don't like to do too many takes. Some actors like to do twenty or thirty takes and try so many different things. I only want one or two. John Travolta, Nic Cage, and Joan Allen all wanted to do more. They wanted to work more. I don't like perfect.

The first couple of takes are very real and natural because the actors are unprepared and just warming up. Sometimes, a little flaw may be a good thing. When they do something wrong, I think they're more interesting. I've got a nickname in the business. They call me "One-shot John." I know what I like and no matter how many times the actors do it I always like the first few takes. If you do it more, it's no longer coming from instinct. It becomes methodical. In Hong Kong, I worked pretty much the same way I do here. I like to use actors who are real. In general, before I start shooting, I like to make friends with the actors and have several conversations with them. I like to see how they feel about everything. I like to hear their story, how they feel about the world, what they love, what they're happy about, and I like to put their experience into the scene and into the character. I write the scene around the actor. Then, they are doing levels of themselves. That's why I like to spend so much time with my actors. I even know their habits. On the set, I like to say, "OK, forget about the script. Forget about the dialogue. Is there any similar experience in your life?" I like to improvise the dialogue. I don't like the typical way of doing things.

I enjoy performers, so while I'm working I forget about story, I forget about other scenes. I only enjoy that particular moment and what the actors are forming in front of the camera. I have no worries about how it's going to fit. If that moment doesn't touch me, then the scene doesn't work. I see myself as one of the audience. I know how people feel. So when that moment really touches me, I know that other people will be touched and that they will like it. They will get the same kind of feeling.

Q: *What is the experience like for an actor when they come in to audition for you?*
A: First, I like to meet the actors. The personal impression I get is the most important thing. Sometimes I watch tape but I like to meet people face-to-face and see how I feel with that person. And I like to listen. I don't so much care about their reading. Every actor can read. I just like to listen to them talk to the casting director. I like to see how they interact. And I like to know a little of their background and their story.

Q: *What makes you ultimately choose someone over someone else?*
A: Personal impressions. Or I'm convinced by the casting directors. I usually trust them. They select some good people to help me make a final decision. The most important thing is I like to find an actor who

really cares about the others. I don't want to work with selfish actors. Some actors only care about themselves or their own image. They can give a performance, but not from the heart. John, Nic and Joan, they really care. They are good human beings.

Q: *Is there anything else that you'd like to say to actors?*
A: They need to be themselves and trust their own instincts. Great actors do that. Great performers think of real life and what comes from their own hearts. I think the director should help the actor to do this. That's very important and that's why I think the director should know the actors well. Actors should believe in the director and trust them. Everything is about love, especially if you are an actor. Actors should have great love for the character they're playing. Believe in the character, and you will give a great performance.

I see my actors as part of my family. They are my heart. And since I love my actors as my own children, I give them the freedom to do what they want. They have freedom of speech, freedom to create, freedom of thinking. I let them improvise everything and then I will shape it. Sometimes the actors have some ideas but they have a problem with expressing them. A good director will give the guidelines to help the performance. Everything that shows on the screen is their acting, not the directing. I've got to keep a very close and good relationship with the actors. That's how I work. And that's how they end up with self-confidence. There is a relationship between an actor and a director that is like a friendship. When an actor has a problem, or they are struck by some personal things, I always like to hear their story and try to help. No matter what the problem, I have time for them; that's the way I work. Or I'll change a scene to use what they're feeling. Sometimes I'll give them some time to work things out and I'll work on something else until they are more comfortable.

Q: *It's so wonderful that you care so much. From your heart, as you say.*
A: I believe that we have to know how to respect each other. I respect the actors, they respect me, I respect my crew. I know people need respect. Acting is an insecure business. Most of the people feel insecure. So you have to make them feel comfortable and make them believe in themselves and in their own charm. Every human being has charm.

They sometimes just don't know how to show it. So my duty is to find the charm: The charm of acting, of the face, of philosophy. If I can help a little bit, I feel happy. A director is not a dictator. A director gives people direction and is there to guide. And the actors sometimes will teach me about life. Sometimes people are built in a different way but deep inside, basically everyone is the same. All of mankind has the same kind of heart.

The Two Sides of John Woo

ROBERT K. ELDER/2002

JOHN WOO loves jazz.

It's obvious as he sits in the smoky neon of Andy's Jazz Club in Chicago, grinning broadly as pianist Wallace Burton kicks into "It Could Happen to You."

It's also apparent in his work. The director/screenwriter made Chow Yun-Fat a jazz musician in his ultra-violent Hong Kong masterpiece, *Hard Boiled*. Music has been an essential element in his films, from a bloody shootout set against "Somewhere Over the Rainbow" in *Face/Off* to a haunting Navajo flute calming World War II soldiers in his latest directing effort, *Windtalkers*, which opens June 14.

For years, he has written scripts under the influence of Miles Davis and Louis Armstrong, shaping his films under a canopy of brassy blue notes.

"Miles gives me a lot of inspiration," says Woo, fifty-six. "His music makes me calm, so relaxed."

Herein lies the dichotomy of Woo: an artist who crafts frenzied action while listening to jazz ballads, an auteur and devout Christian who hates violence but is the master of its portrayal.

"I think he's a man full of contradictions; that's why he's so interesting," said friend and longtime producer Terence Chang.

Beginning his career as a director of Hong Kong comedies in the 1970s, Woo went on to gather a worldwide fan base with "bullet ballets" such as *The Killer* and *Hard Boiled* and inspire cinematic Young Turks of the '90s such as Quentin Tarantino and Sam Raimi.

From the *Chicago Tribune*, 2 June 2002. © *Chicago Tribune*. Reprinted by permission.

Woo's reputation helped him establish an artistic foothold in Hollywood, where he made *Broken Arrow* and *Face/Off*, gunmetal morality tales complete with his signature use of double-gunned protagonists, freeze frame (a nod to François Truffaut), and dramatic slow motion. Violence only heightens the bravery of his heroes, Woo says, to glorify good.

A Hong Kong transplant, Woo has lived in California for ten years, once describing himself as "a falling leaf who doesn't know where home is."

Woo, whose soft-spoken English is often obstructed by a heavy Cantonese accent, says he sees himself as a bridge between cultures. A husband and father of three, he became an American citizen just before filming *Mission: Impossible 2*.

"I always find a way to bring in the good things from the culture in the East. My characters . . . I try to bring them together and make them understand each other," Woo says, articulating the central theme of *Windtalkers*.

He's shy and easy to laugh, so it's difficult to believe that his Hong Kong film crews were afraid of him, calling the director "Old Schoolmaster" and "Black-faced god."

"They called me Schoolmaster in a respectful way. I love to work with young people, to teach them anything about movies. I was pretty strict since I was raised as a Lutheran," Woo says, curling his "L's" into "R's."

Intensity on the Set

When Woo first came to Hollywood to direct Jean-Claude Van Damme in 1993's *Hard Target*, producer Chang had to field questions like, "Why is he so angry?"

"He wasn't angry, he just didn't smile," Chang says. "He was serious on the set and didn't like fooling around."

Woo remains serious on the set but has softened considerably. Hollywood productions aren't the seven-day-a-week, twenty-hour-a-day marathons that whittled his nerves in Hong Kong. Nicolas Cage, who has quickly become part of the Woo canon with *Face/Off* and *Windtalkers*, says he doesn't recognize the earlier descriptions of the director.

"That's not the John Woo I know," Cage says. "He encourages creative thinking on the set; he wants his actors to go beyond the script. He's a humble man, a polite man."

Life-Changing Experience

Adam Beach, Cage's co-star in Woo's latest epic about Navajo code talkers in WWII, adds: "Being in a John Woo film, it'll change your life. He brings you into his life and teaches you respect. The people who work for John would do anything for him."

On the set, Woo says, he sees everyone as family.

"Long, long time ago, they called me a 'Black-faced god' because I never smiled. Of course, I screamed and yelled sometimes," Woo said. "In America, I like to work in a friendly way. People are so nice to me. They really make me change. If I yell and scream, it won't help at all. It only makes things worse."

Chang laughs: "If he's changed at all, I don't think it's America [that's changed him]. It's age. . . . Our roles have sort of reversed now. He used to be the temperamental guy and I always smoothed relationships over. Now I say what I want, and he's the diplomat."

Although Woo's temper has become less volcanic, his movies haven't. *Mission: Impossible 2* managed to deliver signature Woo violence under a PG-13 rating, and *Face/Off* tested the limits of the R with its dark themes and brightly lit bloodbaths.

Still, he's never shot a real gun and repeatedly declines invitations from his prop masters to visit Los Angeles firing ranges.

"It's a little bit of a contradiction, yes. I never wanted to own a gun; I have no desire or curiosity," Woo says, clapping as "Almost Like Being in Love" spends its last few chords at Andy's.

Cage offers another theory of his pacifist friend's penchant for Mexican standoffs and pyrotechnics. It's a catharsis, a purging process.

"Maybe the more violent your art is, the more peaceful your life is because you're getting that out," Cage says. "It's sort of a weird contradiction. What you hate can actually become something very interesting to you artistically. You get power over it."

The fuel of his cinematic catharsis, Woo admits, possibly emanates from a tumultuous childhood. Raised in Hong Kong, Woo (then

Ng Yu-sum) lived in the poorest slums of the city, his family losing their wooden shack to a massive area fire when he was six. For the next two years, his family lived on the street. It was a violent time—Woo saw scores dead after the fire and he witnessed bloody, broken bodies being dragged through the streets during riots.

"The place we lived in was pretty awful; we were living in hell. If you wanted to survive, you had to be strong," Woo says. "I was pretty insecure at the time. My parents took care of me and never let me go wrong, taught me the value of loyalty."

The eldest of three children, Woo says he was a small, thin boy, an easy target for the bullying street gangs that brutalized him. In one instance, he was taken to the hospital after someone threw hot ashes in his face while he was carrying his toddler brother.

"I got beat up almost every day. Whenever I went out of the house or the alley, I had to grab something as a weapon for protection," Woo says. "I had to fight really hard to survive. I never gave up, I fought back."

A Slice of Heaven

Woo's world started to change at age nine when Christian missionaries helped his family get off the streets and found an American family to sponsor Woo's education. He took the name John, in honor of John the Baptist, when his English teacher couldn't pronounce his Chinese name.

"They gave me shelter. I just felt like I was in heaven when I was in the church," Woo says.

He also discovered film. Although his father, a high school teacher, disapproved, Woo's mother took him to the movies, starting with *The Wizard of Oz*. Church became Woo's heaven, but the dark sanctuary of the theater gave flight to his dreams.

"I saw a lot of Chinese movies, American westerns, and cartoons," Woo says.

Because children were admitted free with their parents, Woo and his friends would hold court outside a rundown neighborhood cinema, where they would entreat ticket-holders to pose as parents.

"I hated to sit in the front, loved to sit on the balcony," Woo says. "Once, me and my brother asked a lady to bring us in, and then after we passed [the box office], we walked upstairs."

When the usher got wise to Woo's ruse, he punched the eleven-year-old boy, who again was carrying his kid brother on his back.

"I lost my balance and I was rolling down the stairs with my brother," Woo says. "And then I went out of the theater; I kept watching my movie from the hole in the exit door."

A Different Calling

This stubborn streak, matched with a passion for film, helped Woo jump-start his film career, although it wasn't his original career track. He loved art, music and even taught ballroom dancing in high school, but a shorter left leg kept him from mastering the more graceful waltzes. His first dream was to become a minister.

"My friends in missionary school didn't think I could concentrate on the Bible," Woo says. "They felt I was too artistic, and they encouraged me to go for art rather than be a minister."

A spirited young Woo instead studied film with his friends and climbed his way up the movie industry ladder from production assistant to director, where he directed a string of hit Chinese comedies.

"When I had a chance to direct a movie, I always wanted to make a gangster film or a musical," says Woo. "The studio wouldn't let me do it. They wanted me to make some kind of kung fu films or comedies; they were the biggest markets."

Eventually, Woo's frustration started to seep into his work.

"My comedies became pretty sour because I had so much anger at the time," Woo says. "I wanted to make movies with a lot of meaning. But those kind of comedies were pretty much like cartoons. I was a rebel at the time, so I put that sort of anger and sadness into my comedy. In my comedies, I tried to make people cry, so it didn't work."

His critical breakthrough came with 1986's *A Better Tomorrow*, when Woo cast little-known actor Chow Yun-Fat. With the help of fellow director Tsui Hark, Woo began producing personal stories and galvanizing relationships that would carry him through to success in

Hollywood. *The Killer* (1989) paired him with producer Chang and catapulted Woo to international acclaim.

Fiercely loyal, Woo says friendship remains the central theme to both his work and his life. *Windtalkers*, a bit of a stylistic departure for the director, marks the first film under his Lion Rock Productions with partner Chang. Based on true events, *Windtalkers* is shot in a documentary style, following Navajo code talker Ben Yahzee (Beach) and his shell-shocked partner, Joe Enders (Cage), who must protect the code at any cost.

"I wanted to try something different," says Woo. "I always like a challenge. My hell is war. My nightmares are seeing innocent people get killed."

For his next project, Woo plans to work with Cage again and rekindle his screen collaboration with Chow in *Men of Destiny*, a zero-violence drama about railroad expansion into the West.

Presently, however, the director is searching for old friends.

The chaos of his childhood made him lose contact with the American family that sponsored his education in Hong Kong, a debt of gratitude he'd like to express personally. He only has a name, Janice Knight, and a half-remembered region of the country, perhaps somewhere near San Diego, he says. He's hiring lawyers to assist in his search.

Doing His Part

"I just want to say thank you," Woo says, sipping water while the band finishes its set. "Even though I couldn't get in touch with them, I'm doing the same thing they did for me. Now, I'm sponsoring some kids from different countries, in Africa and China . . . doing it to show my gratitude, to show my respect for that family."

Finding this family will bring him full circle. And having put down roots in California's Pacific Palisades, he no longer sees himself as "a falling leaf."

"I love Hong Kong; I can never forget my home culture. In some way, I still see myself as Chinese . . . but I'm so glad that I get to live here and work here and find so many friends," Woo says. "I found my home here. I've found another heaven."

John Woo: Hot-handed God of Hong Kong Film Directors

PATRICK MACIAS / 2003

WOO'S NEW MOVIE is *Paycheck*, based on a short story by Philip K. Dick. This interview was conducted on Dec. 19, 2003.

PATRICK MACIAS: *Philip K. Dick's writing is often paranoid and uncertain about the future, but* Paycheck *seems to take a different approach.*
JOHN WOO: There are two reasons for this. There are so many problems in this world, so many frustrations. I feel like there's a lot of young people who are very depressed about the future. It seems like there's no hope. This situation is really happening in Asia. Some of the young people in Hong Kong, Taiwan, and Japan become so depressed they even gave up their lives. I feel so sad about it. I wanted to say something to these people and make them realize the future is going to be fine. I also wanted to encourage them. There's always hope and a lot of good people in this world. Just don't give up, you know? So that made me change the script and tone. I talked to the writer about this point to try to make the film more optimistic.

Q: *Were there other major changes made to the script before shooting?*
A: Yeah. Because of the budget. Originally, it was going to be pure sci-fi and a very futuristic movie with a lot of computer graphics and

---

A version of this article appeared on the website *Junk Addicted Pals*, www.japattack.com, December 2003. Reprinted by permission, www.patrickmacias.com.

production design. On the other hand, after I read the original short story, I felt that Philip Dick's characters were very human. There's a lot of humanity in his books. When I watched the movie *Blade Runner*, I was crying when Rutger Hauer died. He had tears in his eyes before he died. I never forgot that speech he makes. And it made me realize that these concepts are about survival, not about looking for death. So that made me feel that we should cut down 80 percent of the sci-fi and put the focus on human drama. I also suggested making the love story bigger. Originally it was a pretty small part. I expanded it a little more and tried to make the rest of the film have a more romantic sensibility.

Q: *How does Ben Affleck compare to other American actors you've worked with?*
A: Well, they are all very different. Ben is very smart and very humble. I like his performance. He's so natural. He never cares about the camera angle. He acts what he feels. When I watched him in *The Sum of All Fears*, it seemed like the other actors were so conscious of the camera angle, but he was not. He never tries to stand out or play for the camera, and I think it's a very natural style. Even though he looks so modern, he also has a classic quality to him. He reminds me of a young Cary Grant.

Q: *Which helps out with the Hitchcock feel in* Paycheck . . .
A: Yeah, yeah. That's why I asked him to dress like Cary Grant in *North by Northwest*. Every actor I work with has a different kind of quality.

Q: *What was Uma Thurman's mental and physical state like after shooting* Kill Bill?
A: She's a wonderful, wonderful lady. I am an admirer of her work. I like her in *Pulp Fiction* and other films. She's very charming. For *Paycheck*, she liked to do most of the stunts by herself, even when huge explosions were going off. During the motorcycle chase, she had to fall off the bike, hit the ground, and do a lot of running. All these explosions were going off really close to her. But she'd refuse to use a double. She wanted to do it herself. She said to me, "John, you have no idea what I've been through on *Kill Bill*. It was the most difficult, dangerous, and awful situation making that film. This is nothing." She came up

with ideas for action during the ending also. She's a really hardworking lady and always wanted to come up with new ideas for the scenes. Uma and Ben also had really good chemistry, so they both made the love story romantic and even funny.

Q: *The action scenes in* Paycheck *are more realistic than we're used to seeing from you.*
A: That was the intention. I wanted to make the film more like a human drama. But on the other hand, the character of Michael Jennings (Ben Affleck) is not a superhero. He's just a computer engineer. Based on that, the action should look more realistic. In this film, I didn't want to go too over the top and make it too violent, since our main character never uses a gun and has no intentions to kill anyone. Even though he almost gets killed by the bad guys, he tries to find a way to survive without becoming a murderer. I wanted to make some of the action scenes more like suspense. When Ben gets chased by the train, I wanted to make it more like Hitchcock.

Q: *Do you feel as artistically satisfied working in the U.S. compared to Hong Kong?*
A: Not as much. Of course, in Hong Kong I had a lot of creative freedom and I could do whatever I felt like. In Hollywood, I still can find similar subjects to work with, but creatively, sometimes, I compromise a little bit. I have to tone down the violence. It's not as much as before. Hollywood is trying to make the kind of movies that can fit into all kinds of countries. For example, for Europe, they really don't want to see violent movies. But Asia really wants to see the action. And in America, violence is always an issue. So I have to consider these kinds of things and make adjustments. But that's OK since I always like a human story and I'm always going to make those kinds of films.

Q: *How about writing your own scripts like before?*
A: I will, but after I feel like I've learned more. For instance, there are two projects I'm working on now. I wrote and developed the story and hired a writer to do the scripts. I think I've got to take it one step at a time. One is an action-musical gangster movie called *The Dancer*. In the 1930s there was this tough guy, but he was also a great dancer and he

was deeply in love with two women. It's based on a true story and the movie will be a combination of *The Killer* and *Cabaret*. The other is a remake of *The Red Circle*. It was made in 1970 and it's one of my favorite films. It's a heist movie directed by Jean-Pierre Melville. I'm working on the treatment and the story.

Q: *I'm curious how things are now between you and (former producer) Tsui Hark?*
A: We are still good friends. Creatively, we think differently. But I'm very grateful to him for helping me to make movies like *A Better Tomorrow* and *The Killer*. Sometimes we worked in different ways, but we are still good friends and I appreciate him.

Q: *Earlier this year, (legendary Hong Kong director to whom Woo was an assistant) Chang Cheh passed away. Do you have any special memories of him?*
A: I was in Hong Kong when he died. The day before I arrived in Hong Kong, he said that one of the people he really wanted to see was me. I thought that after I got off the plane, I could go straight to the hospital and see him right away. But after we landed, I heard that he was already dead. So I was crying. I was very sad. He was my mentor, you know? I really admire his movies and I got so much influence from him. When I first started working for him, I wanted to be an actor. Just like an average young man, I was so confused. I didn't know much about my future. And I didn't see myself much and I didn't know what to do. At that time David Chang and Ti Lung were good friends of mine. They were suggesting me to be the third lead in a film and they recommended me to Chang Cheh. They had hired a cameraman, a lighting man and a makeup person to give me a screen test to convince Chang Cheh to give me the part. But on the day of shooting, he stopped the whole thing. He said to David Chang, "John Woo better focus on directing. He's going to be a good director." I was so moved because at that time I couldn't see myself and I didn't know my future, but he saw it for me. He decided for me. He saw what I couldn't see. So he gave me a lot of confidence. I gave up my acting career to follow what he said to me.

Q: *What are some of your favorite films of his?*
A: So many. *The One-Armed Swordsman, The Boxer from Shangtung, The Assassin,* and *Vengeance.* There's one of his films I'd really like to remake someday, called *Golden Swallow.*

Q: *I'm curious if you've been following how Miramax has been handling Asian films lately.*
A: No. I don't know about that.

Q: *They've been buying up the rights to films like* Hero *and* Shaolin Soccer *and just sitting on them. And when they do release Asian films, they are often recut and rescored. Now they are trying to ban importation of the original versions.*
A: I haven't heard about this. I'm sure they have their reasons, but I don't like this. When some people released *A Better Tomorrow* on DVD and changed some of the music, I was really angry about it. I didn't know why they changed it. I think if you are going to release a movie, it's better to release the original.

Q: *This is a big issue for a lot of your fans. Do you think you could try and look into it?*
A: OK.

Q: *What's going on with your video game company, Tiger Hill Games?*
A: We are working with Sega and Microsoft. The main project right now is with Sega to try and produce very interesting games. It's going to happen sometime soon. There's another project with Microsoft involving cars.

Q: *There's been some talk about you producing a new* Teenage Mutant Ninja Turtles *film.*
A: Not anymore, although we are involved with *He-Man* and *Mighty Mouse* projects. We are negotiating right now. I'll only be involved as a producer.

Q: *What happened to another film project of yours called* King's Ransom *(set to star Chow Yun-Fat and to be shot in San Francisco)?*
A: We're not doing that anymore. That project didn't work out. The script kept changing and changing and it lost the original taste.

Q: *How about* The Devil's Soldier *(based on the adventures of an American mercenary in Qing Dynasty China)?*
A: Not anymore. That would be a very big budget movie. We were trying to make it with Tom Cruise, but it had a budget problem.

Q: *I know you must get asked this question a million times every day, but are there any plans to work with Chow Yun-Fat again?*
A: We have a project we are working on right now called *The Divide*. It's a story about Chinese and Irish immigrants building the railroads in America in the nineteenth century. And there's also two other projects we're working on with Chow Yun-Fat.

Q: *As time goes on, do you see yourself losing interest in the action film genre?*
A: Well, sometimes I would like to try pure drama. Sometimes I want to maintain my own style. But don't worry, I'll never give up using two guns.

John Woo at the Gene Siskel Film Center

BARBARA SCHARRES AND BOB BALABAN/2004

BARBARA SCHARRES. *I remember there was a time when you were debating whether or not you were going to leave Hong Kong and you were talking about the possibility of working in another country. So I'm wondering if you could tell us about that moment of decision when it became clear that you were going to work in the United States. You've made a remarkable transition—not only made a remarkable transition but you have risen to the top of the U.S. industry—something that most directors aspire to and very few achieve.*
JOHN WOO: Well, first of all, I would really like to say I really appreciate everyone giving me such great friendship. [It's] hard to say anything 'cause I want to cry. I found my dream. I found friendship in this country.

Before I made a decision, I had a lot of question marks and I didn't know what I could do here. It's all because of my friend Terence, such a good friend. He had so much confidence in me. He had said to me, "John, I know you can make it." So he gave me the confidence. He gave me help. But so, in the meantime, I really wanted to learn something. I really wanted to learn from the people here. So I tried to prove my kind of work and my kind of a movie. It really could be international, my kind of technique.

And the other thing was that I really wanted to make friends. I just feel real lonely in Hong Kong. My dream was to work in different

---

From the Q&A section of John Woo's award ceremony for the Gene Siskel Film Center's Visionary Award for Innovation in Filmmaking, 12 June 2004. Reprinted by permission of Barbara Scharres and the Gene Siskel Film Center.

countries and in different places, and I always liked to learn from different kind of cultures and people and make a lot of friends.

The other reasons were because of my family. In Hong Kong, we worked like crazy. We work seven days a week, almost over eighteen hours a day. And I never had any time for my children. I didn't have time to have a good look at my wife. We had a big gap in between me and my children and I thought it was pretty dangerous. Over in Hong Kong [my children] hated me. They didn't even want to talk to me. When they needed a father or they needed to see my face, [there wasn't time].

I love my family and I love my children and I wanted it to be normal. After we moved over here to Los Angeles—the people over here only work five days a week and it could allow me to have more time to spend with my children. I was pretty happy; [now] we have had more time to find a way to work together. We communicate with each other. There are so many reasons I like it over here.

BOB BALABAN: *When you were very young is it true that you actually saw a lot of American movies. As a child you went to the movies a lot, yes?*
JW: Yes I've seen a lot of great American films like the *Wizard of Oz*, a lot of westerns, cartoons, musicals. And I'm a big fan of musicals like *Singin' in the Rain*. *Seven Brides for Seven Brothers* was my favorite. Those are my favorites. And I have also seen a lot of [films by] John Ford, Howard Hawks, and Alfred Hitchcock and Sam Fuller. I was also a big fan of Sam Peckinpah. Stanley Kubrick was my idol; [there were] so many.

BB: *I think a lot of people are surprised to find out that you directed a number of comedies, that you were very well known in China for your humor and your comedies. Do you think you might do that again?*
JW: I wish. I'm big fan of Jerry Lewis. He was my idol. I really want to make a movie like Jerry Lewis. . . . I also love Charlie Chaplin and Marx Brothers and all those great actors. Actually I had made seven or eight comedies in Hong Kong. Some of them were pretty crazy; I really love a couple of them.

BS: *We hear that you are going to direct a musical?*
JW: Yeah, I love musicals, I must say. I got great influence from musicals, as I'm sure a lot of people see in most of my action sequences.

Sometimes pretty much it looks like a dance. Actually, I've never learned any martial arts and I have never fired a real gun in my life.

BS: *Never, never?*
JW: And I have never driven a car. So, I just [capture] the musical rhythm and the beauty of action and the beauty of body movement. I use that musical theory to shoot action sequences. I have a project that I [have] wanted to do for so many years. It's an action musical. It's not really a musical; it just has a lot of dancing. It's a gangster film. It's about a gangster who's a tough guy but he's [also] a great dancer. I always wanted to make a movie with combination of dancing and action. Action pretty much looks like a dance, and dance pretty much looks like action. Also, it's a love story. In real life, the guy was in love with two women and also that's a first time for me. I have never been good at love stories in my life.

BS: *Are you writing the script for this yourself or . . . ?*
JW: No, I just give some ideas. We had a very good writer Jeff Pinkner. They say he's very good writer and he's working on a storyline.

BS: *We have some clips here tonight and in a minute we can look at a couple from some of your more elaborate action sequences. . . . Your sequences of this kind are so extraordinarily choreographed and so intricate and so beautiful. How do you get the ideas for this and create them? Does it come into your head first, or in the editing later?*
JW: When I'm deciding on action sequences, it all depends on character and the story first. And I work with my actors and my stunt coordinators very closely. First thing: I need to know my actors. What kind of action they could do? Before we start shooting I have a conversation with them. What kind of action do they like? What is good for them? Like Chow Yun-Fat, he's not an action star but he's very smart, he likes to do some kind of exercises.

BB: *Does he do all his own stunts?*
JW: Most of them. When I look at him, I find he looks so elegant and so charming. Then [I decide] on some action like Steve McQueen or Clint Eastwood, that kind of action is good for him, 'cause he's not a

fighter. So maybe I have him holding a gun like Clint Eastwood, and it looks great. Every actor has a different kind of treatment.

While I'm on the set I usually put myself in the character. I would rehearse a scene and do a scene by myself. While we are shooting the movie *Hard Boiled*, in the teahouse shootout scene, I stood in the middle of the room and I imagined there were maybe about two or three guys on my left side. If they started to shoot at me first, I would throw the gun from my clothes and spin around shooting them, because I used to be a dancer when I was in high school—a ballroom dance instructor when I was about sixteen years old. When I'm choreographing an action sequence, I also feel myself dancing. I'm also figuring some good-looking body movement. . . . Of course, there are lots of moments that I work with the stunt coordinator to come up with a lot more good ideas. I also have a lot of good instincts. When I go to the set, I see what we have. If I see a table, then I will think of how to use the table. If I see a banister, it will give me the idea, "Oh maybe I can use it."

BB: *So you're improvising?*
JW: Yeah, like sliding down from [the banister], shooting two guns. I rehearse the whole scene [with] the coordinator and then if I feel good about it, then I think maybe my actor will feel good about it. That's my specialty. I know how to make a hero.

BB: *John, to me, one of the things that makes your action so interesting is there's so much underneath it. The story is so important for you in your movies. There's a lot of male bonding going on in your films and I'm wondering if this is autobiographical?*
JW: I think there's some. I will say that most of my movies are about friendship. I think that's why [there is] so much interesting in male bonding movies. I love friendship, and I have so much appreciation of all my friends. . . . And friendships are very important in my life. [So when] I made *A Better Tomorrow, The Kilier*, and especially *Bullet in the Head*, there was a very strong friendship theme. But I'm also very interested in making a love story. I also want to make a real heroic female hero movie.

BB: *You were very religious as a child, yes John? I think that is another idea, that as much violence there is in your movies, there's also a great sense*

of right and wrong in them. It's not random. What's going on there can you tell us? Do you mind talking about when you were a child?
JW: Well, when I was raised in a slum, we were living in a very bad neighborhood. In our area there were a lot of drug dealers, prostitutes, gamblers, and gangs. Almost every day I had to deal with a gang, but fortunately I had very strong parents. They led me to go to the right way, telling me what's right and what's wrong.

I also had help from the church. Then whenever I got beat up by a gang, I used to run into the church to talk with the priest, and they comforted me and tried to protect me, so I was so grateful. But in the meantime, I learned something: even those people . . . so [few] care about them. Sometimes, things [are] not so black and white to me. I also found some very good friendships. I have a couple more friends that I put in my movies. *Bullet in the Head* was based on my biography. When I was a kid, I had some gangs that friends were in. I took care of them, and sometimes I even covered for them 'cause they had a lot of family problems. Their parent was a gambler or drug dealer—they just didn't get the love they needed. So I took care of them and tried to change them. Some of them were pretty good and some of them couldn't make it. I also found some good hearts in that kind of world . . .

BS: *Could you tell us something about how different it is working with people in Hollywood as opposed to Hong Kong? I know it is a very different star system in Hong Kong and that [Hollywood] seems like a much more formal way of working. In Hollywood where everyone's working through their agents and it's just more a system of hierarchies. I remember being on your set of* Once a Thief *in Hong Kong and your stars were helping carry the props around, and that doesn't happen here. I don't think Nicolas Cage was carrying the props around for* Windtalkers.
JW: He did.

BS: *He did? Yeah? So what's it been like working with stars in Hollywood and how different is it from working with Chow Yun-Fat in Hong Kong, or some of the other stars you worked with there?*
JW: Well, basically not much big difference. First of all, I'll say that when I'm working with my actors, I like to work with them as a friend before we start shooting. I like to spend some time with them, talk to

my actors. I need to see how they feel about life and what their philosophy about the character—about everything—is. And then also I love [to talk] to my friends.

I need to find out what is his special quality from him, and even what is the best camera angle for my actors. I also like to observe, I like to see some little movement from my actors. I am so much interested to hear their story.

Chow Yun-Fat in *The Killer* he is betrayed by his good friend. And then I talk to him and [I] say, "Is there any similar situation happen in your life?" If he had [been] betrayed by good friend I want him to say what he did, and what he felt. Then he will tell me the story and then he tells me how he felt, and then I will encourage my actors to put their feelings into the scene. I even let them improvise the dialogue and let them say what they would say in their real life.

I used it the same way with John Travolta and Nic Cage. After that conversation, we don't need to talk much on the set. It's so funny when we were working with Nic Cage, especially in *Windtalkers*. Sometimes when he came on to the set after I get everything ready, he looked at me. I look at him, and then he look at me.

"Ready?"

"OK, let's do it."

It's just the eye contact for a few seconds. He knows what I want from him and I know what he wants.

Then when I work with John Travolta . . . I believe the first take is the best take, and have never liked to take more than two takes in action or in drama. I remember when we work together in *Face/Off*, the first day there was a scene with John Travolta and Joan Allen. It was a pretty emotional scene.

And after the first take I said, "OK, good cut. Let's move on."

He said to me, "John, are you sure you're happy with that?"

"Yeah, I'm really happy with that. I felt very natural, that's what I want."

He said to me, "John, they pay me a lot of money, you know, I don't mind doing it thirty or fifty more times."

I said, "I don't care how much they pay you. It's one take."

He was happy, so happy then. From that day they called me, "One Take John."

There's something different working with Chinese actors and American actors. Hong Kong actors: They like to explore themselves. [They] do what they want. They don't care, they have no limit. If they feel like they want to cry, they just cry. They are very emotional. So when I'm working with Nic Cage, I think sometimes [Hollywood actors] like to be a little subtle. Sometimes, some of the actors [don't] get much freedom. They have usually been told you got to do what's on your script, and you can't make any changes.

So when I [was] working with Nic on different scenes: [His character was trying] to convince Joan Allen that he is her real husband [in *Face/Off*]. He was just telling a joke [so she'd know it was him]. Then I would suggest to him, "Can you tell this joke with tears?"

He said, "Can I do it?"

I said, "Yeah, you can do it. If you want to cry, just cry. If you tell a joke with tears, it will feel more bitter. Very effective, it looks more real."

And then "OK."

The second time he was telling the joke with tears, and he feels great. And then I let him make the choice, the one with tears or one without tears. He picked the one with tears. So he feels free. So that's the way I work with them.

I also like Travolta and Cage—they can improvise anything. I like to talk to my actors. Whenever we're on the set, [I say,] "OK. Don't worry about the script. Put it aside." I need surprise, I need to mold it from the script. When I read the script, it seems as [if] I have seen the movie already and then there is not any excitement for me on the set. So whenever we [are] on the set, I try to figure out some new idea. . . . [I] want to make the scene more interesting. Most of the idea depends on my actors because I respect my actors. You know, they are all great. [I] always believe they can give me a lot of surprises. I believe that's one of the joys of making a movie.

BB: *That's interesting. People who often work with Robert Altman often say that one of the reasons actors love working with him is that he gives you the feeling that you can do anything. You don't talk about rehearsing with actors, but you talk about setting up a condition under which they feel they can basically do anything and they feel they will be supported by you and be encouraged by you. It doesn't happen often that directors do that.*

JW: Another thing is, I did start out as an actor on the stage when I was in high school, so I know how the actors feel. I know how they feel, I know what they want. And then . . . most of my Hong Kong films were shot completely without a script. A lot of the scenes, a lot of dialogue, a lot of the moments were created on the set.

BB: *Do you ever have any trouble in Hollywood when you change the dialogue, when you tell people they can just improvise?*
JW: Sometimes I got to shoot two versions; it's a very tricky thing. Sometimes I let the studio people "Oh you added to . . . [a certain scene]." They usually won't care much, but in the cutting room I will use mine. Sometimes I will talk to the studio people to let them know what I'm going to change and, Terence—he's always the one who does the dirty job. I tell Terence and he's got to help me to make it work.

The other thing is the reason I didn't like to use [only] the script is because when I see all the actors, they have their own life. I would like to see how they feel; how they move first. . . . Of course, I have my own vision. I have the idea of a scene and when we get on the set I will talk to the actors and say, "OK . . . do the line. Do the scene. How do you feel?"

. . . I let everyone know what the scene is about. That is the way I work and I never tell the actor how or what to do. Sometimes, I let the actor tell me what to [do], what they want to do and then I try to find something they both have in common. That is how I work, even for the action movies. So that is why in *Face/Off* John Travolta and Nic Cage—every day when they came onto the set, they said, "Oh, we're on vacation." They are so happy.

BB: *There's such an interesting juxtaposition all the time in your films, that fierce anger and this great heart going on all the time. Are you aware of it when it's going on?*
JW: Yeah, sometimes.

BB: *I think it's funny that you get criticized for your violence. I believe to me it's not violence. I have never had trouble watching people getting shot in your movies . . . because it's in the service of something else. I never feel like I'm in danger. When I watch the movie, I always feel like it's part of the story or it's so choreographed, but I always feel it's almost like painting or music. Is that important to you that it should feel that way?*

JW: I think it's important. I like to make everything romantic. I also think, of course, I'm not a violent person. I hate violence. Actually, I also hate war. I hate to see people killing each other; I just do it in movies. The other thing is that I never try to glorify the violence. I try to never use the violence to please the audience. I like to use the action to send a message or sometimes to try to find meaning from the action sequence. If the fight was about love or revenge, it all has a different kind of treatment.

There are a lot of romantic action moments in *The Killer*, because [he] was fighting for love and friendship, so I made it very romantic. And sometimes the action was about the heroic moment, especially for some high spiritual thing. I would like to use the action in the most romantic way. If the scene was about sacrifice—a man scarified himself for his friend or his country—I would like to use a very romantic way to do that.

BB: *On one of your early American movies, the studio was upset with the violence, ironically. As violent as many American movies are, the studio made you cut some of the action sequences . . . why do you think, John?*

JW: Well, maybe I was a little too ambitious at that time. [People] weren't ready for that kind of movie. When I made *Hard Target*, it was my first American movie. There was quite a few scenes that were pretty scary—seeing a guy's ear cut, some people got beat up [and were] bleeding. We had the rating problem, the people from MPAA, and [there was a suggestion] to trim down a lot of the action, the violent shots. Also the studio [made] me cut it seven times to get an R rating. Originally, they tried to give us NC-17. I also maybe learned something from Hollywood: You can do whatever you want, but sometimes you have to know how to behave a little bit. I had to do a lot of adjustment and try not to go too far.

BB: *Are you going to go back and make movies in Hong Kong ever?*

JW: I don't have any plans to make movies in Hong Kong, but I do wish I could make a movie in China. I've been planning to make a historical epic in China. It's about a very famous civil war in China about 2,000 years ago. And at that time China was divided into three parts.

They were all against each other. So I just want to make a movie like *Braveheart*, like [Akira] Kurosawa movies. Like I said, I've always wanted to work in a different place, different country. [I] want to learn some different kind of culture. China is just a beautiful country. It is so many people, a beautiful place. It also has a great history.

Audience Questions

Q: *I was wondering if you were going to work with Chow Yun-Fat anytime soon again?*
JW: Yeah, we do have a plan to work with Chow Yun-Fat again. We have a project called *The Divide*, a story about the early Chinese and Irish immigrants on the railroad. It was based on a true event. Of course, we are still looking at some material. We want to work with Chow Yun-Fat.

Q: *I was wondering if any of you could say your three most favorite movies in the last five years.*
JW: I really love a movie called *No Man's Land* and *Lord of the Rings*, the last one.
   It's so hard. *Boys Don't Cry*.

Q: *My question was the use of the white bird in* Paycheck *and* Mission: Impossible 2 *and what is that symbolic of?*
JW: I think, for me, [the white dove] represents purity, love, peace, spirituality. So that is why I like to use it in a movie. I'm a Christian. When I was in high school, I drew a poster for church every week and I liked to use the picture of the dove for the theme of my drawings.
   And in the early '70s, I was a hippie. I had really long hair; I put flowers in my hair, stuff like that. So I like the symbol of dove. It represents peace and love themes in my movies. . . .
   I use it for meaning in *The Killer*—it's a story about the two guys. They are fighting for justice, they are trying to save the girl, that kind of high spiritual thing. So one is a killer and one is a cop. Even though they work differently, each one of them has a heart. They both have a good heart. Like the cop, he gets shot, we cut to the dove or the candle, like his soul [is] being saved.

Q: *To add on to what she said down there about how did you come up with the style to use Mexican standoffs almost like "Infinite Ammo" flips and slides or when people fly across the room shooting at people in your films?*

JW: I think the ideas came on the set because I never knew it's called a Mexican standoff. I just wanted to make a fun moment. [In] *The Killer* I tried to find a way to emphasize the friend and enemy [dichotomy] and I tried to create a fun moment. Maybe I have [read] too many comics and at that time my favorite comic was *Mad* magazine's *Spy vs. Spy*—the black and white bird that catch each other and actually they are pretty good friends. That gave me the idea to create the scene. I imagine they draw their guns at the same time, pointing to each other . . . [it] would be really dramatic and fun. The other thing is the story of *The Killer* was all about two men in love with the same woman, so that is why I got the idea.

INDEX

Accidentally (1968), xvi, xx, 10, 17–18
Affleck, Ben, xviii, xxxi, 169–70
All the Wrong Clues for All the Right Solutions, 52
Allen, Joan, xxx, 152, 158; in *Face/Off*, 179–80
Allen, Woody, 60
Alliance Franchise, 155
Alphaville Renaissance, 95
Altman, Robert, 180
Amsterdam Kill, The, 31
Anderson, Arthur, xxx–xxxi
Andy's Jazz Club (Chicago), 162
Angels with Dirty Faces, 132
Anna and the King, 153
Antonioni, Michelangelo, 64
Apocalypse Now, 33
Armani, 59
Armstrong, Louis, 162
Assassin, The, 19, 172
Assassins, turning down directing of, 122
Astaire, Fred, 5, 119
Australia, 149–50

Badalato, Bill, xxix
Bailly, Cecile Le, xxvi
Baird, Stuart, 144
Balaban, Bob, 174–84
Bao Hok Lai (Pao Hsueh Li), 15
Batteer, Joe, xxxi
Beach, Adam, xxxi; on John Woo, 164
Beatty, Warren, 27, 63, 142
Bedazzled, 38. *See* Cook, Peter; Moore, Dudley

Bertolucci, Bernardo, 64
Better Tomorrow, A, xvii–xviii, xxv, 23, 32, 35, 53, 55, 76, 78, 89, 92–93, 96, 136–37, 144, 148, 153, 155, 156, 157, 166, 172, 177; filming of, 59–72; genesis of, 48–51; reception of, 49–51, 59–61, 99–101
Better Tomorrow II, A, xxvi, 51–54, 92–93, 99
Better Tomorrow III, A, 54
Big Hit, The, xxxii, 142
Bin Bin, xxv
Black-faced god, 84, 163–64. *See also* Woo, John, black-faced god
Blackjack, xxxi, 148
Blade Runner, 169
Blanford, Larry, xxxi
Blockbuster Video, 110
Bogart, Humphrey, 6
Bond, James, 142, 149
Bonnie and Clyde, 27, 63, 64
Bora, Maseratti, 101
Boxer from Shantung, The, 19, 172
Boys Don't Cry, 183
Brando, Marlon, 158
Braveheart, 183
Brimley, Wilford, xxix
Broken Arrow, xxix, 69, 121, 128, 140, 144, 151–53, 156, 163; budget and schedule, 117; filming of, 114–20
Brooks, Mel, 30
Bugs Bunny, 119
Bullet ballets, ix, 162
Bullet in the Head, xxvii, 23, 68, 84, 89, 91, 93, 99, 114, 118, 120, 155, 177; autobiographical elements, 51, 177; budget and

schedule, 117; genesis of, 51; reception of, 56–57
Bulletproof Monk, xxxii
Burns, George, 46
Butler, Yancy, xxix, 102
Butterfly Murders, The, 52

Cabaret, 171
Cage, Nicolas, ix, xviii, xxx–xxxi, 59, 141, 144, 147, 151–52, 158, 167, 178–80; in *Face/Off*, 151–52, 179–80; on John Woo, 163–64; in *Windtalkers*, 163–64
Cagney, James, 132
Cambodia, 43
Cameron, James, 143
Caro, Mark, 108–13
Carpenter, Russell, xxviii, 94–95, 102–6
Casablanca, 65
Cassavetes, Nick, xxx
Cathay Organization, xvi, 11, 16, 18–19, 21, 91, 99
Catholic imagery, 74, 79. *See also* doves
Censorship. *See Young Dragons, The*
Cercle Rouge, Le, 10. *See also Red Circle, The*
Chai Kittikum Som, xxvii
Chan, Angel, xxii
Chan, Jackie, xvi–xvii, xxi, 21, 24–26, 31, 47, 96, 100, 117, 156; in *Countdown in Kung Fu*, 24–26
Chan, Joe, 9
Chan, Jo Jo, xxiii
Chan, Peter, xxv, 143
Chan, Phillip, xxviii
Chan, Wilson, xxvii
Chan Hing-Ka, xxv
Chan Kai Yat (Chan Kai-yat), xx, 9
Chan Keung Yeung, 9
Chan Pak-cheung, xxiii
Chan Wang Lau, xxiv
Chang, David, 171
Chang, Terence, xi, xviii, xxvii–xxviii, xxix–xxxi, 58, 68, 81–88, 90, 92–93, 96, 98–99, 109, 116, 140, 142, 143, 162–64, 167, 181; on filming of *Hard Boiled*, 81–88; on *Hard Target*, 109; on Hong Kong gangs, 84–85; on ratings in Hong Kong, 87; on Tiananmen Square massacre, 98; on Woo as director, 162–64; on violence, 82
Chang Cheh, x, xvi–xvii, 7, 19, 26–27, 34, 55–56, 64, 76, 99; death of, 171–72;

filming *Just Heroes* for, 55–56; as Woo's mentor, 11–14
Chang Chung, xxi, xxvii
Chang Yau Chung (Chang Yau-chung), xxii. *See also* Cheung, Peter; Cheung Yiu-chung
Chaplin, Charlie, 30, 39, 175
Charlie's Angels, 70
Chase, The (Arthur Penn), 64
Chen Hsun-chi, xxii
Chen Kuan-tai, xxvii
Chen Sing, xxiv
Chen Yue Sang, xxvi
Cheung, Jacky, xxvii
Cheung, Leslie, xxv–xxvi, xxviii, 51, 58, 63, 93, 96, 100
Cheung, Mabel, 97
Cheung, Peter, xxi, xxii–xxiii, xxv
Cheung, Ringo, xxvii
Cheung King-hung, xix
Cheung Sum, 11
Cheung Yiu-chung (Cheung Yiu Chung), xxi
Cheung Yiu-jo, xxiii
Chi Fung Lok, xxvi
Chi Ming Chiang, xxii
Chiang, David (John Chiang), xxvii, 12, 54. *See also* Jiang Dawei
Chiang, John. *See* Chiang, David
Chiao, Roy, xxii, 32
Chicago (musical), 154
Chicago Tribune, xiii, 89–93, 108–13
Chin, Amy, xxviii
Chinese Ghost Story, A (Ching Siu-Tung), 97
Chinese opera, 28–29
Chinese Student Weekly (*Zhonggou Xue Sheng Zhou Bao*), xvi, 7–9, 17
Ching Dynasty Feud, 7
Ching Nai-gun, xix
Ching Siu-Tung, 96
Chiu, Angie, xxii
Chiu Gang Jian, 11–12
Chiu Lui, xxvii
Chiu Tak Hak, xix, 9, 19
Cho, Charlie, xxiv
Cho Chung-lang, xx
Cho Wai-ki, xxvii
Choi Hung, xxvii
Chow, Raymond, xxi–xxiii, xxv
Chow, Stephen, xxvii
Chow, Tony, xxiv

Chow Yun-Fat, xi, xvii, xxv–xxvi, xxviii, 35, 49–51, 54, 58, 59, 65, 73, 75, 78, 80, 81–82, 87–88, 89, 92, 96, 100, 111, 116, 120, 127, 136, 141, 143–45, 147–48, 153, 155, 162, 166, 172–73, 176, 179, 183; in *A Better Tomorrow*, 49–51, 59, 78, 80, 92; future projects with, 167, 172–76, 183; in *Hard Boiled*, 81–82, 87–89; in *The Killer*, 54, 73–78, 179; in *Once a Thief*, 58, 96, 100; in other, non-Woo movies, 153; slow motion time signature, 148
Christian symbolism, xii, 74, 123, 154, 183
Christianity, 74, 84, 165–66. See Lutheran Church
Christiansen, Richard, 89–93
Chronicle of an Assassin, 76
Chu, Emily, xxv–xxvi
Chu, Paul, xxiii, xxvii
Chuan Kin Experimental College, 9
Chun, Janet, xxvii
Chung, Cheri, xxviii, 58
Chung Chang, 24
Chung Siu Fung, xxvi
Chute, David, ix, 73–88
Ciccone, Tony, xxx
Cinema City, xvii, xxii, xxiv, xxvi, 37, 39–40, 47, 51–52, 100; start of, 51–52
Close Encounters of the Third Kind, 39
Close-ups, 77
Coca Cola, 83
Colleary, Michael, xxix, 140
College Cine Club, xvi, 9–10, 17
Comedies, 30–34, 46–47, 52, 130, 166
Concordia Lutheran High School, xvi
Connell, Richard, 101
Cook, Peter, 38
Coppola, Francis Ford, 65
Corruptor, The, 153
Cortes, Rowena, xxii, 32
Countdown in Kung Fu (Hand of Death, Fist to Fist, Hong Kong Face-off or *Shaolin Men*), xvii, xxi, 22, 24–26, 60, 100
Criterion Collection, 17, 73–80, 81–88, 120
Crossing. See *Accidentally*
Cruise, Tom, xviii, xxx, 142–47, 156, 173

Dagort, Phil, xxix
Dancer, The, 170
Daniel, Sean, xxviii
Darkman (Chuck Pfarrer), 101
Davis, John, xxxi

Davis, Miles, 162
Day of the Jackal, The, 76
De Bont, Jan, 122
De Niro, Robert, 153
De Palma, Brian, 148
De Sica, Vittorio, 64
Dean, James, 7
Death Knot (Dead Knot), xvi, xx, 10, 17–18
Deer Hunter, The, 33
Delon, Alain, 49, 58, 59
Demy, Jacques, 12, 131, 133
Devil's Soldier, The, 173
DGA Magazine, The, 114
Di Long (Ti Lung), xxv–xxvi, 12–13, 65, 100
Diamant, Moshe, xxviii
Diaz, Romero, xxvii
Dick, Philip K., 168–69
Dip Hueh Shuan Hung, 75
Directing style, 102–4, 106, 108, 112, 117
Dirty Harry (character), 66, 92
Divide, The, xii, 173, 183. See also *Men of Destiny*
Dorset Street, 9
Double Impact, 104
Douglas, Michael, xxix, 142, 151
Doven, Michael, xxx
Doves, symbolism of, xii, 123, 154, 183
Dragon Tamers, The, xvi, 22–23
DreamWorks, xxxi
Dunaway, Faye, 27, 63

Eastwood, Clint, 59, 176–77
Eckhart, Aaron, xxxi
Elder, Robert K., vii–xiii, 16–58, 162–67
Elrick, Ted, 114–20
Emmerich, Noah, xxxi
Emperor Qin, 34
Enders, Joe. See Cage, Nicolas
Erickson, C. O., xxx
Exorcist, The, 39
Evil One, The (1968), xvi, xix, 10, 16–17, 19
Eyes Wide Shut (Stanley Kubrick), 144, 148

Face/Off, xviii, xxix, 59, 69, 128, 140–42, 144, 148, 151–54, 155, 156, 163, 164; costumes in, 59; Fan Kung-wing, xxiv, xxvi; filming of, 151–54; success of, 140–42; world gross, 153
Fang, Karen, 59–72
Farewell Buddy (The Young Dragons), xvi, 19–20

188 INDEX

Farriss, Andrew, xxx
Fat Chung, xxiii
Faust, 37
Fellini, Federico, 7, 12, 157
Feore, Colm, xxxi
Film Workshop Company, 100
Fist to Fist. See *Countdown in Kung Fu*
Follow the Star, xxii, 32–33
Fonda, Henry, 115
Fong-fong, Josephine. See Siao, Josephine
Ford, John, 175
Fosse, Bob, 154
Freeze frame, use of, 74, 163
French New Wave, 10, 68, 133–35
From Riches to Rags, xvii, xxii, 33–34
Fu Kwok (film studio), 14
Fuller, Sam, 175
Fung Hark on, xix, xxii
Fung Shui-fan, xxiii

Gallotti, Robert "Rock," 106, 112
Games Gamblers Play, 30
Gangs, in Hong Kong, 84–85
Gareri, Joe, xxix
Garland, Judy, 5, 142
Gene Siskel Film Center, The (Chicago), vii, xviii, 89, 174–83
Georgaris, Dean, xxxi
Gere, Richard, 90
Gershon, Gina, xxx
Gfelner, Michael, 104
Giamatti, Paul, xxxi
Gibbs, Michael, xxviii
Goblin, xxiii
Godard, Jean-Luc, 133
Godsick, Christopher, xviii, xxix
Golden Harvest (studio), xvi–xvii, xx–xxv, 20, 22, 37, 40, 43, 99–100
Golden Princess (studio), xxvi–xxviii, 39–40, 52
Golden Swallow, 172
Golden Triangle (Thailand, Vietnam, Cambodia), 43
Goldman, William, 149
Goldwyn, John, 151
Gone With the Wind, 39
Gordon, Mark, xxix, 121
Graham-Rice, Tracie, xxx
Grant, Cary, 58, 153, 169
Greenaway, Gavin, xxx
Gregson-Williams, Harry, xxix

Gross, Holger, xxix, xxxi
Guangxi province, 3, 42
Guangzhou (Canton), China, vii, xv, 3, 42, 91, 144
Gullo, Jeff, xxxi
Gunton, Bob, xxix

Hackett, Michael, xxxi
Hand of Death, xvii, 60–61. See also *Countdown in Kung Fu*
Handover of Hong Kong to China. See Hong Kong, and handover to China
Hard Boiled (*Hard-Boiled*), ix, xii, xxviii, 17, 60–61, 66–67, 81–88, 99, 110, 114, 116, 120, 121, 123, 144, 154, 155, 162, 177; body count in, 110; budget and schedule, 117; ending of, 67; doves in, 154; political significance of, 66–67; shooting of, 81–88, 116, 123, 177; staircase scene, 177; teahouse shootout, 177; Woo on directing, 123, 177. See also *Hot-Handed God of Cops*
Hard Target, xi, xviii, xxviii, 35, 68–69, 87, 94–107, 108–13, 122, 127–28, 143, 150, 152, 163; directing of, 94–113; genesis of, 68–69; lessons from, 127–28, 143, 150, 152, 163; on producers Sam Raimi and Robert Tapert, 35; set reports from, 94–107, 108–13
Hard Times, 90
Harper, Don, xxix
Hau, Tommy, xxvii
Hauer, Rutger, 169
Hawks, Howard, 175
Hawn, Goldie, 154
Heard, Christopher, 33
Heep Woh primary school, 6
Heep Woh secondary school, 6
Hello, Late Homecomers, xxii, 37
He-Man, 172
Henriksen, Lance, xxix, 94, 104, 110
Hepburn, Audrey, 58
Hercules, 35
Hero, 172
Heroes Shed No Tears, xvii, xxv
Hidden Hero. See Chang Cheh
High and Low (Akira Kurosawa), 12, 65
Hill, Walter, 90, 101
Hip Woo primary school. See Heep Woh primary school
Hitchcock, Alfred, 58, 170, 175

Hitchcock, Paul, xxx
Ho, Leonard (Ho Kuan Chang, Ho Guan Chuen), xxiii, 25, 29
Hoi San Lee, xxii, xxiv
Hollywood, 68–69, 77–78, 95, 117, 138, 170, 178
Homoeroticism, 18, 71–72
Hong Kong, x, 3, 10, 125–27, 132–34, 167, 170, 175, 178, 182–83; and handover to China, 41, 65–67, 84, 97, 118
Hong Kong Face-off. See *Countdown in Kung Fu*
Hong Kong Film Archive, vii, xii, 3–15
Hong Kong film industry, vii, 21, 36–37, 70–71, 91–92, 95–96, 101, 107, 113, 117, 125, 135, 138, 141, 170, 178
Hong Kong film scene, vii, 91–92, 95, 98, 101
Hong Kong gangs, 84–85
Hong Kong Hitman, 31
Hong Kong New Wave, 36. See also Hui, Ann; Lam, Ringo; Tam, Patrick; Tsui Hark; Yu, Ronny
Hopkins, Anthony, 144
Horner, James, xxxi
Hsiang-Fei, 40. See also Woo, John
Hsu, Frank, xxv
Hsun Chi Chen, xxii
Hu, King (Hu Chin Chuan), 5, 7
Hu Chin Chuan, 7. See also Hu, King
Hui, Ann, 36
Hui, Michael, 30
Hui, Ricky, xxii–xxiv
Hui, Samuel, xxiii, 30
Hung, Sammo, xxi, 24–25, 31, 47, 100, 127
Hutchence, Michael, xxx
Hutshing, Joe, xxix

Ichikawa, Kon, 7
Indiana Jones and the Temple of Doom, 32
Iraq, invasion of Kuwait, 66
Ishii, Teruo, 7, 74
It's a Mad Mad Mad Mad World, 33

Jacks, Jim (James Jacks), xxviii, 68
Jazz, 162
Ji Han Jae, xx
Jiang Dawei 12–13. See Chiang, David; Chiang, John
Jing Ke, 34

John Woo Film Productions, xxvii, 56
Judo Saga. See *Sugata Sanshiro*
Judo Story. See *Sugata Sanshiro*
Jules et Jim, 58, 74
Julia-Levy, Raul, xxix
Just Heroes, xxvii, 55–56

Kai Kit-Wai, xxviii
Kam Ma, xxv
Kam Ping Hing, 9
Kass, Daryl, xxviii
Kehr, Dave, ix, 81–88
Kelly, Gene, 5, 119
Kemper, Steven, xxx–xxxi
Kill Bill, 169
Killer, The, ix, xii, xviii, 54–56, 67–68, 73–88, 83, 89, 96, 99, 101, 109, 110, 114, 120, 121, 123, 136, 140, 144, 148, 154, 155, 162, 167, 171, 177, 182–84; disputes with Tsui Hark over, 54–55; doves in, 154; endings of, 79–80; filming of, 73–80; genesis of, 54–55, 77; popularity in Hong Kong, 120; proposed remake with Richard Gere, directed by Walter Hill, 90; reception of, 68, 83, 101, 120, 136; success of, 67; Sundance Film Festival 83; violence of, 77–78
Kimball, Jeffrey L., xxx–xxxi
King Hu, 6, 7
King's Ransom, 142, 153, 172
Knight, Janice, 167
Ko, Eddy, xxvi
Ko, Clifton, xxvii
Kon Ichikawa, 7
Kondazian, Karen, 155–61
Kong, Lung, 48–49, 64
Kong Chu, xxvi
Koo, Johnny, xxiii, xxv
Koo, Joseph (composer), xx, xxi, xxvi
Korea, xvi, 22–27, 97
Kowloon Side, 9, 130
Koyama, Keiko, xxxi
Krane, Jonathan D., xxix
Kubrick, Stanley, xvi, 7, 12, 64, 123, 144, 175
Kuk, Linda, xxvii–xxviii, 87
Kuo Sheng, xxii
Kurosawa, Akira, xvi, 7, 12, 24, 34, 65, 183
Kwan, General, 6
Kwan, Teddy Robin, xxv
Kwan Hoi-shan, xxviii
Kwok, Philip, xxviii

Laffredo, Phillip, xxvi
Lai, Alawn, xxvi
Lam, Ardy, xxvii
Lam, Ringo, 36, 142
Lam Bowie, xxviii
Lam Chak, xix
Lam Ching Ying (Lam Ching-Ying), xxiii, xxvi
Lan Law, xxii
Land of Destiny, 173, 183. See also *Men of Destiny*
Lansing, Sherry, 151
Lao, T. C., xxii
Last Hurrah for Chivalry, 34–35, 37, 76
Lau, Catherine, xxvii
Lau, Damian, 35
Lau Chan Sang, xxvi
Lau Hung-Chuen, xxiv
Lau Kar Leung, 13–14
Lau Kong, xx
Lau Shui-Kei, xxiv
Lau Tin-chi, xxii
Laughing Times, xvii, xxiv, 39
Law, Norman, xxiv
Law Kar, 5, 9, 17–19
Lawrence of Arabia, 65
Lazenby, George, 31
Le Bailly, Cecile. See Bailly, Cecile Le
Lean, David, 64
Learning by Doing (1969), xvi, 17–18
Lee, Andy, xxvi–xxvii
Lee, Bruce, 21, 31, 145
Lee, Chris, 144
Lee, Danny, xxvi–xxvii, 73
Lee, Michael, xxiv
Lee, Paul JQ, xxvi
Lee, Waise, xxv, xxvii
Lee Lin Ying (character), 7
Left Hand Gun (Arthur Penn), 64
Lemmons, Kasi, xxix, 105
Leone, Sergio, 77
Leopold, Stratton, xxxi
Lesnie, Andrew, 150
Leung, James, xxvii–xxviii
Leung, Patrick, xxvii, 85–86
Leung, Tony Chiu Wai (Tony Leung or "Big Tony" Leung), xxvii–xxviii, 81, 86, 88, 111, 120
Leung Suk-Wah, xxv
Leung wing-gut, xxi
Levine, Jeff, xxix
Levy, Peter, xxix

Lewis, Brad, xxix
Lewis, Jerry, 30, 175
Lin Nien-tong, 9
Lindo, Delroy, xxix
Ling, Ka, 48
Lionheart, 104
Lion Rock Productions, xviii, 167
Little Apple, 11
Little Big Man (Arthur Penn), 64
Little, Dwight H., xxix
Liu Chiang, xxiii
Liu Mei-ying (mother), xv
Liu Sung Jen, xxiii
Lloyd Webber, Andrew, 154
Lo, Louis, xxii
Lo, Lowell, xxvi
Lo Men, xix
Lo Wei, 26
Lok, Ada, 9
Lone Ranger, 36
Long, Howie, xxix
Lord of the Rings: Return of the King, 183
Lost in Space (TV pilot), xviii, xxxii
Lu Yun Na, 32. See Cortes, Rowena
Lui Chi Ho, 15
Lui Chi-leung, xxv
Lui's Film Company, xvi
Luk Nai, 9
Lung Kim-sung, xxi
Lung Kong, 7
Lutheran Church, 6, 132

Ma, Alex, xxiii–xxiv
Macaulay, Caroline, xxx, xxxi
Macias, Patrick, 168–73
Mad magazine, 184
Magnum Films, xxvi–xxvii
Maguire, Dennis, 104
Maka, Karl, xxiv–xxv, 39
Man from Hong Kong, The, 31
Manchurian, The, 21
Maples, Michele, xxix
Marx Brothers, 175
Masaki, Kobayashi, 7
Mathis, Samantha, xxix, 114, 116, 122
Matrix, The, 70
Matthau, Walter, 46
Matteo Ricci College, xvi, 99
McQueen, Steve, 49, 59, 158, 176
Mean Streets (Scorsese), 57, 74
Melville, Jean-Pierre, 7, 10, 54, 64–65, 123, 133

Men of Destiny, xii, 167, 173, 183
Mexican standoff, 184
MGM, xxx, 144
Microsoft, 172
Mighty Mouse, 172
Milestone Pictures, xxvii–xxviii, 96–97
Ming Ho, xxiv
Mirkovich, Steve, xxix
Mission: Impossible, 148
Mission: Impossible 2, xviii, xxx, 69, 143–54, 156, 163, 164
Mitchum, Robert, 31
Mo, Teresa, xxviii
Money Crazy, xvii, xxi, 30–31, 36, 100
Monkey King, 6
Moore, Dudley, 38
Moreau, Jeanne, 74
Moriarty, Lloyd, 103, 105–6, 112
Most Dangerous Game, The (movie), 110
"Most Dangerous Game, The" (short story), 101
Mui Shuet-shi, xxi
Murawski, Bob, xxviii

Naragawa Kenichi, xxv
Nationalism (Hong Kong), 61, 65, 167
Navy SEALs (Chuck Pfarrer), 101
Nelson, Ralph, 58
New Line Cinema, 68
New York Stories, 37
Newman, Paul, 158
Newton, Thandie, xxx, 149
Newton-John, Olivia, 142
Ni Kuang (Ngai Hong), xxvii, 15
Nicknames, 84, 163–64
Nivola, Alessandro, xxx
Ng, Richard, xxii
Ng, Sui-chan, 57–58
Ng Yu-Sum (John Woo's Cantonese name), xv, 3
Ngai Hong. *See* Ni Kuang
No Man's Land, 183
Nolen, Randy, 104
North by Northwest, 169
Now You See Love (Mabel Cheung), 97

O'Brien, Pat, 132
Old Schoolmaster, 163. *See also* John Woo
Once a Thief, xxvii, xxxii, 57, 91, 93, 96, 178
Once Upon a Time in the West, 115
One-Armed Swordsman, The, 19, 172
One-Armed Swordsman Returns, 19

Osborne, Barrie M., xxix
O'Toole, Peter, 58
Overbey, David, 137
Ozu Yasujiro, 8

Pacific Palisades, 167
Pacino, Al, 158
Pak Ho Street, 3
Palace Cinema, 5
Pan Yin-tze, xxv
Pao Hsueh Li (Bao Hok Lai), 15
Paragon Films, xxv
Paramount Pictures, xxxi, 140, 151
Parents' Heart, The (John Woo High School play), 7
Pau, Peter, xxvi
Paycheck, xviii, xxxi, 168–73
Peckinpah, Sam, x, xvi, 7, 12, 55, 64, 92, 112, 123, 175
Peking Opera, 82, 158
Peking Opera Blues (Tsui Hark), 96
Penn, Arthur, 63–64, 123
Permut, David, xxix
Pfarrer, Chuck, xxviii, 101, 111
Phantom of the Opera, The, 154
Philion, Brittany, vii
Philosophy, 62, 65, 127, 157, 182
Pilferer's Progress, The, 155. *See also Money Crazy*
Pingnan city (Guangxi province), 3
Plain Jane to the Rescue, xvii, xxiv, 40–43, 47, 65, 100, 148
Police Story (Jackie Chan), 96
Politics, 65–67, 84, 113, 118. *See also* Hong Kong, and handover to China; Tiananmen Square massacre
Poon Hang-seng, xxvii
Powell, John, xxx, xxxi
Prince Edward Road, 4
Princess Chang Ping, xxi, 27–29, 36, 136
Pulp Fiction, 122, 169

Qin, Emperor, 34
Queen's Ransom, A, 31

Raimi, Sam, xxviii, 35, 68, 162
Rance, Mark, 73–88
Ratings, xviii, 87, 110, 117, 150, 164, 182
Ray Ban sunglasses, 59–60
Reagan, Michael A., xxx
Rebel Without a Cause, 70
Red Circle, The, 10, 171

Reeves, Keanu, 121
Religious imagery, 74, 79, 133. *See also* doves; Woo, John, on religion
Replacement Killers, The, xxxi, 153
Reuther, Steven, xxix, 151
Revell, Graeme, xxix
Rhames, Ving, xxx, 144
Rice, John, xxxi
Robin, Teddy, 46–47
Rodriguez, Robert, 121, 143
Rolf, Tom, xxxi
Romanticism, 131, 149
Romeo and Juliet, 28
Rosenzweig, Alison R., xxx
Rouse, Christopher, xxxi
Roxburgh, Richard, xxx
Ruffalo, Mark, xxxi
Run Tiger Run, xxv, 40, 46–47
Ryan, Maureen "Mo," 121–24

Sai Sai (Si Si), 10
Samourai, Le, 10, 30, 64
Sandell, William, xxxi
Sanders, Thomas E., xxx
Scharres, Barbara, vii, x, 90, 94–107, 174–84
Schwarzenegger, Arnold, 87
Scorsese, Martin, vii, ix–x, 54–55, 57, 65, 101, 112, 123, 135, 153
Scott, Dougray, xxx, 147; injury, 150
Secret Killer (1968), 17
Sega, 172
Segan, Allison Lyon, xxix
Sek Kei, xvi, xix–xx, 9–10, 18. *See also* Wong Chi Keung
Seven Brides for Seven Brothers, 119, 131, 175
Seven Samurai (Akira Kurosawa), 12, 65
Sex, 30, 45, 110
Shadow War, 153
Shaolin Men. *See Countdown in Kung Fu*
Shaolin Soccer, 172
Shaw Brothers, xvi, 6, 11, 15, 99, 156
Shek, Dean, xxiv–xxvi, 39, 51, 54
Shek Kip Mei, 3
Shum Sham, 31
Siao, Josephine (Josephine Siao Fong-fong), xxiv, 40–41
Si Si (Sai Sai), 10
Simon, Neil, 46
Sin, 39. *See Zu: Warriors of the Magic Mountain*

Singer, Michael, 125–39
Singin' in the Rain, 119, 131, 175
Sit, Louis, xxi, xxii, xxiv
Slater, Christian, xxix, xxxi, 114–15, 121, 122–23
Slow motion, 146–48
Smith, James McKee, xxxi
Smith, John J., xxx
Solomon, David, xxxi
"Somewhere Over the Rainbow," 162
Sons of Good Earth, 6
Spartacus, 65
Speed, 121
Spisak, Neil, xxx
Spy vs. Spy, 78–79, 184
St. Hilaire, Michael, 104
Stallone, Sylvester, 122
Star Wars, 39
Stenta, Richard, xxx
Stevens, Amy, xxx
Sting, The, 31
Stitt, Kevin, xxxi
Stone, Oliver, 68, 101
Story of a Discharged Prisoner, The, 7, 48–49, 64. *See also True Colors of a Hero*
Strick, Wesley, 149
Stromare, Peter, xxxi
Student films, 9–11
Stunts, 24–26, 87–88, 92–93, 96, 112, 123, 145–46, 150
Sugata Sanshiro, 23
Suen Jiawen. *See* Sun Kar Man, Dr.
Sum of All Fears, The, 169
Sunglasses, 50
Sun Kar Man, Dr. (Suen Jiawen), 11, 18
Sun Yueh, xxiv
Sundance Film Festival, 83
Sunset Warrior, The, xvii, 43–46
Sunshine Boys, The, 46
Swain, Dominique, xxx
Sye Hse, xxiii
Szeto Chuek-Hon, xxiii

Tae Kwan Do, 23–25
Taiwan, John Woo sent to, xvii, 11, 40, 46–47, 97–98
Taiwan Golden Horse Film Festival, 53
Takakura, Ken, 49, 59, 75–76
Tam, Patrick, 36
Tan Tao-liang, 24
Tang Siu-Lam, xxiii, xxiv, xxvi

Tao, David, xxiv
Tapert, Robert G., xxviii, 35
Tarantino, Quentin, 83, 121, 143, 153, 162
Taxi Driver, 158
Tears of the Sun, 114, 153. See also *Treasure of the Sierra Madre, The*
Teenage Mutant Ninja Turtles, 172
Ten Thousand Bullets: The Cinematic Journey of John Woo, 33
Teruo Ishii, 75
Thailand, shooting in, 43–46, 97
Thomas, John Ashton, xxxi
Thompson, Anne, xii, 143–54
Three Kingdoms, 6
Throne of Blood, 65
Thurman, Uma, xviii, xxxi, 169
Ti Lung, xxv–xxvi, 12–13, 65, 100
Tiananmen Square massacre, 57, 65, 98, 118
Tien, James, xx, xxi
Tien Ni, xx
Tiger Hill Games (video game company), 172
Time You Need a Friend, The, xvii, 40, 46–47
Ting Hsiao-hui, xxv
To Hell with the Devil, xxiii, 37–39
Tolkin, Michael, 149
Tong, Stanley, 143
Tong Ching, xxiii
Tong Kai, 13–14
Tong Tik-sang, xxi
Toronto Film Festival, xviii
Towne, Robert, xxx, 149
Travolta, John, xxix–xxx, 114–15, 120, 121, 122, 141, 147, 151–52, 158, 179–80; in *Face/Off*, 151–52, 179–80; on *The Phantom of the Opera*, 154
Traxler, Stephen, xxx
Treasure of the Sierra Madre, The, 153
Triad, 78; dealings with, 84–85
True Colors of a Hero, 48–49. See also *The Story of a Discharged Prisoner*
Truffaut, François, vii, x, 7, 10, 12, 64, 123, 133, 162
Tsang, Kenneth, xxvi, xxviii
Tsin Yu, xxi
Tsui Hark, x, xvii, xxv, xxvi–xxvii, 36–37, 39, 48, 51–55, 63, 71–72, 96, 100, 113, 166, 171; disputes with, 53–55, 171; friendship with, 36–37, 52–53; meeting, 36–37; movies of, 39, 52; supporting *A Better Tomorrow*, 48, 51

Twentieth Century Fox, xxix, 68, 114, 121–22
2001: A Space Odyssey, 33, 65

Umbrellas of Cherbourg, The, 12, 131
Universal Studios, xxviii, 68, 110

Van Damme, Jean-Claude, xi, xxix, 68, 94, 102, 104, 108, 110–11, 122, 143, 150, 163
Van Varenberg, Eugene, xxviii
Vengeance, 172
Vietnam, 43, 91, 153
Violence, use of, ix, 77, 82, 87, 102, 182. See also Woo, John, on violence
Vosloo, Arnold, xxix, 94
Voyager Company's Criterion Collection. See Criterion Collection

Wachowski Brothers, 143
Wai Chu-xia, xxiii
Wagner, Christian, xxx
Wagner, Paula, xxx, 148
War, 43–45, 163–67, 182
WCG Entertainment, xviii
Wei Pei, xxiii
Werb, Mike, xxix, 140
Werner, Oscar (Oskar Werner), 74
We're Going to Eat You, 52
West Side Story, 70
Whaley, Frank, xxix
Wild Bunch, The, 70, 92, 118
William Morris Agency, 68
Windtalkers, xviii, xxx, 62, 69, 144, 178; filming of, 162–67
Wizard of Oz, The, 5, 131, 142, 155, 165, 175
Wong, Anthony, xxviii
Wong, Barry, xxviii, 82
Wong, Bill, xxiii
Wong, Carter, xx
Wong, James, xxvii, 140
Wong, Kirk, 142, 143
Wong, Kurt, 36
Wong, Peter, 20. See Wong Hoi Yi
Wong, Raymond, xxiv–xxv
Wong Chi Keung (Wong Chi-keung), 9–10. See Sek Kei
Wong Chung, 13
Wong Hoi Yi, 15. See also Wong, Peter
Wong Ping, 11
Wong Wai, xxiv
Wong Wing-hang, xxv, xxvi–xxviii

Woo, Anne Chun-lung Niu (wife), xvii, 26–27, 36, 41–42
Woo, Angeles Fei-shai (daughter), xvii, 42
Woo, Frank Yee Fong (son), xvii, 41–42
Woo, John: on acting, 152, 157, 158–61, 178; on action, 69–70, 116–17, 122–23, 170, 176–77; as an actor, xxi–xxii, xxviii, 60–61, 156–57; on actors, 120, 152, 158–61, 178, 180; becomes U.S. Citizen, xviii, 163; birth dates, xv; Black-faced god, xi, 84, 163–64; on casting, 158–59; childhood, vii, xv, 3–10, 77, 119, 130–31, 133, 139, 164–67, 177–78; childhood fire (Shek Kip Mei Big Fire), vii, xv, 3; on Chow Yun-Fat, 78, 145, 148, 153–54, 176–77; College Cine Club, xvi, 9–10, 17; comedies of, 30–34, 46–47, 52, 130, 166; on Tom Cruise, 145–48; on difference between Chinese and American actors, 157–58, 180–81; on directing, x–xii, 75, 77, 84–86, 92, 103–4, 116–17, 122–23, 130–31, 147–48, 152, 158–59, 179; discovery of movies, 119, 165–66, 175; education, 124, 133–35, 166; on failure, 137; family of, xv, 3, 8, 42–43, 125–26, 133–34, 164–66, 175, 177; on friendship, x, 52, 62, 68, 71–72, 82, 129, 165, 174–75, 177, 179; high school plays *Ching Dynasty Feud* and *The Parents' Heart*, xvi, 7; on Hollywood, 68–69, 77–78, 95, 117, 138, 170, 178; on Hong Kong, x, 3, 10, 125–27, 132–34, 167, 170, 175, 178, 182–83; on Hong Kong film industry, 21, 36–37, 70–71, 95–96, 101, 107, 113, 117, 125, 135, 138, 141, 178; on honor, x, 73, 118–19; marriage, 36; moving to the U.S., 67–69, 125, 128–29, 141, 163, 174, 177; on musicals, 130–31, 175–76; origin of the name "John Woo," xi, xv, 4, 31–32, 139; philosophy of, 62, 65, 127, 157, 182; politics of, 65–67, 84, 113, 118; on ratings, 87, 182; on religion, ix, xii, 4, 6–7, 33, 119, 131–34, 139; on religious influences, imagery, 74, 79, 119, 124, 133, 154; school sponsorship, 119, 132, 167; on slow motion, 146–48; social life of, 126–27; student films of, xix, xx, 9–10, 16–18; on Tiananmen Square, 65–67, 98, 118; on John Travolta, 145; values of, 118–19, 125–26, 131–33, 138–39; on violence, 43–45, 77–78, 116–17, 123, 181–82
Woo, John J. S., xvii, xxi–xxiii, 31
Woo, Kimberly Hsiang-fong (daughter), xvii
Wood, Oliver, xxix
Wright, John, xxix
Wu, Amy, 140–42
Wu, David, xxv, xxvi–xxviii
Wu Chuk-wen (father), xv–xvi, 8, 134, 138–39
Wu Hsiang-Fei (pseudonym), xvii, xxiv. See also Woo, John
Wu Ma, xxvii
Wu Yusen (Wu Yu-sen). See Woo, John
Wu Yu-Sheng (Wu Yu Sheng), vii, xv, 32, 114, 123. See also Woo, John

Yahzee, Ben, 62, 167. See also Beach, Adam
Yam, Simon, xxvii
Yam, Yolinda, xxvii
Yau Chung Chang, xxii–xxiii
Yaun Tung-chun, xxi
Yee Tung-lung, xxvii
Yeh, Sally, xxvi, 73, 80
Yeoh, Michelle, 143
Yik Ka, xxii–xxiii
Yim, William, xxviii
Yojimbo, 12
Yost, Graham, xxix, 115, 121
Young Dragons, The, xvi, xx, 12, 15, 20–21, 99, 156
Young Girls of Rochefort, The, 12, 131
Young People, 13
Yu, Ronny, 36
Yu Yang, xx
Yuen, Bill, 24
Yuen, Fennie, xxvii
Yuen Wah, xx
Yuen Woo Ping, 14

Zimmer, Hans, xxix–xxx
Zhongguo Xue Sheng Zhou Bao, 7–8. See also *Chinese Student Weekly*
Zu: Warriors of the Magic Mountain, 39. See *Sin*

CONVERSATIONS WITH FILMMAKERS SERIES
PETER BRUNETTE, GENERAL EDITOR

The collected interviews with notable modern directors, including

Robert Aldrich • Pedro Almodóvar • Robert Altman • Theo Angelopolous • Bernardo Bertolucci • Tim Burton • Jane Campion • Frank Capra • Charlie Chaplin • Francis Ford Coppola • George Cukor • Brian De Palma • Clint Eastwood • John Ford • Terry Gilliam • Jean-Luc Godard • Peter Greenaway • Alfred Hitchcock • John Huston • Jim Jarmusch • Elia Kazan • Stanley Kubrick • Fritz Lang • Spike Lee • Mike Leigh • George Lucas • Sidney Lumet • Roman Polanski • Michael Powell • Jean Renoir • Martin Ritt • Carlos Saura • John Sayles • Martin Scorsese • Ridley Scott • Steven Soderbergh • Steven Spielberg • George Stevens • Oliver Stone • Quentin Tarantino • Lars von Trier • Orson Welles • Billy Wilder • Zhang Yimou • Fred Zinnemann

www.ingramcontent.com/pod-product-compliance
Lightning Source LLC
Chambersburg PA
CBHW021840220426
43663CB00005B/338